The Politically Incorrect Guide™ to the
CIVIL WAR

The Politically Incorrect Guide™ to the

CIVIL WAR

H.W. Crocker III

Since 1947
REGNERY
PUBLISHING, INC.
An Eagle Publishing Company • Washington, DC

Copyright © 2008 by H.W. Crocker III

Library of Congress Cataloging-in-Publication Data

Crocker, H. W.

The politically incorrect guide to the Civil War / H.W. Crocker III.

p. cm.

Includes bibliographical references and index.

ISBN 978-1-59698-549-0

1. United States—History—Civil War, 1861-1865. 2. United States—History—Civil War, 1861-1865—Campaigns. 3. Generals—United States—Biography. 4. Generals—Confederate States of America—Biography. 5. United States—History—Civil War, 1861-1865—Biography. 6. Political correctness—United States. I. Title.

E468.9C77 2008

973.7—dc22

2008039431

Published in the United States by
Regnery Publishing, Inc.
One Massachusetts Avenue, NW
Washington, DC 20001
www.regnery.com

Manufactured in the United States of America

10 9 8 7 6 5 4 3 2 1

Books are available in quantity for promotional or premium use. Write to Director of Special Sales, Regnery Publishing, Inc., One Massachusetts Avenue NW, Washington, DC 20001, for information on discounts and terms or call (202) 216-0600.

To the Keydets of VMI

"America and the whole world is
crying out for the spirit of the Old South."
—G. K. Chesterton

CONTENTS

Part I

★ ★ ★ ★ ★ ★ ★ ★

WHY THE SOUTH WAS RIGHT

Chapter One

A COUNTRY OF THEIR OWN

Y ou have to imagine the scene. On 20 December 1860, the streets of Charleston, South Carolina, erupted in joy.

Think of the state in which you live, a state you're proud to call home. What if you and many of your fellow Virginians, or Californians, or Texans—and your state legislatures—felt that for decades your state had been provoked and derided by the federal government? What if you—and your state legislatures—concluded that the federal government no longer served your state's interests? What if your state asserted that it existed as an independent entity before it joined the Union, that it had ceded its autonomy only in part, to promote the general welfare, and that when the federal government failed to serve the ends of the people of Virginia, or California, or Texas, these people, in their states, were entitled to rescind their voluntary cession of authority to the federal government because anything else would be submission to tyranny? What if your state suddenly, proudly, declared itself independent and reclaimed its inherent, sovereign rights?

South Carolina had done just that. South Carolinians had declared themselves a nation once again.

Guess What?

❦ Southern secession in 1861 was better founded in law than the secession of the American colonies in 1776

❦ Alexis de Tocqueville thought racism was far more prevalent in free states than in slave states

❦ Jefferson Davis and Robert E. Lee expected slavery to fade away naturally

Artillery batteries fired salutes over Charleston harbor. Church bells pealed from the many spires of "the Holy City." Brightly dressed bands and militia (for this was the South where every man felt a martial calling) marched in celebration. And South Carolinians rejoiced in a new birth of freedom—of government of the people, by the people, and for the people of South Carolina.

A special Convention of the People of South Carolina had declared by unanimous vote, 169 to nil, "that the Union now subsisting between South Carolina and other States, under the name of 'The United States of America,' is hereby dissolved," and that, echoing the language of the Declaration of Independence, the "State of South Carolina has resumed her position among the nations of the world, as a separate and independent State; with full power to levy war, conclude peace, contract alliances, establish commerce, and to do all other acts and things which independent States may of right do."[1]

An audacious action, certainly—its authors, however, were not a body of red-hot revolutionaries, but a convention of eminentoes from the state, including five former governors, four former United States senators, a former Speaker of the United States House of Representatives, and men of local prominence—from clergymen to planters—all of whom felt their patriotic sap rising.

It was 1776 all over again.

In their new Declaration, the delegates reminded folks up north that the Declaration of Independence of 4 July 1776 was the precedent for their action. It had affirmed what South Carolina was reaffirming now, that the colonies were, "and of right ought to be, FREE AND INDEPENDENT STATES; and that, as free and independent States, they have full power to levy war, conclude peace, contract alliances, establish commerce, and to do all other acts and things which independent States may of right do."[2]

South Carolina had reclaimed these sovereign rights—and did so on the very same grounds that Jefferson had laid out eighty-four years before:

whenever any "form of government becomes destructive of the ends for which it was established, it is the right of the people to alter or abolish it, and to institute a new government."[3] For the people of the Palmetto Republic, that time had come.

And who could not wish them well? A short month later they were joined in secession from the United States by Mississippi (9 January 1861), Florida (10 January), Alabama (11 January), Georgia (19 January), Louisiana (26 January), and soon thereafter by Texas (1 February). Before Texas had even fully seceded, South Carolina and its sister states of the Deep South had met and created a new confederation of states. They called it the Provisional Government of the Confederate States of America, with its capital in Montgomery, Alabama.

A new country, a new republic, had sprung up in North America. It was based—despite what Yankees like Henry Adams would say—not on

States' Rights = The American Way

When, in 1861, South Carolina reasserted that it was a sovereign state, it was on firmer ground than Thomas Jefferson had been in 1776 when he drafted the Declaration of Independence proclaiming that the colonies were sovereign states. In fact, they were not; they were British colonies under colonial charters. It was the "crown in parliament" that was sovereign over the colonies. But the Declaration, the Continental Congress, the Articles of Confederation, and the Constitution all rested on Jefferson's asseveration that the colonies were free and independent states, (which is why states, rather than a mass majority vote of all the people in all the states collectively, approved the Constitution). State sovereignty was a cornerstone of America's political philosophy, and given these precedents, South Carolina's declaration of independence was a much less radical step than the Declaration of Independence.

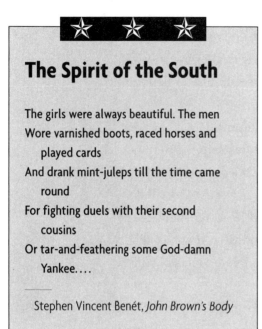

The Spirit of the South

The girls were always beautiful. The men
Wore varnished boots, raced horses and
   played cards
And drank mint-juleps till the time came
   round
For fighting duels with their second
   cousins
Or tar-and-feathering some God-damn
   Yankee....

Stephen Vincent Benét, *John Brown's Body*

treason, but on patriotism. Its members so loved their respective sovereign states, were so jealous for their freedom, that they had embarked on the perilous if exhilarating course of founding a new nation.

It was a nation that did not seek a *novus ordo seculorum*, but rather the preservation of the life, liberty, and pursuit of happiness of South Carolinians, Mississippians, Floridians, Alabamans, Georgians, Louisianans, and Texans. The new nation was created out of motives of preservation, not destruction, of conservatism rather than revolution. For inspiration, the South looked to its past; one Georgia delegate wanted the new nation to be named "The Republic of Washington." Instead, George Washington ended up on the Great Seal of the Confederacy.

And the man chosen to be Washington's successor—the father of this new country and first president of the Confederate States of America—would not be a Robespierre or a Napoleon. Instead, he would be a pillar of rectitude and principle, of constitutionalism and liberty, of Christian stoicism and political conservatism.

Jefferson Davis was a United States senator from Mississippi at the time of secession. He believed in secession's legality, while working to prevent its necessity—as one might believe in the legality of divorce, while doing everything possible to preserve a marriage. A graduate of West Point, a distinguished colonel of the Mississippi Rifles in the Mexican War, a former member of the United States House of Representatives, and perhaps the finest secretary of war the United States ever had, Davis was also a planter, a man of education, and a man devoted to his state.

When he rose in the United States Senate to announce that he would follow Mississippi's withdrawal from the Union, he said, "It is known to senators who have served with me here, that I have for many years advocated, as an essential attribute of State sovereignty, the right of a state to secede from the Union....If I had thought that Mississippi was acting without sufficient provocation....I should still, under my theory of government, because of my allegiance to the State of which I am a citizen, have been bound by her action."[4]

He did not fear, in fact he relished, the prospect of being arrested and tried in a federal court on charges of treason, so confident was he that he could prove the absolute constitutionality of secession. For him—as for many Southerners, especially in the Upper South—secession was a remedy justified only *in extremis*. But that point had manifestly been reached when state governments in South Carolina, Mississippi, and other Southern states promulgated their ordinances of secession. Once these sovereign states had made their decision, men like Jefferson Davis felt bound by it—to do otherwise, to prefer loyalty to a federal *government* rather than to the state, the soil, the land, and the people to which one belonged, and which in Davis's case had sent him to the United States Senate, *that* would have been treason.

He pointed out to the United States Senate that the people of the Deep South "tread but in the paths of our fathers when we proclaim our independence and take the hazard...not in hostility to others, not to injure any section of the country, not even for our own pecuniary benefit, but from the high and solemn motive of defending the rights we inherited, and which it is our duty to transmit unshorn to our children."[5]

In his inaugural address as president of the Confederate States of America, Davis assured his listeners that they had performed no "revolution." They had merely "formed a new alliance, but within each State its government has remained, and the rights of person and property have not been disturbed. The agent, through whom they communicated with foreign nations, is changed; but this does not necessarily interrupt their international relations."[6]

Far from disturbing "the rights of person and property" the Confederate government sought liberation from northern tariffs, an expansion of free trade, and the protection of a most peculiar form of property—slaves.

Was the war really all about slavery?

In the sense that the South was defined by slavery, yes. The Southern states were the slave states. But so too were the border states of Maryland, Delaware, Missouri, and Kentucky. Slavery was also legal in the federal capital, Washington, D.C. It was constitutional, and certainly no innovation as it had existed in America for more than two centuries. It had even, only a few years before (1857), been reaffirmed as a constitutional right by the Supreme Court, and in the early days of the war, it was a right that United States President Abraham Lincoln upheld. During the federal occupation of Missouri in 1861, Lincoln summarily removed General John C. Frémont from command when the abolitionist general refused to rescind a proclamation confiscating the property—and freeing the slaves—of active Confederates.

Lincoln, after all, had embarked on the war *denying* that his presidency endangered slavery in the South. In his First Inaugural Address (4 March 1861) Lincoln reassured Southerners that "I have no purpose, directly or indirectly, to interfere with the institution of slavery in the States where it exists. I believe I have no lawful right to do so, and I have no inclination to do so."[7] This, said Lincoln, was his constant policy.

True to his word, he reiterated it in a letter to Horace Greeley, an abolitionist and editor of the *New York Tribune*, on 22 August 1862, "My paramount object in this struggle is to save the Union, and is not either to save or to destroy slavery. If I could save the Union without freeing any slave I would do it, and if I could save it by freeing all the slaves I would do it; and if I could save it by freeing some and leaving others alone I would also do that."[8]

Lincoln, however, was a lawyer and politician of remarkable slipperiness. Southerners remembered when Lincoln campaigned for the Senate in 1858 against Stephen Douglas and made his famous proclamation: "A house divided against itself cannot stand. I believe this government cannot endure permanently half slave and half free. . . . Either the opponents of slavery, will arrest the further spread of it, and place it where the public mind shall rest in the belief that it is in the course of ultimate extinction; or its advocates will push it forward, till it shall become alike lawful in all the States, old as well as new—North as well as South."[9]

Nevertheless, the stated aim of the Lincoln administration in 1861 was *not* the abolition of slavery; it was the forcible reunification of the Union. In Lincoln's early presidential view, a house divided against itself by slavery could stand, if it was reinforced by enough bayonets. And the use of bayonets, cannons, sabers, muskets, and rifles to subjugate the South certainly did not constitute a state of war. Indeed,

Books Yankees Don't Want You to Read

The Southern Tradition at Bay: A History of Postbellum Thought, by Richard Weaver (Regnery, 1989). A brilliant, classic dissertation on the South's view of itself; what Weaver called, "the last non-materialist civilization in the Western world."

Lincoln asserted that the conflict between North and South was a legal matter to be resolved by the police—a domestic dispute.

On 15 April 1861, Lincoln issued an order for 75,000 volunteers to subdue in the South "combinations too powerful to be suppressed by the ordinary course of judicial proceedings, or by the powers vested in Marshals by law." Marshals? Judicial proceedings? In the canny imagination of Abraham Lincoln, the Confederate States of America simply did not exist—and thus could not be recognized by foreign governments. The Southern states, he reckoned, had never seceded, because secession was a legal impossibility. All that had happened in South Carolina, Alabama, and the other Southern states, was a large-scale riot that needed a larger than usual body of marshals and judges to straighten out.

While denying that he meant to abolish slavery, Lincoln simultaneously chided the South, denying its claims to high principle, by asserting that "One section of our country believes slavery is *right* and ought to be extended, while the other believes it is *wrong* and ought not to be extended. This is the only substantial dispute."[10]

★ ★ ★ ★ ★

Extending Slavery?

Jefferson Davis believed the phrase "the extension of slavery"—used by Northerners to besmirch Southern motives—was a "most fallacious expression." The South had never sought to extend slavery, he said.

Au contraire:

"The question was merely whether the slaveholder should be permitted to go with his slaves, into territory (the common property of all) into which the non-slaveholder could go with his property of any sort. There was no proposal nor desire on the part of the Southern States to reopen the slave-trade, which they had been foremost in suppressing, or to add to the number of slaves.... Indeed, if emancipation was the end to be desired, the dispersion of the negroes over a wider area among additional Territories, eventually to become States, and in climates unfavorable to slave labor, instead of hindering, would have promoted this object by diminishing the difficulties in the way of ultimate emancipation."

Jefferson Davis, *The Rise and Fall of the Confederate Government* (Collier Books, 1961), 27.

Unfortunately for the South, Lincoln was lent support by the Confederacy's own vice president, the Gollum-like Alexander Stephens, who embarrassed the cause of Southern Independence by asserting, "Our new government is founded . . . its foundations are laid, its cornerstone rests, upon the great truth that the negro is not equal to the white man; that slavery, subordination to the superior race, is his natural and normal condition."[11]

In this, Stephens was not entirely at odds with Lincoln. Lincoln certainly opposed slavery, but he also said in one of the Lincoln-Douglas debates: "I will say then that I am not, nor ever have been, in favor of bringing about in any way the social and political equality of the white and black races—that I am not, nor ever have been, in favor of making voters or jurors of Negroes, nor of qualifying them to hold office, nor to intermarry with white people; and I will say in addition to this that there is a physical difference between the white and black races which I believe forever forbid the two races living together on terms of social and political equality. And in as much as they cannot so live, while they do remain together there must be the position of superior and inferior, and I as much as any other man am in favor of having the superior position assigned to the white race."[12] One of his proposed solutions to the problem of slavery was setting up colonies, either in Africa or Latin America, for American blacks; ideally, he wanted to free the slaves and then send them somewhere else.

One man that Vice President Alexander Stephens certainly did not speak for was President Jefferson Davis, whose roseate view of slavery, shaped by his own experience as a planter, was of slaves who were "contented, well provided for in their physical wants, and steadily improving in their moral condition." Slavery as it existed in the South, he believed, was guided by providence to lift heathen blacks to Christianity; its end might be "the preparation of that race for civil liberty and social enjoyment"; and "it is quite within the range of possibility that the masters" would eventually, of their own volition, desire to free the slaves "when their slaves [themselves] will object."[13]

Jefferson Davis, then, saw the abolition of slavery as something that would happen peaceably in due course. This view was shared by the pre-eminent Confederate general, Robert E. Lee, who wrote to his wife shortly after Christmas in 1856, "In this enlightened age, there are few I believe, but what will acknowledge, that slavery as an institution, is a moral and political evil in any Country. It is useless to expatiate on its disadvantages." Like Davis, he believed, "the blacks are immeasurably better off here than in Africa, morally, socially and physically," and that while "we see the course of the final abolition of human slavery is onward, and we must give it all the aid of our prayers and all justifiable means in our power," Lee concluded that "emancipation will sooner result from the mild and melting influence of Christianity than from the storms and contests of fiery controversy."[14]

For Davis and for many of the great generals of the Confederacy—who were the real leaders of the new nation—arguments over slavery, and the claim of Northern moral superiority, were nothing more than a cynical Yankee ploy. The North, which had had few slaves in any event, had dispensed with slavery when it was no longer economically viable; the South would do the same—and indeed, might already be headed in that direction: slave owners, though influential, were a small minority in the South, and Southern workingmen, like Northern workingmen, had every reason not to want to compete against slave labor.

Indeed, outside of the minority of abolitionists, this was the driving force behind anti-slavery sentiment in the North: the preservation of the status of white labor. As Lyman Trumball, United States senator from Illinois, proclaimed: "we, the Republican Party, are the white man's party. We are for the free white man, and for making white labor acceptable and honorable, which it can never be when Negro slave labor is brought into competition with it."[15]

Or, in Lincoln's own words: "Whether slavery shall go into Nebraska, or other new territories, is not a matter of exclusive concern to the people who may go there. The whole nation is interested that the best use shall be made of these territories. We want them to be homes of free white people. This they cannot be, to any considerable extent, if slavery shall be planted with them. Slave states are the places for poor white people to move from."[16]

The appeal of Free States, in other words, was that they might be free of blacks. Perhaps this was why Alexis de Tocqueville noted that "Race prejudice seems stronger in those states that have abolished slavery than in those where it still exists, and nowhere is it more intolerant than in those states where slavery was never known....In the South, where slavery still exists, less trouble is taken to keep the Negro apart: they sometimes share the labors and the pleasures of the white men; people are prepared to mix with them to some extent; legislation is more harsh against them, but customs are more tolerant and gentle."[17] Many Northerners had a view of an all-white future; Southerners did not.

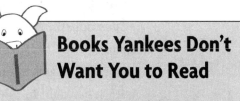

Books Yankees Don't Want You to Read

The Rise and Fall of the Confederate Government, by Jefferson Davis (Collier Books, 1961). Jefferson Davis's defense of the Southern cause is irrefutable, and this one-volume condensation, "abridged for the modern reader," makes it a relatively easy read.

In addition, if slavery were a moral trump card, if it decided who was right and who was wrong, then Britain had held moral superiority over the American colonists in 1776, for the Crown was willing to free black slaves as a wartime measure against the rebels, just as Lincoln would later do. The real issue, the real battle, was over the rights of the sovereign states, and their protection from Northern invasion.

As Confederate General Richard Taylor, the son of President Zachary Taylor, put it after the war, the people of the Confederacy "struggled in all honorable ways, and for what? For their slaves? Regret for their loss has neither been felt nor expressed. But they have striven for that which brought our forefathers to Runnymede, the privilege of exercising some influence in their own government." In bitter repudiation of Alexander Stephens, Taylor added: "Yet we fought for nothing but slavery, says the world, and the late vice-president of the Confederacy, Mr. Alexander Stephens, reechoes the cry, declaring that it was the corner-stone of his Government."[18]

The New Republic

But the real cornerstone of the Confederate government was the United States Constitution, modestly modified to meet the needs of the Southern people. The Confederate Constitution guaranteed the right to slavery, but the United States Supreme Court had already ruled that slavery was a constitutional right in the *Dred Scott* case (1857). No great change there. The Confederate Constitution also banned the importation of slaves. There would be no Confederate slave ships. The Constitution guaranteed freedom of speech and religion and incorporated the bill of rights into its basic

The Old Southern Gentleman

"For the aristocrat of Old Dixie, with all his faults and inconsistencies, did understand what the gentleman of Old Europe generally did not. He did understand the Republican ideal, the notion of the Citizen as it was understood among the noblest of the pagans. That combination of ideal democracy with real chivalry was a particular blend for which the world was immeasurably the better; and for the loss of which it is immeasurably the worse. It may never be recovered; but it will certainly be missed."

G. K. Chesterton (and Lawrence J. Clipper, editor), *Collected Works of G. K. Chesterton Volume XXXV, The Illustrated London News, 1929-1931* (Ignatius Press, 1992), 218.

structure. It limited the president to a single six-year term, granted him a line-item veto to prevent pork-barrel spending, and prohibited the Confederate Congress from issuing any tariffs or otherwise spending money on "internal improvements," except for basic necessities for navigation, harbor development, and commerce. The Confederate States of America, in short, had formed a republic with a limited government that guaranteed individual and state rights; and unlike the republic up north, didn't insist on subjugating states that didn't want to be a part of it. The Confederacy might have had slavery, as the United States did, but it was no tyranny.

What the Confederate Constitution sought to do was to preserve what Southerners believed was the original intent of the Constitution, which the North had tried to overturn. To the framers of the Confederate Constitution, sovereignty resided in the people of the states. That's how it had been in the colonial period, and how it was under the Articles of Confederation and under the Constitution of the United States. The North, however, had adopted a view not of sovereign states affiliated within a union, but of a sovereign majority of an American people, represented in the federal government.

To Southerners, this interpretation of the Constitution was flat-out wrong. The Constitution, Jefferson Davis pointed out, did not create a new *American* people; sovereignty continued to reside with the people within their respective states. "The monstrous conception of the creation of a new people, invested with the whole or a great part of the sovereignty which had previously belonged to the people of each State," Davis argued, "has not a syllable to sustain it in the Constitution."[19]

And you don't have to take Jefferson Davis's word for it. Alexis de Tocqueville said much the same in his book *Democracy in America*: "The confederation [the Union] was formed by the free will of the states; these, by uniting, did not lose their nationality or become fused in one single nation. If today one of those same states wished to withdraw its name from the contract, it would be hard to prove that it could not do so."[20]

This constitutional nicety, this guarantee of liberty (in the Southern view), is often treated in one of two ways—either it is ignored (and thus the main constitutional defense of the South is neglected) or it is dismissed, as the celebrated British military historian Major General J. F. C. Fuller dismissed it in 1932: "from the purely legal point of view," he wrote, Jefferson Davis was correct; "consequently, when in 1861 the Southern States seceded they had the law on their side. But what Jefferson Davis did not see was that the great industrial revolution was rapidly merging the individual states into 'one great consolidated State,' and that forces of circumstances had in fact replaced law."[21]

The South, being an old-fashioned place, did not bow to this progressive view; it refused to accept a future as an agricultural subsidiary of an industrious and industrial North; it thought it had a civilization of its own worth defending: one that had, over the long course of history, from the very first settlement of the Continent, diverged ever more widely from the civilization of the Northern states. And in thinking all this, the South was right.

The older, more settled parts of the South would recognize themselves in the description that Confederate veteran George Cary Eggleston penned of his memory of old Virginia:

> It was a soft, dreamy, deliciously quiet life, a life of repose, an old life, with all its sharp corners and rough surfaces long ago worn round and smooth. Everything fitted everything else, and every point in it was so well settled as to leave no work of improvement for anybody to do. The Virginians were satisfied with things as they were, and if there were reformers among them, they went elsewhere to work their changes. Society in the old Dominion was like a well-rolled and closely packed gravel walk, in which each pebble had found precisely the place it fits best. There was no giving way under one's feet, no

uncomfortable grinding of loose materials as one walked about over the firm and long-used ways of Virginia social life....The Virginians were born conservatives, constitutionally opposed to change. They loved the old because it was old, and disliked the new because it was new; for newness and rawness were well-nigh the same in their eyes.[22]

> ## The Spirit of Antebellum Virginia
>
> "Such was Virginia before the blast of war swept over her hills and down her dales—a mint-julep stirred with a sword-blade."
>
> Major General J. F. C. Fuller, *Grant & Lee: A Study in Personality and Generalship* (Indiana University Press, 1982), 25.

Granted, in the West, on the frontier, newness and rawness were to be expected. But the goal of Southern life was leisure and what Bagehot called "the conservatism of enjoyment." Men did not focus their energies on industry, but on manners. They did not seek change and reform and progress—and Southern men-folk were as politically minded as any on the planet—but rather preservation of an existing system. They were not led by divines who had left Christian doctrine behind and become Unitarians or transcendentalists or preachers of a social gospel that included abolitionism among its causes. Antebellum Southern religion was, in Professor Richard Weaver's words, "a simple acceptance of a body of belief, an innocence of protest and heresy which left religion one of the unquestioned and unquestionable supports of the general settlement under which men live."[23]

North and South were, in fact, divided in the most profound way, almost as separate civilizations, though sharing the same language and the same federal government—something that was recognized as early as the founding of the United States by John Taylor of Caroline (of Caroline County, Virginia), who was an ally of Thomas Jefferson, supporter of ratifying the Constitution, and a United States senator. He referred to the sovereign states as "state nations" (whose rights were protected by the Constitution) and to the United States as the "United Nations."

Both men envisioned the possibility of secession. Jefferson wrote to James Madison in 1798 that if the federal government could not be restrained from enforcing such laws as the Alien and Sedition Acts, the best course would be for states like Virginia and Kentucky "to sever ourselves from the union we so much value rather than give up the rights of self-government."[24] One can easily, then, imagine, had he still been alive, Jefferson supporting the Confederate States of America, with John Taylor of Caroline rallying his follow Southerners with the cry: "CSA out of the UN."

Some sixty years after the Civil War, the Southern poet Allen Tate wrote in bold historical strokes about the differences between the antebellum North and South: "In a sense, all European history since the Reformation was concentrated in the war between the North and the South. For in the South the most conservative of the European orders had, with great power, come back to life, while in the North, opposing the Southern feudalism, had grown to be a powerful industrial state which epitomized in spirit all those middle-class, urban impulses directed against the agrarian aristocracies of Europe after the Reformation."[25]

Those were the stakes: two visions of civilization, each of which despised the other. The South considered the North an unprincipled, money-grubbing, self-righteously intolerant leviathan, and thought of itself as a liberty-loving agricultural Sparta of gracious gentlemen, classical culture, and feudal order.

The North, on the contrary, considered the South a backward land of hot-tempered planter-aristocrats who kept a booted heel and a master's whip on the backs of slaves, tainted the Union with its "peculiar institution," and dragged it into wars against Mexico only to expand its hateful "slave power." The North, in its own view, was enlightened, practical, and business-like, and consequently wealthy, forward-looking, reforming, and the obvious moral superior to a region that kept imported Africans in bondage.

In the North they read *Uncle Tom's Cabin*, and waxed furious at intolerable Southern slavery. In the South they read *Ivanhoe* and dreamt of chivalry.

The North believed in Free Soil, Free Men, and industry supported by high tariffs—and in stifling the creation of slave states that would perpetuate the South's "unfair" advantage in representation (unfair because slaves counted as three-fifths of a person for representation's sake). The South believed in a free association of sovereign states, in free trade, and in the freedom of slave-owners to settle in new territories (and thus create more slave states to preserve a regional balance of power).

A Minority Institution

★ Seventy-five percent of white Southern families did not own slaves.

★ Half of all slave owners owned only one to five slaves.

★ Fewer than 1 percent of slave owners owned more than fifty slaves.

★ Not all blacks in the South were slaves. About 10 percent of blacks in the Upper South were free and made their living as laborers or small tradesmen. Less than 2 percent of blacks in the Deep South were free, but they tended to be rich and own slaves themselves.

The North believed in an indissoluble Union, led by itself—since it had the wealth, the banking, the industry, the population, and indeed the future of the country in its hands. The South believed the North was trying to extinguish the South's liberty, its prosperity, and its own vision of the future.

More than that, in the famous words of Mary Chestnut, wife of United States senator James Chestnut of South Carolina, "We separated from the North . . . because we have hated each other so."[26]

———◆◆◆———

Chapter Two

THE GUNPOWDER TRAIL

Powder kegs had been stacking up in the North and South for generations. Even in colonial days one could recognize that the Pilgrims and Puritans of New England, the free thinkers of Rhode Island, the Quakers of Pennsylvania, the landed gentlemen of Anglican Virginia, the Scotch-Irish immigrants of the back country, and the rest of the American motley were very different folk. Most of them spoke the same language, they were united first under the Crown, as members of the British Empire, and could unite in common cause, but no one would ever mistake a Northerner for a Southerner.

New England had frequently felt at odds with Southern ambitions—whether the issue was the Louisiana Purchase, the War of 1812, the annexation of Texas, or the Mexican War, all of which were considered in the Southern interest rather than the Northern. There had even been New England secessionist movements. After the Louisiana Purchase in 1803, some misfit New England Federalists, led by Senator Timothy Pickering of Massachusetts, supported the secession of New England and New York as "a new confederacy" that would be "exempt from the corrupt and corrupting influence and oppression of the aristocratic Democrats of the South."[1] In 1814, while the War of 1812 was still being fought, delegates from the New England states met at the Hartford Convention, called by

Guess What?

◆ Leading Northern abolitionists considered the Constitution "a covenant with death and an agreement with hell"

◆ Before Nat Turner's Rebellion, there were at least three times more anti-slavery societies in the South than in the North

◆ "Landslide Lincoln" won the election of 1860 with less than 40 percent of the popular vote

An Abolitionist on the Constitution

"Resolved, that the compact which exists between the North and the South is a covenant with death and an agreement with hell—involving both parties in atrocious criminality—and should be immediately annulled."

William Lloyd Garrison, head of the Massachusetts Anti-Slavery Society, 1844. His resolution was approved. As an additional dramatic gesture, he burned a copy of the Constitution and proclaimed: "So perish all compromises with tyranny!"

the Massachusetts state legislature, to discuss secession from the Southern and Western states. In the 1840s, many Northern abolitionists had similar ideas.

Likewise, South Carolina had long been a home to fire-eaters. In 1832, South Carolina had threatened secession over the "Tariff of Abominations," after asserting the state's right to nullify federal legislation noxious to its interest.

South Carolina couched its argument in the language of Thomas Jefferson and James Madison, who had supported the right of states to nullify federal laws they deemed unconstitutional. Jefferson had done so in the Kentucky Resolutions and Madison had done so in the Virginia Resolutions of 1798. The nullifiers also spoke for the economic interests of the agricultural South, which in the 1830s—thanks to high tariffs—was financing more than 70 percent of the cost of the federal government. But in 1832, South Carolina stood alone among the Southern states in threatening to nullify federal law or secede from the Union. In 1861, South Carolina was not alone. The tensions in the country had grown more severe as the sectional stakes had been ratcheted up.

As was shown by the Kentucky and Virginia Resolutions (which sought to overturn the Alien and Sedition Acts), Timothy Pickering's plot for a New England confederacy (in opposition to the Louisiana Purchase), the Hartford Convention (opposed to the War of 1812 and the trade embargo with Britain), and the nullification crisis (in opposition to high tariffs), the conflict between North and South was about more than slavery.

But, of course, it was about slavery too. Northern abolitionists were shrill in their condemnations of the South—and had been ever since 1818 when debate erupted over whether Missouri should be admitted to the Union as a slave state (of which there were currently eleven) or as a free state (of which there were also eleven). The Missouri Compromise of 1820 seemed to settle the issue. Missouri came in as a slave state, but was balanced off by the entry of Maine as a free state, and Missouri's southern border became the official dividing line—states created north of that border would be free states, beneath it would be slave states.

Thomas Jefferson did not welcome the Compromise because he thought it portended the death of the Union. The line drawn by the Missouri Compromise was all too obviously a battle line, for a "geographical line, coinciding with a marked principle, moral and political, once conceived and held up to the angry passions of men, will never be obliterated; and every new irritation will mark it deeper and deeper." He also believed that Congress had acted unconstitutionally, because it was not within Congress's power "to regulate the condition of the different descriptions of men composing a state. This certainly is the exclusive right of every state, which nothing in the Constitution has taken from them and given to the general government." For Jefferson, the Compromise was "like a firebell in the night, [which] awakened and filled me with terror. I considered it at once as the knell of the Union. It is hushed, indeed, for the moment. But this is a reprieve only, not a final sentence." Slavery was the cause, and while Jefferson believed that eventually "emancipation and *expatriation* could be effected; and gradually, and with due sacrifices . . . as it is, we have the wolf by the ears, and we can neither hold him, nor safely let him go. Justice is in one scale, and self-preservation in the other."[2]

Abolitionists help abolish the Union

Many Southerners agreed with Jefferson that slavery had left them holding a "wolf by the ears." Why? One reason was the Haitian Revolution, a slave uprising that lasted from 1791 to 1804, and that was full of gruesome stories of black slaves mutilating, raping, and murdering the French colonists, until every white man, woman, and child was extirpated from the island.

Before the Haitian Revolution, many Southerners accepted slavery as an unfortunate inheritance. After the Haitian Revolution they regarded it as an unfortunate necessity. The Francophile Thomas Jefferson, who was

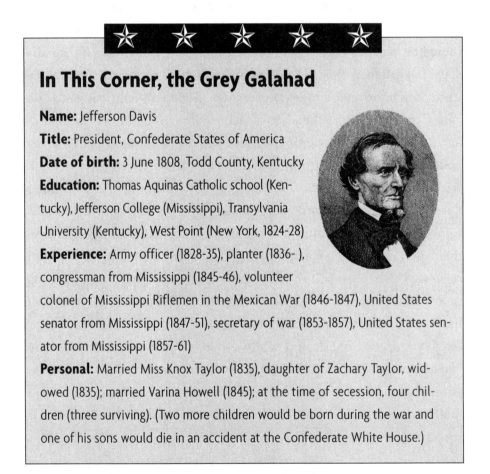

In This Corner, the Grey Galahad

Name: Jefferson Davis

Title: President, Confederate States of America

Date of birth: 3 June 1808, Todd County, Kentucky

Education: Thomas Aquinas Catholic school (Kentucky), Jefferson College (Mississippi), Transylvania University (Kentucky), West Point (New York, 1824-28)

Experience: Army officer (1828-35), planter (1836-), congressman from Mississippi (1845-46), volunteer colonel of Mississippi Riflemen in the Mexican War (1846-1847), United States senator from Mississippi (1847-51), secretary of war (1853-1857), United States senator from Mississippi (1857-61)

Personal: Married Miss Knox Taylor (1835), daughter of Zachary Taylor, widowed (1835); married Varina Howell (1845); at the time of secession, four children (three surviving). (Two more children would be born during the war and one of his sons would die in an accident at the Confederate White House.)

president from 1801 to 1809, was as alarmed as any Southern slaveholder by the ferocity of the rebels. He supported Napoleon Bonaparte's attempts to crush them. Before the Haitian Revolution, he had privately toyed with the idea of a gradual emancipation; now he hardened himself against it.

While the Haitian Revolution had led to the deaths of more than 80,000 whites and an untold number of blacks, a far fewer number—fifty-seven white men, women, and children—were killed in Nat Turner's Uprising of 1831. But it was much closer to home, in the green and pleasant land of Virginia. Southern slaveholders often told themselves that their blacks were content and well taken care of—and in many cases they might have been. But on plantations across the South, in counties where blacks could easily outnumber whites, memories of Nat Turner and the Haitians flickered and the nightmare remained.

Being a kind master was no salvation. Turner acknowledged that his own master had been kind. Nor was freeing the blacks an obvious solution:

In This Corner, the Blue Bomber

Name: Abraham Lincoln

Date of birth: 12 February 1809, Nolin Creek, Kentucky

Title: President, United States of America

Education: Self-educated

Experience: Clerk, three months in the state militia, ran a town store that went bust, postmaster, surveyor, Illinois State legislator (1834-42), lawyer (1836-60), congressman from Illinois (1846-48).

Personal: Married Mary Todd (1842), four sons, two surviving. (One died in 1862 at the White House.)

Turner had seventy followers, some of whom were free blacks. Nor was education or Christianity apparently any help. Turner had been taught to read, became a Baptist preacher, fancied himself a prophet, and felt inspired by a vision to kill every white person he could find. In short, he was mad.

He bore, in fact, a striking resemblance to another mad man—this one white, and a darling of the abolitionists—who began a campaign of murder in the hope of sparking a massive slave insurrection in the South: John Brown.

Turner and Brown helped convince Southerners that they had no friends in the North. Before Turner's uprising, as memories of Haiti faded, there was widespread abolitionist sentiment in the South. In 1827, there were 130 anti-slavery societies in the United States—more than 100 of those were in the South, and drew their support from Southern evangelical Christians. They had political clout too. In 1830, Thomas Jefferson's grandson (Thomas Jefferson Randolph, later commissioned a colonel in the Confederate Army) opened a debate in the Virginia Assembly on manumitting the slaves. Immediately after Turner's rebellion, the Virginia legislature actually considered—and nearly approved—freeing and deporting the state's slaves, but opted instead for what seemed the more practical alternative: imposing stringent laws that, among other things, denied slaves the right to an education so that they could not preach an unholy gospel, as Turner had done. A man who would later gain fame in Confederate grey—Thomas Jonathan "Stonewall" Jackson—was one of the most prominent breakers of this law, running a Sunday school for blacks that taught them to read and write.

If Nat Turner's rebellion helped erase Southern anti-slavery sentiment, the effect of John Brown's raid on Harpers Ferry was worse. Southerners had always been appalled at the violence of Northern abolitionist rhetoric. They regarded such Northerners as imperious know-nothings who would bear none of the consequences of abolition and simply, captiously, demanded that it be done—as if overturning the economic, social, and political structure of the South was a trifle. They were, in Southern eyes, would-be arsonists, fanning flames that could ignite a holocaust. John Brown seemed to personify the abolitionist as arsonist, terrorist, and murderer. Even Lincoln, to his credit, thought Brown a fanatic, but to the dismay of Southerners, many Northern abolitionists considered Brown a martyr.

Brown first came to national attention in another North-South conflict. This one was caused by Stephen Douglas's Kansas-Nebraska Act of 1854, which repealed the Missouri Compromise. Douglas's scheme was to repeal the Compromise in order to win Southern votes for the transcontinental railway that would run through Nebraska and Kansas (and his home state of Illinois) rather than take the Southern route—the shortest route and the one favored by Secretary of War Jefferson Davis—running from San Diego to New Orleans. The United States had already made the Gadsen Purchase, buying additional Mexican territory through which the railway would run if it took the Southern route.

Books Yankees Don't Want You to Read

The History of the Confederacy, 1832-1865, by Clifford Dowdey (Barnes & Noble Books, 1989, originally published as *The Land They Fought For*). Dowdey is one of the best historians of the War.

Under the Kansas-Nebraska Act, the Nebraska Territory would divide into the states of Kansas and Nebraska, and these states could decide for themselves whether they would enter the union as free states or slave states. The Act was an attempt of bribery on Douglas's part. While Nebraska's fate was essentially already decided—it would be a free state—Douglas dangled the prospect of Kansas, which under the Missouri Compromise should also have been a free state, as a potential slave state. It was a terrible idea, which only turned Kansas into "bleeding Kansas," as "free-soil" partisans and pro-slavery partisans rushed not to settle the territory but to unsettle it: Northern "Jayhawkers" on the one side, Southern "border ruffians" on the other.

Northerners held the numerical upper hand—indeed, did so overwhelmingly—because Southerners wealthy enough to own slaves were generally content to stay where they were, and certainly not eager to risk their wealth in a violent new territory. But the border ruffians from Missouri gave the pro-slavery faction a political head start. They ensured that pro-slavery gunmen staffed the polling places so that Southern rights were respected.

Northern immigration to Kansas became a crusade, attracting men like John Brown. Brown responded to the border ruffians with a declaration of holy war against them—or against innocents who happened to look like them. In 1856, at Pottawatomie Creek, Brown and his accomplices kidnapped five innocent pro-slavery settlers and—like the later Lizzie Borden—gave them the equivalent of forty whacks. This was Brown's warm-up for his raid on Harpers Ferry, Virginia, in 1859.

Not content with murder in Kansas, John Brown aimed to foment a slave insurrection in Virginia. His first target, however, was not a slave owner but the slaveless federal arsenal at Harpers Ferry. Brown and his twenty men crept into Harpers Ferry before dawn, killed two men (one of them a free black), and easily captured the rifle works and an extremely well-stocked armory. To strengthen his hand he seized sixty hostages among the townspeople (including Colonel Lewis Washington, a kinsman of George Washington). Then he waited for a wave of slaves to well up and form his Mameluke army with which he would sweep away the "peculiar institution" in a purgation of blood.

But his rebellious slaves never came. Instead, the Maryland militia came and trapped Brown and his men within the town's fire-engine house adjacent to the armory. The War Department in Washington summoned Colonel Robert E. Lee[3] to command a detachment of Marines. Lee ordered the Marines to attack the firehouse with sledgehammers (to break into it) and bayonets; their muskets were unloaded in order to avoid civilian casualties.

Brown was captured and put on trial—giving him a forum to become a hero to abolitionists—and then hanged. One of Brown's gifts was a mesmerizing presence and a biblical eloquence; even those who knew him to be a fanatic were impressed by his words and his self-possessed dignity in the court room. He told the court that not only was he willing to give his life to free the slaves, he was willing to give the lives of *millions* to free the slaves. "Now, if it is deemed necessary that I should forfeit my life for the furtherance of the ends of justice and mingle my blood further with the blood of my children and with the blood of millions in this slave country whose rights are disregarded by wicked, cruel, and unjust enactments, I say, let it be done."[4]

Radicals in the North now had their martyr. The South, which, initially, had not been troubled by Brown's crime—Lee had dismissed it as a riot—was shocked at the outpouring of Northern abolitionist rhetoric proclaiming the virtues of a murderer and would-be terrorist who welcomed the death of millions if it would end slavery. The North's reaction to Brown's execution convinced the South that the United States was indeed a house divided, and that the South had better fortify its half of the estate.

Lincoln's dilemma

That was 1859. There was a presidential election in 1860, and on election day, there were four candidates for president: Abraham Lincoln of the Republican Party (founded 1854), the party of the moral majority whose political platform pledged its opposition to both slavery and polygamy (an issue because of Mormon Utah); Stephen Douglas of the Democrat Party, which stood for nothing but opportunism; John C. Breckinridge, James Buchanan's vice president, running as a "National Democrat" (which really meant "Southern Democrat"); and Tennessean John

Bell who ran under the banner of the Constitutional Union Party, which represented "the anti-extremist Old Gentleman's Party" of the Upper South.

The results were definitive. Lincoln swept Maine, New Hampshire, Vermont, Massachusetts, Rhode Island, Connecticut, New York, Pennsylvania, Ohio, Michigan, Indiana, Illinois, Wisconsin, Iowa, Minnesota, and Oregon, and squeaked out a victory in California, where the vote totals divided into near even thirds between Lincoln, Douglas, and Breckinridge. Stephen Douglas won only Missouri and three of New Jersey's seven electoral votes (the other four went to Lincoln). Breckinridge won in Texas, Louisiana, Arkansas, Mississippi, Alabama, Florida, Georgia, South Carolina, North Carolina, Maryland, and Delaware. The great John Bell took the gentlemanly bourbon-sipping electors of Tennessee, Kentucky, and Virginia. More telling than the tally of states was the tally of electoral votes. Lincoln had won more electors (180) than his combined opponents: Breckinridge (72), Bell (39), and Douglas (a measly 12).

The new president, however, did not enjoy a political honeymoon; he confronted what he had predicted, a house divided, and with his manly rail-splitter sinews, he tried to squeeze it back together.

In his First Inaugural speech, delivered 4 March 1861, one month after the creation of the Provisional Government of the Confederate States of

Landslide Lincoln

In the election of 1860, Abraham Lincoln won slightly less than 40 percent of the popular vote. Stephen Douglas took almost 30 percent of the vote, John C. Breckinridge had 18 percent (and won almost all the Southern states), and John Bell had more than 12 percent (winning three states of the upper South). If the Democrats had been united, they still would have lost, shifting only the electoral votes of California and Oregon, which shows just how outnumbered in electoral college votes the South had become: a Democrat candidate could have taken 60 percent of the popular vote and still lost the election.

America, he asserted his right to execute federal law in every state that participated in the 1860 federal election and to "possess the property and places belonging to the government, and to collect the duties and imposts." He proposed to do this, in other words, in states that had not only declared their independence from the Union, but had formed a new Southern Confederacy. If Lincoln ever felt sympathy for King George III, it would have been understandable. He was trying to enforce his authority over a people who denied it.

He added what amounted to a declaration of war that denied it was a declaration of war: "In *your* hands, my dissatisfied fellow-countrymen, and not in *mine*, is the momentous issue of civil war. The government will not assail *you*. You can have no conflict without yourselves being the aggressors. You have no oath registered in heaven to destroy the government, while I shall have the most solemn one to 'preserve, protect, and defend' it."[5]

Lincoln said that if the South was dissatisfied with the result of the election, it had two choices: "Whenever they shall grow weary of the existing Government, they can exercise their *constitutional* right of amending it or their *revolutionary* right to dismember or overthrow it."[6] But it was disingenuous in the extreme to uphold revolution as a right, and not secession. When the colonists had declared their independence from the Crown in 1776 they had seceded from the British Empire; they did not seek to storm Buckingham Palace or the Parliament at Westminster. So too, Jefferson Davis and his fellow Southerners had no desire to overthrow the government of the United States or conquer those who wished to belong to it. The South merely wanted to go its own way, which is why the Civil War should really be called the War for Southern Independence or the War of Northern Aggression. President Jefferson Davis, in his first message to the Confederate Congress, put the South's case in eight simple words: "All we ask is to be let alone."[7]

Lincoln's position was especially disingenuous given that he had once held secession—referring specifically to Texas's secession from Mexico—as a fundamental, universal human right: "Any people anywhere, being inclined and having the power, have the right to rise up and shake off the existing government and form a new one that suits them better. This is a most valuable—a most sacred right—a right, which we hope and believe, is to liberate the world. Nor is this right confined to cases in which the whole people of an existing government, may choose to exercise it. Any portion of such people that can, may revolutionize, and make their own, of so much of their territory as they inhabit."[8]

What then, was the problem? Well, circumstances had changed, and Lincoln now sided with Santa Anna rather than the Texans. There was still, however, the need for a *casus belli*. During the Mexican War, which Congressman Lincoln opposed—and in which men like Jefferson Davis, Robert E. Lee, and Thomas Jonathan Jackson fought—Lincoln demanded to know at precisely what spot, on which side of the border, American blood had been shed to justify the war. Now he earnestly wanted to wage war against his former fellow countrymen. But to do so he needed the fulfillment of his previous "Spot Resolutions." He needed the South to fire on Union troops.

"Fort Sumter's been fired upon, my regiment leaves at dawn"

There were some in the North who thought the Union should let its "erring sisters depart in peace." Fort Sumter changed all that. Though no one died at Fort Sumter, though Lincoln could not point to the fort and say that Union blood had been shed, the roar of cannons against the fort was echoed by a roar of Northern fury to preserve the Union. Lincoln had successfully goaded the South into firing the first shot, and reaping the unfortunate consequences.

Of course, things looked rather different from the landward side of Charleston Harbor. Fort Sumter could not exist in South Carolinian waters with its canons pointing at Charleston. It, like other federal properties on Southern land or in Southern waters, had to be surrendered. In exchange, the South offered not only to pay for the properties, but to pay the South's portion of the federal debt of the United States.

These Southern offers, however, were solutions Lincoln did not want to hear. Nor did he desire to meet with Southern representatives sent to defuse the crisis, despite the intervention of two associate justices of the Supreme Court on their behalf. The issue was first principles. The South could not secede. It was irretrievably bound to the United States. While Fort Sumter was, one would think, erected for the protection of the people of Charleston, it must now remain as a federal fort directed *against* the people of Charleston and their desire to be free of federal authority.

Sumter's importance was in part symbolic. It and Fort Pickens at Pensacola, Florida, were the only two Federal forts in the new Confederate republic that had not

Books Yankees Don't Want You to Read

The Story of the Confederacy, by Robert Selph Henry (Da Capo Press, reprint, no date; foreword by Douglas Southall Freeman). Originally published in 1931, it remains a classic history.

surrendered to the Confederate States of America. Had Fort Sumter been peaceably surrendered, the initial crisis confronting North and South would have been defused. But as a Federal citadel in Charleston Harbor, the seat of secession, it was regarded as an intolerable provocation, irritant, and threat.

The issue was not just Charleston harbor, of course. Lincoln had vowed to collect "duties and imposts"—tariffs—in the South. Tariffs amounted to 95 percent of federal revenue, and the Morrill Tariff of 1861 (signed into law by President James Buchanan) had more than doubled tariff duties. The

South had opposed the tariff, the North had supported it, and now, though South Carolina had left the Union, Lincoln proposed to enforce it.

Ratcheting up the pressure, on 6 April 1861, Lincoln announced that he was sending men and supplies to Sumter—men who would not fire, he pledged, unless fired upon. It was apparent now to the Confederates that if they were to take possession of the fort, they could not wait. On 12 April 1861, after gentlemanly negotiations between Confederate General P. G. T. Beauregard and the fort's commander, Kentucky-born Major Robert Anderson, failed to win surrender of the fort, Beauregard ordered his artillerists to open fire on Fort Sumter. Two days later, the fort was his.

The South had won the stand-off over Fort Sumter, but it had also handed Lincoln the victory he sought—the South had fired first. Lincoln now had his righteous cause—to put down the rebel insurrection.

Lincoln had closed his inaugural speech by saying: "We are not enemies, but friends. We must not be enemies. Though passion may have strained it must not break our bonds of affection. The mystic chords of memory, stretching from every battlefield and patriot grave to every living heart and hearthstone all over this broad land, will yet swell the chorus of the Union, when again touched, as surely they will be, by the better angels of our nature."[9]

Beautiful sentiments, but one has to wonder whether seeking to wage war on one's fellow Americans, as Lincoln was committed to do, is actually a reflection of the better angels of our nature. Arkansas, Tennessee, North Carolina, and Virginia thought it wasn't, and rather than join in the suppression of the Southern states, they seceded as well—and the Confederate government swiftly moved from Montgomery, Alabama, to Richmond, Virginia.

For these Southern states, the "mystic chords of memory" were strong indeed. Robert E. Lee spoke for them when he declined command of the Union forces, "stating as candidly and courteously as I could, that though opposed to secession and deprecating war, I could take no part in the invasion of the Southern states."[10] Earlier he had confessed, "a Union that can only be maintained by swords and bayonets...has no charm for me....If the Union is dissolved and government disrupted, I shall return to my native state and share the miseries of my people and save in defense will draw my sword on none."[11] He made good on that promise and took the position that every humane man can echo: "With all my devotion to the Union and the feeling of loyalty and duty as an American citizen, I have not been able to make up my mind to raise my hand against my relatives, my children, my home."[12] So spoke a man who had served the flag of the United States his entire adult life, a West Pointer, a former superintendent at West Point, a veteran of the Mexican War.

But Abraham Lincoln—the man who thought the Mexican War wrong, even if it had brought the United States California, Utah, Nevada, and Arizona, and parts of Colorado, Wyoming, and New Mexico, as well as a greater Texas, with little resistance in those territories—thought it perfectly

We're All Confederates Now

Put yourself in Robert E. Lee's shoes. If the South seceded today, how many of us would think the proper response would be for the federal government to send tanks over the bridges spanning the Potomac into Virginia, to blockade Southern ports and carpet bomb Southern cities? If we don't, it's because we see the United States as the Confederacy saw it, *as a voluntary union.* The idea that we have to keep California, Mississippi, Minnesota, and Maine together by force would probably strike us as ridiculous. And if it came to that, it would probably strike us as horrendous and wrong.

right to wage war, total war, against his fellow Americans. It would last four years and be the bloodiest war in our history.

Pride versus power

On paper, the war was decided before it was fought. The Federal forces had a four-to-one advantage in available fighting manpower (counting only white males) and an industrial base that outweighed the South by an even larger proportion. In terms of manufactured goods, Massachusetts alone produced 60 percent more than the entire Confederacy. Other Northern states—New York and Pennsylvania—produced double the Confederacy's total. Likewise, banking and ready capital belonged to the North, not the South, by a ratio of three to one. Nine-tenths of Southern savings were, in fact, in Northern banks.

Books Yankees Don't Want You to Read

Their Tattered Flags: The Epic of the Confederacy, by Frank E. Vandiver. (Texas A&M University Press, 1989). A spirited retelling, Vandiver was a military historian and president of Texas A&M.

The North had 22,000 miles of railroad track laid, to only 9,000 for the South—and much of the South's track ran on differing gauges, which made transportation difficult, as did the comparative lack of roads. The South had 3,000 miles of coastline, but shipbuilding was a Yankee art and shipping a Yankee business. In fact, just about everything was a Yankee business. The Deep South had virtually no factories. Only the secession of Virginia gave the South a foundry to cast artillery. The South had few pharmacies either, and the North declared medicines contraband, so whiskey became the Southern anesthetic of choice.

The South was wealthy in only three commodities—cotton (nine-tenths of the world's supply came from the South), tobacco (good for spitting in the eyes of Yankees), and pride (a conviction that any Johnny Reb could whup any three, or possibly ten, Billy Yanks).

The South initially thought that if it withheld its "white gold" for sale on world markets, it could compel powers like France and Britain to intervene on its behalf—what it really did was assist the United States Navy. On 19 April 1861, Lincoln ordered Southern ports blockaded, an act of war that the United States Navy was not yet large enough to enforce. Nevertheless, the South, with its typical courtesy, kindly did the Navy's work for it by not exporting its cotton. It eventually realized its error, but too late—relying on daring blockade-runners to try to bring goods into Southern ports. As the blockade tightened, the South was left with only one partially opened port in Wilmington, North Carolina. Southerners were never as clever as Yankees when it came to money.

It was its martial prowess—its men born to the saddle and to arms, the military tradition of its aristocrats, and the raw-boned rebel yell of its small farmers, workingmen, and frontiersmen in which the South trusted. It had never claimed to be an industrial power like the North. It had disdained Northern efficiency in favor of manners and charm. Yet when Lincoln's armies crossed the Potomac, the South was ready with serried ranks of armed, equipped, and uniformed men led by more than competent generals. The Federals would find that Southern fighting prowess was no trifling matter.

Part II

★ ★ ★ ★ ★ ★ ★ ★

THE HISTORY OF
THE WAR IN SIXTEEN BATTLES
YOU SHOULD KNOW

Chapter Three

———◆◆◆———

DIXIE RISING,
1861-1863

Most wars start with a mixture of trepidation and excitement. For the North, the trepidation came not only from the prospect of war, but from Southern sympathizers known as "Copperheads" (because they sometimes wore copper pennies so they could recognize each other in public). Pro-Southern Democrats were plentiful in the Border States of Maryland, Missouri, and Kentucky, but also as far afield as Ohio and New York City. Maryland's were especially worrisome, because between them and Confederate Virginia, the more nervously inclined Washingtonians could feel surrounded. But Lincoln's deft suspension of civil liberties, imposition of martial law, and jailing of suspected secessionist sympathizers (including Baltimore's mayor and police chief, thirty-one Maryland state legislators, and the grandson of Francis Scott Key, author of "The Star Spangled Banner") alleviated most of the trepidation. The Supreme Court protested that the president had no right to suspend the writ of habeas corpus. Lincoln replied that he had a war to fight. As he had the army on his side, and the Supreme Court did not, Lincoln won the argument. It is a mode of debate that other presidents might want to try with the Court. All told, Lincoln's administration jailed more than 13,000 political prisoners—a fact you won't find in most history books (but you've found it here).[1]

Guess What?

✦ The official newspaper of the Vatican editorialized on behalf of the South

✦ The idea of bombing people "back to the Stone Age" got its start with the Federal siege of Vicksburg

✦ The Emancipation Proclamation did not free a single slave— and caused draft riots in the North

Holy Horses, Batman!

Visitors to historic Southern churches might be surprised at the frequency with which they find a marker that reads: "Union cavalry stabled their horses in the church." This is true from The Falls Church (Episcopal) in Virginia (where Founding Fathers George Washington and George Mason where vestrymen) to The First Presbyterian Church of Holly Springs, Mississippi. Whether this represented the high regard they had for their horses, ("Take a pew, Trigger."), or their low regard for Southern churches is open to question. It's fair to note, though, that they occasionally used churches for target practice too. Some of Southern, or Christian, inclinations might find such behavior a trifle impious.

The excitement came from the fact that the rebel capital was only a hundred miles away. The Federals already had advanced footholds in pro-Unionist western Virginia (which would be annexed as the separate state of West Virginia) and in Alexandria and Arlington, Virginia, where they occupied the home of Robert E. Lee, with the design, in due course, of turning it into a national cemetery.

The Federal plan was to march to Richmond but Confederate armies were forming to block their way. The flashpoint was the railroad junction at Manassas, a mere thirty miles from Washington.

First Manassas (21 July 1861)

The Background:

The Confederate commanders were generals Joseph E. Johnston and P. G. T. Beauregard. Johnston, the highest-ranking U.S. Army general to join the Confederacy, was a Virginian, a West Pointer, and would prove himself the most adept retreater in Confederate service. If there were a decoration for "Retreater-in-Chief with Oak Leaf Cluster," he would have deserved it. The Louisiana-born Beauregard was a man of many talents. He designed the Confederate battle flag, he was an engineer who had graduated second in his class at West Point, and he was the shortest-lived superintendent in the history of West Point, serving all of five days (23 to 28 January 1861) before it became apparent that having a Confederate in charge of training officers for the Union might be a mistake.

Against the Confederates was mustered the largest army ever seen on the North American continent. Under the command of General Irvin McDowell, another West Pointer, an Ohioan whose buckeye horizons had been broadened by a French education, was the Union army of Northeastern Virginia (which became the more famous Army of the Potomac). The Federal troops were inexperienced, but gaily dressed—some as French-Moroccan Zouaves, others as imitation Highlanders—and Lincoln was eager to see them put into action. So were civilians from Washington who turned out to picnic and watch the battle. They were given a heck of a show.

The Battle:

McDowell's men struck the Confederates on the hot, humid morning of 21 July 1861, and steadily pushed back the Confederate left until South Carolina General Bernard Bee saw, over the ridge of Henry Hill, General Thomas Jonathan Jackson's Virginians waiting to repel the Federals. Bee rallied his men with the cry: "There is Jackson standing like a stone wall! Let us determine to die here and we will conquer! Follow me!"[2] At least that's how he's sometimes quoted. The National Park Service prefers: "There stands Jackson like a stone wall. Rally behind the Virginians," which certainly has a better ring to it. And there are some ignoble fellows who believe Bee's actual sentiment was: "There's Jackson standing like a dadburned stone wall! Why the heck doesn't he do something!"

In fact, Jackson's bayonets thwarted the blue-belly tide.

Hit on both flanks (William Tecumseh Sherman was hitting the Confederate right), the lines reformed around Jackson, who coolly appraised the enemy and intended to "give them the bayonet." Confederate artillery proved useful too, as did musketry and saber thrusts. Jackson forced the federals back with a ferocious charge, but a sort of bloody equilibrium had been reached with the Federal and Confederate lines receiving continuous reinforcements. Finally, in the afternoon, the Yankees heard a banshee rebel yell piercing through the reverberating gunfire; then they saw Confederate Colonel Jubal A. Early's men smashing into their right flank. Stunned and exhausted, the Federals fell back, and at the prodding of Confederate artillery, the retreat accelerated until it become a pell-mell Federal flight to the capital—soldiers with their rifles and packs; civilians with their picnic baskets.

What You Need to Know:

At the end of the battle, President Jefferson Davis rode to Henry Hill, where Confederate wounded, including Jackson, were being treated, and ordered: "I am President Davis! All of you who are able follow me back to the field!" Davis, who always preferred to ride to the sound of the guns, wanted to take his commander in chief responsibilities rather more literally than most presidents. The wounded "Stonewall" Jackson was game. He said: "Give me ten thousand men and I will take Washington tomorrow."

It's Not the Stars and Bars

"The Stars and Bars" is the nickname of the First National Flag of the Confederacy. But when people think of the "Confederate flag" what they usually have in mind is the Confederate battle flag, with its familiar St. Andrew's Cross. The battle flag, designed by General P. G. T. Beauregard, has thirteen stars, though only eleven states seceded. This is because Missouri and Kentucky, which had pro-Confederate governors, were considered Confederate states by the Confederate Congress. It was also of symbolic benefit, reminding the South that its thirteen states were rebelling against King Lincoln as the thirteen colonies had rebelled against King George.

But rain began to fall, mud began to form, and cooler—and wronger—heads thought that the dispersed and tired Confederates needed to rest and reform, not harry the retreating Yankees. In one way, it didn't matter. If shocking the North was the intention, the North was well and truly shocked. The Northern war of aggression would be no picnic. In another more important way it did matter. What would have been the outcome had Stonewall Jackson ridden into Washington and captured Honest Abe at gunpoint? One can only wonder whether the North wouldn't have said to the Southern states, "Er, gosh, sorry for the invasion of Virginia. Why don't we call this whole war thing off? Oh, and may we have our president back?"

Shiloh (6-7 April 1862)

The Background:

In Virginia, Stonewall Jackson kept the Federals baffled in the Shenandoah Valley and fearful of a possible Confederate attack on Washington; that, and the fact that General George McClellan was now in command of Federal forces, meant stasis on the Eastern front.

In the West, things were going badly for the Confederacy. Confederate General (and Episcopal bishop) Leonidas Polk had been the first to trespass troops into officially neutral Kentucky (which had a pro-Confederate governor and a pro-Union legislature), but the Federal counterthrust put much of the state in Union hands. Missouri was a goner too, and Federal troops were on the march in Arkansas and Tennessee.

The Union hero of the West was Ulysess S. Grant—a fighting general whose victory at Fort Donelson, Tennessee, 16 February 1862 had won him the nickname of "Unconditional Surrender" Grant. Grant was now at Pittsburgh Landing, Tennessee. Grant's Union army of the Tennessee had 42,000 troops (37,000 immediately at hand, 5,000 a short march away) and he was looking to combine his forces with General Don Carlos Buell's Army of the Ohio, numbering about 50,000 men, who were occupying Nashville.

Before these two giant Union armies merged, Confederate General Albert Sidney Johnston wanted to smash one of them. A Kentucky-born, Louisiana-raised West Pointer, before the war Johnston had been considered the finest Southern officer in the Army. As the Confederate West crumbled, his reputation had crumbled too. Attacking Grant was to be his redemption; the result was the battle of Shiloh.

The Battle:

Beauregard, Johnston's second-in-command, had drawn up the plan, and at dawn, Sunday, 6 April 1862, Johnston's rebel-yelling Confederates put it into action, bursting upon the unprepared Union encampment, announcing themselves by shooting dead an aide standing next to General Sherman. The Confederates drove the Federals back: Sherman was on the Union right, General John McClernand holding the Union center behind the Shiloh church. On the Union left was General Benjamin Prentiss, whose troops found a sunken road forming a natural trench where they could reform and mow down charging Confederates. The rebels dubbed this part of the Yankee line "the Hornets' Nest." The Confederate attack all along the line was so powerful that Grant thought he was facing 100,000 men—and it is proof of his mettle that he resolved to fight it out.

The Hornets' Nest held together—even under Confederate artillery attack—but no other part of the Union line did, as Sherman and McClernand continued their fighting retreats. With Confederates encircling the nest, and more than half of his men dead, Prentiss finally surrendered. As daylight petered out, Beauregard called off any further advances. Albert Sidney Johnston was dead—killed leading a charge against a heavily fortified peach orchard near the Hornets' Nest—but the Confederates had won the field. Beauregard thought his men needed to be regrouped; they could finish off Grant's army in the morning.

But Grant was resolute. In the morning, with 26,000 reinforcements, he counterattacked, and in a military *danse macabre*, the battle of the day before was repeated, though this time it was the rebels who fought on the retreat. By mid-afternoon, the Federals had pushed all the way back to their original lines, and Beauregard conceded the ground.

What You Need to Know:

There were more casualties—24,000—at Shiloh than there had been in the American War of Independence, the War of 1812, and the Mexican War *combined*, and yet the battle itself was a bloody draw. After Shiloh, Grant said: "I gave up all idea of saving the Union except by complete conquest."[3]

The Shenandoah Valley Campaign (1862)

The Background:

General McClellan had assembled a massive 150,000 man army to attack Richmond, but before he launched his men down the Peninsula, he needed to deal with Stonewall Jackson in the Shenandoah Valley. As long as Jackson roamed the Valley, the government in Washington could not rest easy. General Nathaniel Banks and his 38,000 troops were given the job of destroying or dispersing Jackson's forces and then joining McClellan for the "on to Richmond" campaign.

The Campaign:

In practice, it didn't work out that way. Jackson's swift-moving infantry, or "foot cavalry," never numbered more than 6,000 men, but their mysterious marches, countermarches, and sudden attacks, were enough to mislead, surprise, and defeat the enemy throughout the Shenandoah Valley campaign of 1862 in the battles at Kernstown (23 March, a tactical

★ ★ ★ ★ ★ ★ ★

The *Monitor* and the *Merrimac*

Naval warfare was supposed to favor the Federals—seafaring, after all, was associated with New England. But it was the Confederacy that sent the first ironclad ship into battle, the *Virginia* (built on the remains of the sunken *Merrimac*). The *Virginia*, though extremely slow, with a creaky engine and without much firepower (only ten guns), proved extremely efficient in its first encounter with the enemy on 8 March 1862. It sank the USS *Cumberland* (which packed thirty guns), defeated the USS *Congress* (a fifty-gun frigate), which ran aground and struck its colors, and survived the attacks of a fleet of gunships and shore batteries at Newport News. It also gave a serious fright to the U.S. Secretary of War Edwin Stanton who blubbered,

> "The Merrimac will change the whole character of the war: she will destroy, seriatim, every naval vessel; she will lay all the cities on the seaboard under contribution. I shall immediately recall Burnside; Port Royal must be abandoned. I will notify the governors and municipal authorities in the North to take instant measures to protect their harbors.... Not unlikely, we shall have a shell or cannonball from one of her guns before we leave this room."*

In the event, nothing so dramatic happened. The next day the Federals hurried their own ironclad, the USS *Monitor* (which actually had seniority, launching a little over a month earlier), to battle the Confederate sea beast, and the two ironclad ships fought to a draw. And that was the last battle fought by the CSS *Virginia* that Stanton so feared would ravage the entire Union coastline and send a cannonball into the White House. The CSS *Virginia* tried to bring the *Monitor* to battle again, but the nimbler Union ship dodged every attempted attack. Finally, on 11 May 1862, after the Federals occupied Norfolk, the *Virginia*'s crew scuttled her. She had a short, if gallant, fighting career.

---

* Quoted in Robert Selph Henry, *The Story of the Confederacy* (Da Capo, 1964), 109.

defeat but a strategic victory because it diverted troops from McClellan's Richmond campaign), McDowell (8 May), Front Royal (23 May), Winchester (25 May), Cross Keys (8 June), and Port Republic (9 June).

What You Need to Know:

Not only did Jackson save the Valley, he deprived Union General McClellan of tens of thousands of troops he wanted for his offensive against Richmond, as Federal forces in the Valley were reinforced and sent to capture Jackson. The only troops that slipped out of the Valley to fight near Richmond were Jackson's own, when Robert E. Lee, taking due note of the clever commander of the Valley, summoned him to Richmond's defense at the battle of Seven Days.

The Seven Days (25 June to 1 July 1862)

The Background:

Richmond remained the prize that captured the Federals' imagination. With McClellan's enormous army, surely it could be taken, and the war swiftly won. True, McClellan's 150,000 men had been whittled down to 100,000, with troops diverted to defend Washington or fight Stonewall Jackson. But this was still more than double the size of any Confederate army that could be turned against them, though McClellan could never believe that he faced so few when they fought so well.

McClellan, regarded as a military genius, a young Napoleon, had a plan: he would not be a military primitive. He would not slog straight down from Washington to Fredericksburg to Richmond against heavy Confederate resistance. No, he would employ the Navy to land his troops at Fort Monroe on Virginia's coastline. From there he had a march of only seventy-five miles to the Confederate capital, and the Navy could support him along the James River.

The landing was an enormous operation—more than 120,000 men were eventually landed—and conducted extremely well. An Englishman who saw it said it marked "the stride of a giant."[4] The giant, however, found his way blocked by fewer than 15,000 Confederates at Yorktown. Presumably, he could have brushed this force aside, so mighty was his right hand, but the Young Napoleon was, as ever, cautious about the dangerous Johnny Rebs and spent a month in elaborate siege of a Confederate force that marched up and down behind its entrenchments successfully convincing the Yanks that its numbers were legion. When they finally got footsore and withdrew, the Young Napoleon advanced again.

He had hoped the Navy would advance with him, but Confederate defenders at Drewry's Bluff, seven miles from the rebel capital, convinced the Federals that the James River was impassable as it approached the city. So McClellan was on his own—or as on his own as he could be with more than 120,000 troops now under his command. He marched them to a point five miles from the city. The blue-coated infantry could see the spires of the church steeples—and Confederate General Joseph E. Johnston could see the Federal forces massing before him. He had about 40,000 men to meet the Federals at the Battle of Seven Pines (or Fair Oaks) on 31 May 1862. On that day he did the best service he ever did the Confederacy: he managed to get wounded badly enough that Robert E. Lee took command. (Johnston himself said as much: "The shot that struck me down is the very best that has been fired for the Southern cause yet."[5])

After Seven Pines, both sides withdrew. Lee set his men to building trenches, earthworks, and fortifications—so that he could defend the city with fewer men—and shaped his new Army of Northern Virginia to attack. McClellan was waiting for him, and lobbing shells at the Confederate lines.

The Battle:

Lee amassed about 70,000 troops. He left 25,000 of them to defend Richmond, and threw the rest in an unceasing offensive against McClellan's invaders. Lee's initial intention had been to "drive our enemies back to their homes"[6] but that intention had evolved into an aggressive campaign to destroy McClellan's army in what became known as the Seven Days campaign (25 June–1 July 1862).

During the Seven Days Lee kept the army surging forward in a series of battles (the major ones were Mechanicsville, 26 June; Gaines' Mill, 27 June; Savage's Station, 29 June; Glendale or Frayser's Farm, 30 June; and Malvern Hill, 1 July) until General McClellan was driven back a full twenty-five miles, in what McClellan tried to term a strategic withdrawal, but which became known popularly, and more accurately, as "the great skedaddle."

What You Need to Know:

The Seven Days was a Confederate victory, but a brutally costly one. Confederate General D. H. Hill said of the Confederate attack on Malvern Hill against flaming Union artillery: "It was not war, it was a murder."[7] Nearly a third of the Confederate army of Northern Virginia went down as casualties. Their sacrifice, however, was not in vain. Not only was Richmond safe, but it would be three years before Federal troops again would be that close to the Confederate capital. That was three years for the South to try to win its independence.

Second Manassas (28-30 August 1862)

The Background:

To win Southern independence, the Confederates first had to liberate Northern Virginia, which was occupied by Federal General John Pope. The blustery Pope bragged that his headquarters would be in the saddle where, Confederates joked, most people kept their hindquarters. He had 50,000 men sitting on Northern Virginia's railway lines. Worse, in Lee's opinion, was Pope's declaration that his army would live off Southern civilians. All Southern male civilians in territory occupied by Pope were subject to immediate arrest; only those who could prove their loyalty to the Union would be paid for confiscated goods; and any Southerner—male or female—who tried to communicate with a son or a husband in the Confederate army could, by Pope's orders, be executed as a spy or a traitor.

One can say, as Northern sympathizers routinely do, that restoring the Union required just such measures of total war—and perhaps it did. But that doesn't answer the question of why restoring the Union—if this was the only way of restoring it—was such a morally commendable act.

For Southerners like Lee, the example of uncivilized warfare offered by "the miscreant Pope" had to be "suppressed."[8] It was a type of warfare that Confederates were beginning to identify with Union occupation—and it justified and underscored all their antebellum complaints about Yankee officiousness, arrogance, and a moral imperiousness that amounted to self-righteous immorality. For instance, in May 1862, Federal General Benjamin Butler, in charge of the Union occupation forces of New Orleans, issued his notorious General Order No. 28, which specified that any Southern belle caught treating a Yankee soldier with contempt would be treated as a prostitute. This earned him the epithet of "Beast" Butler. (He was also known as "Spoons" Butler because—in another common complaint about Yankees occupying Southern homes—he allegedly had a habit of making off with the silverware.)

Butler was too far from Lee's reach, but Pope was a blackguard who could be taught Southern manners. Most men in Lee's position would have been cautious. General McClellan was still not far away, at Harrison's Landing, and he outnumbered Lee even more than he had before the Seven Days. Pope's numbers were also greater than Lee's. Yet Lee daringly divided his forces, confident that McClellan would remain in his position on the James River until ordered to leave by Lincoln's new general in chief, Henry "Old Brains" Halleck.

The Battle:

Lee ordered Stonewall Jackson and 24,000 men north to harass Pope, (whose army was roughly three times that size). After Halleck recalled McClellan's army to Washington, Lee rushed up another 31,000 Confederates under General James Longstreet to crush Pope.

Lee ordered Jackson to put his troopers between Pope and the Federal capital, a maneuver that was sure to bring the Union commander to battle. Jackson had already clashed with a portion of Pope's force at Cedar Mountain (9 August 1862), where he had rallied his men by waving his sword in one hand and the battle flag in the other while under heavy enemy fire. Now Jackson maneuvered his army behind Pope's and further annoyed the Union general by burning his supply depot at Manassas Junction. Confederate cavalry commander J. E. B. Stuart offered his own insult by raiding Pope's camp and making off with Pope's dress coat.

Pope mistakenly thought he had "bagged" the slippery Jackson. "I see no possibility of his escape," said Pope. But while Jackson held Pope's attention, Lee and General Longstreet rode up to the rescue. Jackson tenaciously defended his position in what became the battle of Second Manassas. Two of Jackson's best commanders (General William Taliaferro and General Richard Ewell) went down with wounds; some of his men, their ammunition expended, were reduced to swinging their muskets as clubs, desperately hurling stones, and lunging with bayonets; but Jackson held on.

When General Longstreet arrived on the flank, he waited for just the right moment to strike. He kept his full complement of troops drawn up and made a careful survey of the land, unhurried by the obvious pressure on Jackson or by Lee's repeated suggestions that he expedite his assault. Finally, Longstreet smashed the exposed Union line with an artillery barrage that lifted the pressure on Jackson. Then, at Lee's command, Longstreet sent his troops charging into the Federals, rolling the bluecoats up, while Jackson's own troopers jumped over their defensive positions, screaming the rebel yell. Under attack from two sides, Pope's army broke into flight—running all the way to Washington, where it met McClellan's tardy relief force.

Jackson's and Longstreet's combined corps totaled 55,000 men; they had defeated 75,000 Federals (about 63,000 of whom had been engaged); and in the words of a Union army historian, Pope "had been kicked, cuffed, hustled about, knocked down, run over, and trodden upon as rarely happens in the history of war. His communications had been cut; his headquarters pillaged; a corps had marched into his rear, and had

How the War Was Fought

In assessing the moral rights and wrongs of the Civil War, it might be worth bearing in mind how the two sides fought the war. Jefferson Davis saw the conflict in terms of defending the borders of the Confederate States of America. Robert E. Lee saw his job as the defense of his home state of Virginia, and of isolating Union armies and destroying them. Both men saw the best prospect for Confederate victory in European intervention (though Lee was more pessimistic that it would actually materialize). Davis hoped to achieve such intervention by diplomacy, Lee with his victories on the battlefield. What neither man would countenance was war as the Federals conceived it—a war against civilians, a war of subjugation. A recent author has even criticized Lee and Davis for abiding by such gentlemanly rules of warfare, saying that is why the South lost the war, though he welcomes Southern defeat in any event. According to him, "The elimination of slavery and the aristocrats who fed on it was a glorious and long-overdue advance,"* which is true if you think "glorious" the killing of 600,000 Americans, the destruction of the South, the practice of total war against Southern civilians, and the elimination of the class that produced the Southern founding fathers like George Washington, Thomas Jefferson, George Mason, and for that matter, Lee's father, "Light Horse Harry" Lee.

Men like Robert E. Lee and Jefferson Davis would not consider waging war on civilians. Lee once wrote to

52

encamped at its ease upon the railroad by which he received his supplies; he had been beaten and foiled in every attempt he had made to 'bag' those defiant intruders; and, in the end, he was glad to find refuge in the intrenchments of Washington, whence he had sallied forth, six weeks before, breathing out threatenings and slaughter."[9]

What You Need to Know:

If First Manassas had given the Federals a shock, Second Manassas was worse, because it showed the Confederacy had real staying power.

his son Custis: "I am opposed to the theory of doing wrong that good may come of it. I hold to the belief that you must act right whatever the consequences."[†] Another author (and Union partisan) criticizes Lee for not becoming the military dictator the South allegedly needed, instead deferring always to the elected government of the Confederacy.[‡]

If abiding by the law of a free republic and fighting a defensive war solely against armed combatants be flaws, the South had them, and the North did not. Lincoln ignored the law, the Constitution, and the Supreme Court when it suited him. His armies waged war on the farms, livelihoods, and people of the South, not just against their armies. That's what it took to trample out the vintage where the grapes of wrath are stored.

---

* Bevin Alexander, *How the South Could Have Won the War: The Fatal Errors that Led to Confederate Defeat* (Crown, 2007), see Introduction.

† See the discussion of this in H.W. Crocker III, *Robert E. Lee on Leadership: Executive Lessons in Character, Courage, and Vision* (Primal Forum, 1999), 190.

‡ Major General J.F.C. Fuller, *Grant & Lee: A Study in Personality and Generalship* (Indiana University Press, 1982), see especially 122.

More than that, at least in the Eastern theatre, the Federal army had been dramatically outfought and outgeneraled. In the three months since Robert E. Lee had held field command, he had broken the imminent siege of Richmond, ended the Confederate retreat, and driven two Union armies—Pope's and McClellan's—across the Potomac. It was the Federal capital that now feared a siege, that was preparing to evacuate govern-

All for Dixie, St. Andrew, and the Papacy!

No country ever recognized the Confederate States of America, but the Papal States came the closest. The official papal newspaper, *L'Osservatore Romano*, editorialized on the South's behalf, British diplomat Odo Russell reported that the pope "would not conceal from me the fact that all his sympathies were with the Southern Confederacy and he wished them all success,"[*] and after the war, when Jefferson Davis was held a prisoner by the Federals at Fort Monroe, the pope sent him a crown of thorns, which he had woven with his own hands.

Unlike Protestant denominations, which divided into northern and southern branches, the Catholic Church stayed united, and if the pope preferred the South, it is easy to see why: the South was a rural, hierarchical, more traditionally religious society than the North.

The Church also deprecated nationalism—the centralizing, aggressive power of the state—that was everywhere crowding out the Church and those subsidiary institutions the Church believed were essential as buffers between the individual and the state. The Church, in other words, was the natural ally of feudalism, federalism (or states' rights), and conservatism. Given a choice between a religiously ambiguous nationalist (Lincoln) and a Catholic-educated defender of states' rights (Jefferson Davis), it was no contest for the pope.

Vivat Dixie!

[*] Quoted in James Hennesey, S.J., *American Catholics: A History of the Roman Catholic Community in the United States* (Oxford University Press, 1981), 156.

ment property to New York, and that was readying clerks for the defense of the city.

Lee's success had liberated not only most of Virginia, but also, indirectly, the North Carolina coastline. In the Old Dominion itself, western Virginia was now under only tenuous Federal occupation, and in the words of Lee's Pulitzer Prize-winning biographer Douglas Southall Freeman, except "for the troops at Norfolk and at Fort Monroe, the only Federals closer than 100 miles to Richmond were prisoners of war and men busily preparing to retreat from the base at Aquia Creek."[10]

Sharpsburg (or Antietam) (17 September 1862)

The Background:

Having liberated most of the Old Dominion, Lee took his troopers on a campaign into Maryland, with his eyes on Pennsylvania, hoping to draw out another Union army and defeat it. This was an election year, and if Lee could bring Confederate troops to Maryland and Pennsylvania, perhaps Northern voters would return a congressional majority that would recognize Southern freedom.

Lee issued a proclamation as his army crossed into Maryland—a state where Lincoln had suspended habeas corpus and imposed martial law[11]—emphasizing that the South stood for the principle of freedom, free association, and tolerance. In contrast to Pope's threats against Southern civilians, Lee's proclamation said: "No constraint upon your free will is intended: no intimidation will be allowed within the limits of this army, at least. Marylanders shall once more enjoy their ancient freedom of thought and speech. We know of no enemies among you, and will protect all, of every opinion. It is for you to decide your destiny freely and without constraint. This army will respect your choice, whatever it may be; and while the Southern people will rejoice to welcome you to your natural position among them, they will only welcome you when you come of your own free will."[12]

Lee's troops were vulnerable, traveling in Federal territory, and in one of the great turning points of the war, Union troops found three cigars wrapped in a sheet of paper. The paper was a duplicate of Lee's Special Orders No. 191 belonging to one of General D. H. Hill's staff officers. The orders were delivered to McClellan, who now knew not only Lee's entire plan of maneuver, but recognized how dangerously divided were Lee's forces. "Here is a paper," exclaimed Little Mac, "with which if I cannot whip Bobby Lee I will be willing to go home."

The Battle:

Lee was surprised at McClellan's sudden alacrity—as if he knew Lee's route and dispositions, which of course he did. McClellan was bringing 75,000 men to the attack. Lee's full strength was only 38,000 men, and he could bring that number to the field only if Jackson's corps returned in time from recapturing Harpers Ferry. Lee dispatched 15,000 men to impede McClellan's advance through a gap in Maryland's Catoctin Mountains. He brought the rest of his army to the Maryland town of Sharpsburg on Antietam Creek, where he intended to meet McClellan's thrust.

The battle was engaged on 17 September 1862. The odds against Lee narrowed with the clock. Each advancing hour brought more Confederates from the march to the battle line. In the morning, as Lee arranged his men at Sharpsburg, he brought barely a quarter as many troops as McClellan to the field. By afternoon, with the arrival of Jackson, he had shaved the odds to three to one against him. And at full strength, which he did not have until the battle was nearly over, he was still outnumbered by two to one.

The battle was desperate. In the first four hours of combat, 13,000 men in blue and grey fell as casualties in the bloodiest day of the war.

Twice, the Confederate line was almost overwhelmed: first at Bloody Lane, where the Confederates, mistakenly thinking they had been ordered to retreat, nearly allowed their forces to be divided; and then late in the day when Lee's right flank, which he had continually stripped to support his left, began to give way under a fierce, sustained attack by Union General Ambrose Burnside. As the flank finally dissolved under Federal fire, Burnside had a clear field to destroy Lee's army.

But then, bang on time, after a seventeen-mile forced march, came Confederate General A. P. Hill's men from Harpers Ferry. Hill brought only 3,000 men to field—2,000 others had either fallen out or been left straggling behind—but with serendipitous precision, they arrived exactly when and where the Confederates needed him most, on Burnside's flank. Despite the rigors of the march, Hill's men tore into the Federals, scattering the Union assault. The day of battle was over.

That night, Lee ordered no retreat. His men made camp, rested, and held their ground—daring the Federals to attack them again the next day. McClellan declined the opportunity. So, with nightfall, Lee pulled the men out of their lines and led them back across the Potomac to the safety of Virginia, with A. P. Hill smacking a contingent of pursuing Federals into the north bank of the Potomac, providing, in the words of historian Shelby Foote, "a sort of upbeat coda, after the crash and thunder of what had gone on before."[13]

What You Need to Know:

The Battle of Sharpsburg is often considered a Confederate defeat, because it ended Lee's invasion and thwarted his plans. So it did, but Lee and the Army of Northern Virginia deserve credit for what was also a brilliant tactical victory in the battle itself. The Confederates had held their ground against overwhelming odds, and held it again without challenge the next day. And if Lee could not take his army farther north, J. E. B. Stuart took his cavalry as far north as Chambersburg, Pennsylvania. President Lincoln was certainly not well pleased. He relieved General McClellan from command.

Fredericksburg (11-13 December 1862)

The Background:

President Lincoln, frustrated at this litany of defeat in the Eastern theater, now took a more active role in directing Union strategy, along with his Secretary of War Edwin Stanton. With General Ambrose Burnside they plotted a straight course from Washington to Fredericksburg to Richmond. The only thing that stood in their way was the army of General Robert E. Lee.

The Battle:

Lee prepared defensive positions on the hills to the east of the city, in a seven-mile line facing the Rappahannock River. He relied on the high ground and carefully positioned artillery, rather than trench works; and, as usual, he was badly outnumbered. He had about 78,000 men to Burnside's 120,000.

Lee's frontline defenders were Mississippi and Florida riflemen who sniped at the Federals as they bombarded Fredericksburg. The Federals then crossed the Rappahannock River and moved into the city. Lee's Mississippians, under the command of General William Barksdale, were gallant in slowing the Union advance, but by evening the Mississippians and Floridians were withdrawn (some of the Mississippians had to be removed forcibly, even under arrest, because they were reluctant to yield the ground), and the Federals were, for the moment, uncontested occupiers of Fredericksburg, looting and vandalizing the houses. They would receive a terrible punishment the next day.

The morning opened with a fog so thick that cavalry commander J. E. B. Stuart and an aggressive Stonewall Jackson thought the Confederates should launch a surprise attack under its cover. But Lee demurred. Then the Union guns belched smoke and thunder, trying, largely unsuccessfully, to find the Confederates. As the fog slowly lifted, the artillery battle became a duel—a duel between an entire line of Union cannon and a single Confederate

The Emancipation Proclamation

Contrary to popular opinion, the Emancipation Proclamation did not free the slaves. The first thing to remember is that a president cannot simply issue a proclamation overturning established law. A dictator can do that, but the president of a democratic republic cannot. So the Emancipation Proclamation was in no sense "law." Nor did it even purport to free all the slaves. Issued 22 September 1862 and made effective 1 January 1863, it left untouched slavery in the Border States or in parts of the South occupied by Federal forces (like New Orleans). Instead, the Emancipation Proclamation announced that slavery was hereby abolished in areas in rebellion against the United States. It might take a dictator to issue edicts abolishing constitutional rights (as established by the Supreme Court), but it certainly takes a dictator of extreme presumption and effrontery to abolish established rights in another country.

Of course, Lincoln did not look at it that way, but nor were Lincoln's motives solely to achieve the abolition of slavery. He issued the proclamation after the battle of Sharpsburg (Antietam), and by doing so he changed the nature of the war from that of restoring the Union (or achieving Southern Independence) to a war fought over the morality of slavery. (It also allowed the enrollment of free blacks in the Union army.) This did not make the war more popular in the North (in fact, it had the opposite effect), but it did put the kibosh on British or French intervention on the side of the South. Neither of these governments wanted to fight a war in favor of slavery—Southern independence, perhaps; slavery, no.

But there is yet another way to look at the Emancipation Proclamation, and that is through Southern eyes. With so many Southern men in Confederate grey, and planters serving as officers, it was the planters' wives who ran the plantations: a single white woman and her children and slaves. In Southern eyes, then, the Emancipation Proclamation was the ultimate in Yankee perfidy—an attempt to incite slave uprisings against Confederate women and children.

Happily, while the proclamation did encourage slaves to seek their freedom, there were no slave uprisings, no murders of women and children—which might say something good about Southerners too, both white and black.

59

artillery officer, Captain John Pelham, with two guns, one of which was quickly disabled. J. E. B. Stuart sent orders for Pelham to retire, but like the Mississippi sharpshooters before him, Pelham had to be compelled with three sets of orders, and then withdrew only after he ran out of ammunition. Lee called him "the Gallant Pelham" and said of his performance at Fredericksburg: "It is glorious to see such courage in one so young."[14]

The Federal artillery barrage intensified. Then the Federal infantry began testing the Confederate line, advancing uphill in force. The Confederates waited until the Union soldiers were well in the open before unleashing a deadly artillery barrage of their own. The Federals fell back, only to come again and again at the Confederate line, and to be repulsed again and again.

While Jackson had some hard fighting on Lee's right, Burnside massed the bulk of his forces for an almost obsessive assault on Lee's left at Marye's Heights. Lee saw the Federals were taking a horrible beating, but warned Longstreet that the Union concentration was so heavy that it might break through. Longstreet, who preferred to fight on the defensive, was phlegmatic: "General, if you put every man now on the other side of the Potomac on that field to approach me over the same line, and give me plenty of ammunition, I will kill them all before they reach my line."[15] The Union soldiers came on, and were shot down, all day.

As night fell, Lee finally ordered his men to dig in. Burnside talked about launching another attack, but his subordinate officers talked him out of it. They had had enough. Federal casualties for the battle of Fredericksburg were more than 12,000 men; Confederate casualties were more than 5,000. A month later, Burnside tried to regain the offensive with what became known as "the Mud March," which went nowhere. He offered to resign and was reassigned to Ohio.

What You Need to Know:

Fredericksburg helped to build the reputation of the apparently invincible Robert E. Lee and the Army of Northern Virginia that repeatedly thwarted Union generals, their massive armies, and their plentiful supplies. It also highlighted Lee's awareness of the cost of war. Lee had witnessed the women, children, and old men of Fredericksburg evacuate the city, trudging through the snow and bitter cold. When the Federals bombarded the city, he said, "These people delight to destroy the weak and those who can make no defense; it just suits them."[16] It was also at Fredericksburg that Lee, overlooking the slaughter on Marye's Heights said, memorably, "It is well that war is so terrible—we should grow too fond of it."[17]

Murfreesboro (31 December to 2 January 1862)

The Background:

While the Confederacy amassed victories in East, the news was almost always bad in the West. The difference was leadership. In Virginia, the Confederacy had the better generals. In the West, Union generals like Ulysses Grant, William Sherman, Phil Sheridan, and George Thomas, were more than a match for the likes of Confederates Albert Sidney Johnston, Braxton Bragg, Leonidas Polk, and P. G. T. Beauregard.

In October 1862 the Confederates had both failed to retake Corinth, Mississippi, and been routed from Kentucky at the battle of Perryville (8 October 1862). The intolerable Braxton Bragg—the loser at Perryville, and unfortunately a favorite of Jefferson Davis—regrouped his forces at Murfreesboro, where he met Union General William S. Rosecrans in battle on 31 December 1862.[18] Bragg had about 34,000 men, Rosecrans about 44,000.

The Battle:

The Confederates moved first, driving into the Federal right, overwhelming it, and swarmed ahead until they ran into Union General Phil Sheridan. Sheridan held the line, counterattacked, and then set up a new defensive line on the Federal right. His men fought hard, but when they ran out of ammunition, they had to fall back again, and the Union right began folding onto the Union left, like the blade of a pocket knife returning to its handle. Rebel yells pierced the air, and again butternut and grey

★ ★ ★ ★ ★ ★ ★

The New York Draft Riots

While not technically a battle, the New York Draft Riots of 13-16 July 1863 had the moral effect of one. While the Emancipation Proclamation added a bounce to the step of the abolitionists, it offended many other Northerners who saw no reason to alter the Constitution and had no desire to encourage black emigration to the North. "Preserving the Union" was far the better recruiting slogan. In fact, the Emancipation Proclamation led to draft riots—the biggest and most destructive of which was in New York City. One might think of New York as being a quintessential Union state, but it had a Democratic governor (Horatio Seymour) who hated Lincoln and had been elected on an anti-war platform, and New York City was full of Irish immigrants. The Irish were fully willing to fight for their new country, but they would be damned if they would fight to free slaves, who would then migrate North and drive down their wages. And they didn't much like the idea that rich people could buy their way out of the draft. Other New Yorkers were simply tired of a bloody and seemingly endless war.

The result was rioting, with 50,000 New Yorkers spreading havoc in the streets. An estimated 100 people were killed (including free blacks, who were lynched), another 300 were injured, and the city suffered more than a million dollars' worth of property damage. The rioters had to be put down with artillery, bayonet charges, and the imposition of martial law. So many federal troops were diverted to deal with the riots that they were, in the words of historian Samuel Eliot Morison, the "equivalent to a Confederate victory."[*]

* Samuel Eliot Morison, *The Oxford History of the American People: Volume Two: 1789 through Reconstruction* (Mentor Books, 1972), 451.

uniforms surged ahead, even though many Confederates, their rifles fouled by rain, charged with sticks in their hands instead of guns.

The day could have been won by the Confederates had Generals Bragg, John C. Breckinridge, and Leonidas Polk committed themselves now *en masse*, but they did not. Instead, Bragg ordered Breckinridge's men into the center of a well-defended Union line bristling with artillery, and General Polk, who directed the attack, sent the troops in piecemeal, which is how they were destroyed.

The Union army survived the first day of battle—and it was the only day that mattered. New Year's Day was a day of inactivity, and an attempt to dislodge the Federals on 2 January was repulsed with heavy Confederate casualties. Bragg then abandoned the city of Murfreesboro. Both sides suffered casualties of about 13,000 men, but the Confederate losses had apparently been for nothing.

What You Need to Know:

Had Bragg delivered a Confederate victory to match Lee's successes, the Union, as Lincoln noted in his letter of congratulations to Rosecrans after the battle, "could scarcely have lived."[19] As it was, Bragg's failure at Murfreesboro meant that North and South entered 1863 with no end of bloodletting in sight.

Chancellorsville (1-3 May 1863)

The Background:

After the Union disaster at Fredericksburg, President Lincoln replaced Ambrose Burnside as commander of the Army of the Potomac with "Fighting Joe" Hooker. Hooker had a reputation as a hard-drinker. Charles Adams, a Union cavalry officer (and Henry Adams's son), remarked that Hooker's headquarters was "a place to which no self-respecting man liked to go, and no decent woman could go. It was a combination barroom and brothel."[20] Like many men who spend their time in barrooms and brothels, Hooker was a braggart. He let it be known: "My plans are perfect, and when I start to carry them out, may God have mercy on General Lee, for I shall have none."[21]

The Battle:

Hooker's plan was to advance on Fredericksburg, then divide his massive army of 134,000 men, and trap Lee's much smaller force (60,000) between his two wings (both of which would outnumber Lee), crunching the Confederates in a Union vise. It didn't work out that way.

The Federals' maneuver worked well enough initially—it was the Confederate response that was stunning. Lee left a small holding force of 10,000 men at Fredericksburg to hold off about 23,000 Federals. But then, to Hooker's amazement, the Confederates, far from panicked at the 73,000 Federals forming up behind them, attacked, and drove the bluecoats back. Hooker called for reinforcements and ordered his men to dig entrenchments.

But Hooker was in for another nasty shock. Lee kept a mere 17,000 men to occupy the attention of the dug-in Federals who outnumbered him more than four to one. Meanwhile he sent Stonewall Jackson, with another 26,000 men, on a bold flanking movement against the Union right.

While Hooker imagined he had Lee trapped, it was Hooker who fingered his collar and decided to skedaddle when Jackson's troopers came roaring into the Federal lines. The Confederates forced both sides of Hooker's pincer movement back across the Rappahannock River, in a humiliation of the boastful Union commander.

One Union officer confessed: "They have beaten us fairly; beaten us all to pieces; beaten us so easily." In New York, in the newspaper offices of Horace Greeley, the reaction was worse: "My God, it is horrible—horrible! And to think of it—130,000 magnificent soldiers so cut to pieces by less than 60,000 half-starved ragamuffins!" Worse still was the reaction in Washington. Senator Charles Sumner of Massachusetts exclaimed, "Lost—lost. All is lost!" Lincoln moaned: "My God! My God! What will the country say?"[22]

What You Need to Know:

Chancellorsville was the greatest Confederate victory of the war, won against the longest odds, but for which the Confederacy paid an enormous price in the death of Stonewall Jackson, Lee's most trusted and effective lieutenant. In the gloomy dusk, scouting ahead of his lines to see how he

Stonewall's Body Lies a Mouldering in the Grave

Visitors to Virginia driving down Highway 95 might be astonished when they see a road sign announcing "Stonewall Jackson Shrine." Yes, you read that right: "Shrine." The shrine is simply the building where he died. It was then part of the property of the Chandler Plantation at Guinea Station. It is now maintained by the National Park Service. Interestingly, Jackson has two burial places. His left arm was amputated at a Chancellorsville field hospital in the hope of saving his life. The arm was buried by Jackson's chaplain at Ellwood, a house owned by the chaplain's brother near Chancellorsville. It too is now a property of the National Park Service. A marker rests on what is the presumed burial place of the arm. The rest of Jackson is buried at the Stonewall Jackson Memorial Cemetery in Lexington, Virginia.

could capitalize on his smashing success, Jackson and his staff officers were shot by Confederate troopers who mistook them for a Federal patrol.

Vicksburg (29 March to 4 July 1863)

The Background:

Vicksburg, sitting on the Mississippi River, was the "Gibraltar of the Confederacy." Lose it, and the Confederacy was cut in twain. Hold it, and the South had access to the grain and men of the lower South and the West. Or, in Lincoln's words: "We may take all the northern ports of the Confederacy and they can still defy us at Vicksburg. It means hog and hominy without limit, fresh troops from all the states of the far South, and a country where they can raise the staple without interference."[23]

With the Federals working their way down from the north, and already occupying the river's southern outlet at New Orleans, a siege of Vicksburg was almost inevitable. But taking Vicksburg was an imposing challenge. Its big guns kept the river clear of Union blue, and the city's marshy landward approaches were tough-sledding at best for an attacker, and were made even more perilous by Confederate snipers and saboteurs.

In 1862, Admiral David Farragut tried repeatedly to capture Vicksburg along the Mississippi, but the big guns chased him back. General Grant tried the landward approaches and had no better luck. With General Sherman defeated at Chickasaw Bluffs (in December 1862) and Confederate cavalry ravaging Grant's communications and supply lines, the Federals were forced to withdraw. But in 1863, Grant came again. His plan this time was to skirt the big guns through elaborate engineering works—building a canal, diverting the river—all of which came to naught.

But in March 1863, Grant decided on a bold maneuver. He would march his men down the Louisiana side of the river, cross it well south of Vicksburg and then swing round and attack—marching all the time through enemy territory. Rear Admiral David Porter, meanwhile, would reinforce his gunboats and, in a perilous gamble, run them by the fortress at night. On 16 April and 22 April 1863, Porter made his two daring passages under the guns of Vicksburg with spectacular success. The air was lit with fire and flame, but his losses were minimal. The focus now shifted to Grant.

The Campaign:

Grant's plan was to isolate Vicksburg, marching first to Jackson, Mississippi, cutting off the citadel's line of retreat and source of supply, and then invest the rebel fortress. Starting with 50,000 troops (a number that would grow to 77,000), divided into five corps, Grant faced 30,000 Confederates who were strung out defending too many points with too few men.

Of the major battles of this campaign, four deserve attention. The Battle of Port Gibson (1 May 1863), conducted one day after Grant landed his men across the Mis-

Bombing Americans Back to the Stone Age

That's what the Federals did to the inhabitants of Vicksburg, where their shelling drove people into caves. The Federals also cut off food to the city. As for medicine, throughout the war, the Federals regarded it as contraband, so the Confederates made due with whiskey.

sissippi River at Bruinsburg, led to the Federals achieving a foothold twenty-five miles south of Vicksburg. The Confederates had mounted a gallant defense, but had been outnumbered three to one. At the battle of Raymond (12 May), near Jackson, the bluecoats again outnumbered the Confederates three to one (and in artillery seven to one) and again the Confederates withdrew but only after a stiff fight. At the Battle of Jackson (14 May), Grant marched into Mississippi's capital city, which Confederate general Joseph E. Johnston had decided to abandon, and destroyed its railways and industry.

The climactic battle before the siege of Vicksburg was at Champion Hill (16 May) twenty miles east of the city, where 32,000 Federals, under General Grant, collided with 22,000 Confederates, under General John C. Pemberton. In a hard fought contest, a Confederate counterattack nearly reached Grant's headquarters. Saving the day for the Federals was General Marcellus Crocker (leader of "Crocker's Greyhounds") who threw two brigades of bluecoats against the rebels and saved the Federal line. The Confederates retreated to Vicksburg.

Grant first tried to take Vicksburg by storm. But he underestimated the strength and stubbornness of the Confederate defenders. After five days of knocking Federal troops against the Confederate wall, Grant decided to shell and starve the Confederates instead, while continuing offensive probes and calling for reinforcements. The shelling of Vicksburg was so intense that its citizens dug a system of caves in which to live.

By July Confederate General Pemberton realized the game was up. He had been waiting for reinforcements from General Joseph E. Johnston, who despite having orders and reinforcements to save the city, would take no such risk. Pemberton wanted to fight his way out, but his subordinate generals thought this quixotic, given how ill fed and badly outnumbered the men were. Pemberton conceded this and on 4 July 1863, nearly 30,000 Confederates—and the city of Vicksburg—were surrendered to U.S. Grant. The 4th of July became a day of mourning, rather than celebration, in Vicksburg.

What You Need to Know:

Losing Vicksburg meant the loss of the Confederate West. The Mississippi River belonged entirely to the Federals, who captured the last remaining Confederate strongpoint, the besieged Port Hudson, Louisiana, on 9 July.

Gettysburg (1-3 July 1863)

The Background:

General Robert E. Lee wanted to isolate a Union army and destroy it. That, he believed, was the quickest way to convince the North to allow the Southern Confederacy its freedom. So he marched his men out of war-ravaged Virginia through Maryland and into Pennsylvania.

The Battle:

The battle was fought over three days: 1-3 July 1863, with the final troop totals equaling close to 95,000 Federals and 75,000 Confederates. As the initial skirmishes began, almost accidentally, Kentucky-born Union General John Buford, an old Indian fighter, secured the high ground for the Federals.

The Confederates could have won the battle the first day. They pushed the Federals from their advanced positions in front of Gettysburg and along Seminary Ridge. The subsequent Union position—known as the

The Ghosts of Gettysburg

"For every Southern boy fourteen years old, not once but whenever he wants it, there is the instant when it's still not yet two o'clock on that July afternoon in 1863, the brigades are in position behind the rail fence, the guns are laid and ready in the woods and the furled flags are already loosened to break out and Pickett himself with his long oiled ringlets and his hat in one hand probably and his sword in the other looking up the hill waiting for Longstreet to give the word and it's all in the balance...."

From William Faulkner's *Intruder in the Dust*

"fish hook"—eventually formed like the base of the letter J at Cemetery Hill and Culp's Hill, extending straight down Cemetery Ridge to Little Round Top and Big Round on the Union left.

Lee asked General Richard Ewell to attack the base of the fishhook, in order to sweep the Federal line, "if practicable." Ewell, to Lee's dismay, didn't think it was, though Confederate General John B. Gordon knew otherwise: "The whole portion of the Union army in my front was in

★ ★ ★ ★ ★

Was Pickett's Charge a Mistake?

Pickett's Charge is often held up as one of Lee's few battlefield blunders. But it wasn't. On the retreat to Virginia, Lee told cavalry commander John B. Imboden:

> "I never saw troops behave more magnificently than Pickett's division of Virginians did today in that grand charge upon the enemy. And if they had been supported as they were to have been—but for some reason not yet fully explained to me, were not—we would have held the position and the day would have been ours. Too bad! Too bad! Oh, too bad!"[*]

The reason they had not been supported as they should have been was Longstreet's stubborn delay of the advance. Lee was, in fact, badly served by many of his officers at Gettysburg who were not on their best form. Ewell was jittery, Longstreet reluctant, A. P. Hill was sick, and J. E. B. Stuart was riding his cavalry on a pointless circumnavigation of the enemy when his cavalry should have been Lee's eyes and ears. On their best form, the Army of Northern Virginia could have won the battle, and in Lee's mind, they should have won the battle.

---

[*] Quoted in Shelby Foote, *The Civil War: A Narrative, Fredericksburg to Meridian* (Random House, 1963), 581.

inextricable confusion and in flight . . . my troops were on the flank and sweeping down the lines. The firing upon my men had almost ceased. Large bodies of the Union troops were throwing down their arms and surrendering . . . .In less than half an hour my troops would have swept up and over those hills . . . .It is not surprising that . . . I should have refused to obey that order [to retreat]."[24]

On the Union side of the line, it had been a lucky escape, but with heavy casualties. I Corps had lost nearly 10,000 men and some units had been virtually annihilated (the 24th Michigan suffered casualties of 80 percent). But arriving at midnight was the Army of the Potomac's new commander, General George Meade, who inspected his defensive positions and found them solid.

That was one opportunity lost for the Confederate army. Another came on the second day, when Lee's plan was to "attack the enemy as early in the morning as practicable"[25] at the opposite end of the fish hook. The attack was entrusted to General James Longstreet. Longstreet, however, disliked Lee's plan, preferring, according to his later testimony, to maneuver the Confederate army into a defensive position that would force the Yankees to attack it.

Longstreet delayed the attack until near day's end, waiting for reinforcements. By that time, Union troops under General Daniel Sickles had advanced, contrary to General Meade's orders, into an area known as the Peach Orchard, the Wheat Field, and Devil's Den, smack in front of Longstreet's long-delayed advance.

Confederate General John Bell Hood, dispatched scouts to see if it was still possible to flank the Union left, as originally planned. The answer was yes, if the Confederates moved their attack around to the hills of Little Round Top, which had no more than a Union observation unit, or unoccupied Big Round Top.

Hood reported this intelligence to Longstreet, but Longstreet refused to alter the plan of attack. He sent his men charging, *en échelon*, uphill, into spewing Union fire. Still, the Union line began to dissolve, and the Confederate attack spilled over to Little Round Top.

There the Confederates met the hastily formed line of the 20th Maine led by Colonel Joshua Chamberlain. Chamberlain's thin blue line forced back the Confederate attacks, and trusting to courage against numbers, he counter-charged with fixed bayonets, stunning the Confederates into retreat and hundreds of surrenders.

But everywhere else on the center-right of the Union line, furious fighting continued. General William Barksdale, pushing his Mississippians to almost pierce the Union line, was killed. Union General Sickles lost a leg (smashed by a cannon ball), but nonchalantly lit up a cigar as though it were nothing. The 1st Minnesota regiment, rushing to plug a gap in the Union line, sustained 82 percent casualties, but did its duty and held the position. Cemetery Ridge remained in the hands of the bluecoats.

Twice, fate—in the form of reluctant generals—had deprived Lee of the victory he thought was possible at Gettysburg. On day three, Lee resolved on a daring stratagem.

That night, at the Union council of war, Meade and his officers resolved that they would hold their ground and brace for Lee's next move. Having attacked the Federals on both flanks, Meade suspected that Lee would attack dead center. Meade was the first general to read Robert E. Lee exactly right.

Lee planned for Ewell to lead a diversionary attack on the Union right while Longstreet made the main attack under cover of the largest artillery barrage ever attempted by the Confederate army. Longstreet, however, wanted to renew his argument from the day before. He wanted either to renew his flanking attack or have the entire army shift to the Union left and establish a defensive line that would compel the Federals to attack.

Lee listened patiently, but rejected Longstreet's arguments and told him to get his men into position. Longstreet, however, delayed all the morning through the afternoon. Indeed, by the time he got his men moving, the artillery, which had barraged the enemy, was depleted of ammunition.

The Confederates now had the challenge of crossing a mile of open ground with minimal artillery support to suppress federal fire. They did not flinch. The charge would be led by the brigades of General George Pickett. Officers to the front, General Lewis Armistead—whose father had been a general and whose uncle had been the lieutenant-colonel commanding the defense of Fort McHenry in the War of 1812—shoved his

Meade the Victor?

After the Battle of Gettysburg, Meade was harried with telegrams from Washington urging him forward, but Meade waited ten days before he moved. As one Confederate staff officer wrote, the Federals "pursued us as a mule goes on the chase after a grizzly bear—as if catching up with us was the last thing he wanted."[*]

Lincoln held Meade responsible for letting the Confederates escape. In a letter to the Union general that Lincoln wrote but did not send, he said: "I do not believe you appreciate the magnitude of the misfortune involved in Lee's escape. He was within your easy grasp, and to have closed upon him would, in connection with our other late successes [like Vicksburg], have ended the war. As it is, the war will be prolonged indefinitely. Your golden opportunity is gone, and I am distressed immeasurably because of it."[†]

* Quoted in Emory M. Thomas, *Robert E. Lee: A Biography* (W.W. Norton & Company, 1997) 305.
† Quoted in James McPherson, *Gettysburg* (Rutledge Hill Press, 1993) 109.

black hat over the tip of his sword and waved his men forward. With him were Pickett's other brigade commanders: James Kemper, a former member of the Virginia House of Delegates whose grandfather had served on George Washington's staff, and Richard B. Garnett, a West Pointer suffering from a bad knee and worse fever. He advanced on horseback, however obvious a target that made him.

The Confederates marched forward as if on parade, even stopping at one point to adjust and straighten their lines, oblivious to the holes being torn in their ranks by the Union fire. Of Pickett's Virginians, Brigadier Garnett was shot off his horse, dead. Brigadier Kemper, calling for Armistead's men to support his brigade, collapsed, shot in the groin.

Armistead waved his men to come on, they were close enough now to the Union line to break into a jog—and they were blasted by canister. But through the storm of smoke, artillery fire, and minié balls, the Union front *was* suddenly pierced. Chasing a line of retreating Federals was Armistead himself, still waving his black hat on his sword, shouting, "Come on boys! Give them the cold steel! Follow me!" They surged forward into hand-to-hand combat, Armistead and his troopers running straight into two Federal regiments rushing to close the line. Armistead, arm outstretched to a silent Federal cannon, went down, mortally wounded, falling at a point on the battlefield now called "the high tide of the Confederacy." On another part of the front, the University Greys, made up entirely of students from Ole Miss, managed to plant their colors no more than a yard from the Union line before the devastating Union fire killed every last one of them.

Now it really was over. The Confederate lines wavered and buckled. As one rebel commander said, "The best thing the men can do is get out of this. Let them go."[26] As the shattered Confederate units drifted back, Lee rode forward to meet them. "All good men must rally....General Pickett...your men have done all that men could do; the fault is entirely my own....All this has been my fault—it is I that have lost this fight and you must help me out of it the best way you can."[27] The Confederate soldiers cheered Lee. They even begged another chance. But Lee waved them down, and prepared them—with a newly revitalized Longsteet—for a counterattack that didn't come.

Both sides licked deep wounds. The Union army had suffered 23,000 casualties. The statistics were even grimmer for the Confederates. Twenty-eight thousand men were lost, more than a third of Lee's army, and among them a high proportion of senior officers whose talents and experience could not be replaced. Lee's officers had sacrificed their lives in the battle they hoped would secure Southern freedom.

What You Need to Know:

Gettysburg and Vicksburg were the turning points of the war. The hopes of the Confederacy would never again rise so high as they did on the battlefield in Pennsylvania.

The Gettysburg Address

"Four score and seven years ago our fathers brought forth on this continent, a new nation, conceived in Liberty, and dedicated to the proposition that all men are created equal.

"Now we are engaged in a great civil war, testing whether that nation, or any nation so conceived and so dedicated, can long endure. We are met on a great battlefield of that war. We have come to dedicate a portion of that field, as a final resting place for those who here gave their lives that the nation might live. It is altogether fitting and proper that we should do this.

"But, in a larger sense, we cannot dedicate—we cannot consecrate—we cannot hallow—this ground. The brave men, living and dead, who struggled here, have consecrated it, far above our poor power to add or detract. The world will little note, nor long remember what we say here, but it can never forget what they did here. It is for us the living, rather, to be dedicated here to the unfinished work which they who fought here have thus far so nobly advanced. It is rather for us to be here dedicated to the great task remaining before us—that from these honored dead we take increased devotion to that cause for which they gave the last full measure of devotion—that we here highly resolve that these dead shall not have died in vain—that this nation, under God, shall have a new birth of freedom—and that government of the people, by the people, for the people, shall not perish from the earth."

Of course it was not clear how government "of the people, by the people, for the people" was endangered by Southern independence. Some might say that's exactly what Southerners were fighting for.

Chapter Four

THE LONG GOODBYE, 1863–1865

After defeat at Gettysburg, the Southern cause—short of foreign intervention—was doomed. The South did not have the resources to fight a long war. In their most important resource—men—the South had no shortage of courage and determination. But courageous and determined men fell and died, and were not easily replaced. By the end of the war, *one quarter* of the draft-age white male population of the South was dead. Moreover, the war, in the words of historian Gary Gallagher, "cost the Confederacy two-thirds of its assessed wealth . . . killed 40 percent of its livestock, destroyed more than half its farm machinery, and left levees, railroads, bridges, industry, and other parts of the economic infrastructure"—not to mention entire cities—"severely damaged or ruined."[1]

At the outset of the war, the North numbered some 20 million people; the South had only nine million, four million of whom were slaves. The North was also open to immigration—which the blockaded South wasn't—which opened a whole new field of military recruiting. More boys in blue (more than 364,000) were killed than boys in grey (260,000), but while Northern families grieved, Lincoln's government could better afford the loss—better afford a war of attrition—than could the government of Jefferson Davis. By war's end, nearly 625,000 Americans lay

Guess What?

→ Douglas MacArthur's father, Arthur MacArthur, was a hero at the Battle of Chattanooga

→ The cadets of the Virginia Military Institute helped turn back a Yankee army at the Battle of New Market

→ The Federals waged a war against Southern civilians (destroying their crops, their cities, and their homes)

dead—more American servicemen than were killed in World War I, World War II, the Korean War, and the Vietnam War *combined*. And that does not even factor in the untold losses in Southern civilians.

Northern victory would eventually come, but it would take nearly two more years of hard fighting, and the deaths of many a gallant soldier to achieve.

Chickamauga (18-20 September 1863)

The Background:

Confederate General Braxton Bragg retreated from Knoxville and Chattanooga, Tennessee, without a fight, with the supposed intent of setting up a masterful counterattack. He was pursued by hard-drinking (he was a Catholic convert), hard-swearing (his brother converted too and became a bishop), Yankee General William S. Rosecrans ("Old Rosey"—a West Pointer who had graduated fifth in his class).

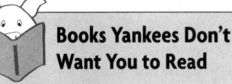

Books Yankees Don't Want You to Read

The Civil War: A Narrative (three volumes), by Shelby Foote (Random House, 1958-74). A richly rewarding history of the War, full of lively anecdote and detail, that puts to shame shallow, politically correct simplifications.

The Battle:

The armies collided in a deeply forested area near Chickamauga Creek. Visibility and room to maneuver were minimal, and the fighting was fierce with virtually every unit committed to combat. After a bloody but inconclusive opening round, Rosecrans pulled his men back under cover of nightfall, tightened the Union lines, built up log breastworks, and took up defensive positions.

Bragg, meanwhile, planned to flank the Federal left, which, unfortunately for him, was exactly the point that Rosecrans decided to reinforce.

Bragg, however, now had another hammer to bludgeon the Federals: James Longstreet had arrived, detached from Lee's command. Longstreet's journey from Virginia had been detoured and delayed because of the Federal capture of the railroad at Knoxville. He finally found the battlefield by riding through the dark and asking directions from Federal troops—neither side recognizing the other in the black night.

At daybreak, the attack on the Federal left was pushed hard but went nowhere. The morning's fighting was another bloody stalemate, until the Federals mistakenly left a gap in the center-right of their line. Confederate General John Bell Hood—riding to battle with one arm in a sling, and suffering a wound that would cost him a leg—led a charge against the Federal right flank. As the Federal right dissolved, Longstreet shifted his own men to the right and charged through the gap, shattering the Union line and driving Rosecrans and the Federal army into flight.

Union Major General George H. Thomas saved the day for the Federals, becoming "The Rock of Chickamauga."[2] He regrouped the Federals on the high ground at Snodgrass Hill, from which the Confederates couldn't dislodge them until dusk. Thomas gave ground so stubbornly that the Confederates, exhausted, finally stopped pressing him. Thomas then withdrew his men in good order to Chattanooga.

What You Need to Know:

Chickamauga was Longstreet's return to form after Gettysburg. His aggressive performance earned him the nickname, "Old Bull of the Woods." At Chickamauga the Confederates for once outnumbered the Federals, 65,000 to 62,000 men. They also took the worse casualties: more than 18,000 to more than 16,000. Though a Confederate victory, it was a victory that, because of poor generalship by Braxton Bragg, achieved little, except to reassure the Southern people that all was not lost in Tennessee.

Chattanooga (24-25 November 1863)

The Background:

Rosecrans had performed badly at Chickamauga, fleeing the field. Grant sacked him and appointed the Rock of Chickamauga, General Thomas, to replace the Runner of Chickamauga. General Thomas had the task of holding Chattanooga at all costs—and Lincoln made sure he was plentifully reinforced, which was easy to do because Braxton Bragg besieged the city with his usual incompetence; as Longstreet said: "We were trying to starve the enemy by investing him on the only side from which he could not have gathered supplies."[3]

The Battle:

By 23 November 1863, 70,000 Federal troops were amassed in Chattanooga. The Federal breakout began with General Thomas seizing Orchard Knob from the Confederates, and driving the Confederate line back. The next day, Joseph Hooker led the Federal attack at the Battle of Lookout Mountain, known as the "The Battle above the Clouds," and used his six-to-one advantage in men to defeat the Confederates.

But the key battle was the Battle of Missionary Ridge. It was begun on 24 November and engaged with a fury on 25 November. Again the Federals had six to one odds in their favor, but the three Confederate lines ascending the steep ridge threw back Federal attacks all day—at times in hand to hand combat.

General Thomas, however, refused to be denied victory. He brought up 23,000 Federals on a two mile-long line and sent them charging a full mile under fire. The bluecoats crashed into and overwhelmed the 3,200 Confederates in the rifle pits at the base of the ridge. As retreating Confederates scrambled out of the way, fire poured down on the Federals from the Confederate second line: artillery fire, musket fire, an inferno of blazing fire. The Yankee junior officers on the spot thought they had no choice: they had to charge straight up the mountain through that avalanche of artillery shells and bullets.

Grant, seeing the blue uniforms move up, thought it was suicide and demanded to know who had given the order to attack up the ridge. No one knew, but the bluecoats kept moving, dodging behind whatever cover they could find as they made their ascent. Soon they had captured the second line of Confederate rifle pits, the defenders scrambling higher to the final line. Though the fire remained fierce and deadly, the Union troops got a break. As the Federals ascended, the Confederate artillery's field of fire diminished to nothing, it being impossible to depress the barrels any farther. The Confederate gunners were reduced to lighting fuses on canister shells and rolling them and cannon balls down the ridge.

Grabbing the flag of the 24th Wisconsin from an exhausted color sergeant, eighteen-year-old Lieutenant Arthur MacArthur (father of future general Douglas MacArthur) led the final charge: "On Wisconsin!" he cried. Soon the Federals were over the top, and as MacArthur planted his regiment's colors in front of what had been Braxton Bragg's headquarters he was greeted with the sight of Confederate uniforms melting away down the reverse slope of the ridge.

Destruction and Reconstruction

"Lincoln may have been right in thinking that he was bound to preserve the Union. But it was not the Union that was preserved. A union implies that two different things are united; and it should have been the Northern and Southern cultures that were united. As a fact, it was the Southern culture that was destroyed. And it was the Northern that ultimately imposed not a unity but merely a uniformity."

G. K. Chesterton (and Lawrence J. Clipper, editor), *Collected Works of G. K. Chesterton Volume XXXV, The Illustrated London News, 1929-1931* (Ignatius Press, 1992), 217.

Phil Sheridan led the Federals' pursuit, which continued the next day. Only the fighting courage of Patrick Cleburne's shielding division (Cleburne was known as "the Stonewall Jackson of the West") allowed the Confederates to escape. The charge up Missionary Ridge had decided the contest. Told that Confederate generals had considered Missionary Ridge impregnable, Grant replied, "Well, it *was* impregnable."[4] But the bravery of men like Arthur MacArthur and Phil Sheridan had changed that.

What You Need to Know:

The Battle of Chattanooga at last led to General Braxton Bragg's removal from command. Unfortunately, Jefferson Davis replaced him with another general who specialized in retreat: Joseph E. Johnston.

Atlanta (7 May to 2 September 1864)

The Background:

Grant, now a lieutenant general, turned the middle theatre of the war over to William Tecumseh Sherman with orders to "get into the interior of the enemy's country as far as you can, inflicting all the damage you can against their war resources."[5] Sherman, in return, made his famous pledge: he would "make Georgia howl!"

Amassed under Sherman's command were 100,000 excellently supplied men against Joseph E. Johnston's 65,000 Confederate defenders, many of whom suffered shortages of clothing, ammunition, and food. As Sherman pursued them, they proved wily opponents, blocking all flanking attacks and erecting impromptu earthwork defenses. But the salient fact was that the Confederate line kept drawing southward, toward Atlanta. The entire month of May 1864 was spent in fighting retreat from north Georgia to just north of the Chattahoochee River, beyond which was the prize city. Johnston finally drew up his forces at Kennesaw Mountain, where he was prepared to make a stand. As Sherman noted, Johnston had made the area "one vast fort...Johnston must have fifty miles of trenches."[6]

Sherman tried to take Kennesaw Mountain by storm on 27 June 1864, and suffered a bloody repulse, losing 2,000 men to 500 Confederates. Unable to break Johnston, Sherman maneuvered around him, crossing the Chattahoochee and forcing Johnston to fall back on Atlanta. Johnston had done what Johnston always did: executed tactically brilliant retreats. Jefferson Davis suddenly awoke to the fact that if this continued, Johnston would be executing his tactical brilliance all the way to the Gulf of Mexico. If the Confederacy was going to survive, Sherman had to be defeated, not parried. Davis relieved Johnston and put the gallant Texan John Bell Hood (now with only one leg and one useful arm) in command. Hood, a West Pointer, had been an aggressive and courageous division and corps commander and knew what was expected of him.

The Battle:

Many of Hood's fellow officers thought he had been promoted beyond his abilities, and Hood's performance argued that they were right. His initial attacks were well planned, but they failed badly in execution and horribly in casualties. He attacked at Peachtree Creek on 20 July 1864 and lost nearly 5,000 men while inflicting well fewer than half that many Union casualties. Two days later, he surprised Sherman with another attack. If delivered properly, it could have been a body blow to Sherman's army. Instead it was an ill-coordinated glancing blow that cost the Confederates another 10,000 men to fewer than 4,000 Federals. Six days later, Hood fought at Ezra Church and lost 5,000 more men. Aggressive he was, but the one-armed, one-legged general was suffering amputations of his army. And it was to no avail. Atlanta was besieged for a month, and then Hood had to evacuate the city. On 2 September 1864, the Federals occupied Atlanta.

What You Need to Know:

If defeat at Vicksburg and Gettysburg brought premonitions of doom to the Confederacy, the fall of Atlanta—severing Virginia and the Carolinas from the rest of the Confederacy—made defeat virtually inevitable.

The Virginia Campaign of 1864

The Background:

After Gettysburg, Lee no longer had the men, the horses, or the provisions to attempt another invasion of the North. He was now compelled to fight on the defensive. His task: repel the invader at every turn. His opponent, the best general the Union had: Ulysses S. Grant.

Grant's plan was simple. Sherman's fiery "March to the Sea" would ravage Georgia and then cut north through the Carolinas and Virginia; Phil Sheridan would go on a farm-burning crusade in the Shenandoah Valley; and the U.S. Navy would tighten its grip on the South's blockaded ports. Meanwhile, Grant and Meade and the Army of the Potomac, about 120,000-strong, would march relentlessly down to Richmond slugging it out against Robert E. Lee's army of roughly 62,000 men until the Grey Fox was pummeled and beaten into submission.

The Campaign:

Grant's first major clash with Lee was at the Battle of the Wilderness (5-6 May 1864). The Confederates hit the Union army as it marched through "the Wilderness" west of Fredericksburg. Lee hoped to trap the Army of the Potomac in this dense forest where its numerical superiority would be negated by the impossibility of maneuver.

On the first day of fighting, Confederate general A. P. Hill—outnumbered nearly three to one—caught and held the Federals at his front. So the Confederate trap was set, if the thin grey line could hold. Lee's plan was for Longstreet's fresh corps, a day's march away, to deliver a crushing attack on the Federal flank.

Longstreet, however, was slower than the Federals were. At 5:00 a.m., a massive Federal assault tore into the ragged Confederate lines compelling Lee to ride forward and rally his men. Just at that moment, when it looked as though the Confederates would break, Longstreet's corps burst onto the scene. He might have been late, but he made up for it by pressing the battle aggressively, not merely repelling the Union charge, but crumpling the Federals' left flank.

So effective was the Confederate countercharge that it appeared the momentum would be completely turned—that the moment of absolute Confederate danger might become an amazing Confederate triumph. But Longstreet, riding ahead of his lines, was badly wounded by friendly fire. With Longstreet down, Lee rode to the front to direct the Confederate attack, but he found the forward surge of the Confederate line had already stalled. The moment of redirecting it had passed.

Thwarted once, Grant was determined to continue after Lee, no matter what the cost. He would shift his men to the south and attack, shift to the south and attack, forcing Lee to keep moving with him to block the Federal army of the Potomac from advancing against Richmond.

Blue and grey clashed again, only two days later in a two-week-long struggle at Spotsylvania Court House, where Lee set his men to digging what his biographer Clifford Dowdey has called "the most elaborate system of field fortifications then seen in world warfare," designing "what amounted to mobile forts."[7] Twice, during the fierce fighting, Lee had to be restrained from charging into the fray. When it was over, the results for Grant were as bad as they had been in the Wilderness. In both battles he had lost nearly two men for every one of Lee's, while also outnumbering Lee by nearly two to one (110,000 Federals to 63,000 Confederates at Spotsylvania).

Grant swore that he would "fight it out on this line if it takes all summer,"[8] which it would—and more. Two days after the last fighting at

Books Yankees Don't Want You to Read

Lee, by Douglas Southall Freeman (abridged from four-volume original by Richard Harwell), (Charles Scribner's Sons, 1991)

Lee, by Clifford Dowdey (Stan Clark Military Books, 1991)

Robert E. Lee: A Biography, by Emory Thomas (W. W. Norton & Company, 1997)

Gray Fox: Robert E. Lee and the Civil War, by Burke Davis (Burford Books, 1956)

These are four of the best books on Robert E. Lee (the last more narrowly focused than the others). Yankees don't want you to read them, because if you do, it'll be hard to imagine that he was on the wrong side.

Spotsylvania Court House, Lee checked Grant again at North Anna River (23 to 26 May 1864) in a well-executed tactical defense that Lee hoped to turn into another trap for Grant's army, but Lee was too sick to direct his counteroffensive and had no worthy lieutenant to carry it out. So the armies repeated their mirrored shifts to the south, confronting each other at Cold Harbor.

Grant, frustrated at Lee's continual thwarting of his advance, decided to rely on the sheer weight of his two-to-one superiority in numbers to end this bloody minuet. He hurled his men in a straightforward charge against Lee's newly and hastily erected fortifications.

For Grant, at least in human terms, it was a terrible mistake. The Union soldiers ran into blistering musketry and artillery fire, blue uniforms falling in grotesque, bloody clumps. Grant ordered assault after assault, thinking he had shaken the Confederates. In fact, he had only demoralized his own men. The Battle of Cold Harbor (31 May to 3 June 1864) was a Union disaster. Federal casualties were 10,000 men to Confederate losses of 4,000 men. While Grant's steady stream of reinforcements kept his army above 100,000 troops, it was *his* men who were wondering how long this could go on and *his* officers who feared political reaction to the staggering bill in casualties. In a month's worth of fighting, Grant had lost 50,000 men. Nearly 1,700 Federal soldiers had sacrificed their lives or been wounded every day in Grant's war of attrition.

What You Need to Know:

Though he fought for a lost cause, Lee's brilliance shone during the Virginia Campaign of 1864. Every one of its major battles was a stunning tactical victory for Lee. In the battle of the Wilderness, Grant lost nearly two men for every one of Lee's (Union casualties were 18,000 to not quite 11,000 for the Confederates). At Spotsylvania Court House it was the same story, with Union casualties of 18,000 to no more than 10,000 Confederates. Again at Cold Harbor, it was always Grant's troops who got far the worst of the fighting. But in brutalitarian terms, these were casualties that Grant could afford, and Lee could not.

Petersburg and Appomattox
(15 June 1864 to 9 April 1865)

The Background:

Grant gave up trying to get around Lee to Richmond, and instead opted to lay siege to Petersburg and cut Richmond's supply lines to the south. Lee had foreseen this probability, but was powerless to prevent it. He also knew what it meant for the Confederacy. Lee confessed to Confederate general Jubal A. Early that if Grant were to cross the James River and attack Petersburg, "It will become a siege, and then it will be a mere question of time."[9]

A siege meant that Grant's war of attrition would be ratcheted up a notch, but Lee held Grant at Petersburg for ten months, during which time the Union general could spare no men for an attack on Richmond. If this delaying action could be counted a victory, it was certainly a Pyrrhic one, because it was also during these ten months of successful defense that Lee witnessed the rest of the Confederacy wither, put to the torch by Sherman's men who marched from Atlanta to Savannah to South

Go VMI!

In the Shenandoah Valley, at the Battle of New Market (15 May 1864) cadets from the Virginia Military Institute (marching eighty miles in four days) joined Confederate forces under General John C. Breckinridge to expel the Federal invaders. Ten cadets were killed (including a descendant of Thomas Jefferson), but Union general Franz Sigel and his bluecoats were put to flight and pulled out of the Shenandoah Valley. In memory of their gallant performance, cadets from VMI—where Stonewall Jackson taught and George C. Marshall graduated—reenact the march every year.

Carolina to their last major engagement at Bentonville, North Carolina (19-21 March 1865) where Sherman defeated the ever-retreating Joseph E. Johnston.

In Tennessee, Confederate General John Bell Hood fought his army to the point of effective annihilation between the battles of Franklin (30 November 1864) and Nashville (15-16 December 1864).

In the breadbasket of Virginia, Union General Phil Sheridan executed Grant's orders to reduce "the Shenandoah Valley [into] a barren waste . . . so that crows flying over it for the balance of this season will have to carry their provender with them."[10] By the time Sheridan was done, the fertile Valley's wheat, flour, hay, cattle, sheep, pigs, and chickens were either destroyed or in Federal hands; the farmers left with nothing but burnt offerings, not even their tools were spared.

That meant that the Confederacy's hopes—such as they were—rested entirely on General Robert E. Lee and the Army of Northern Virginia.

The Campaign:

Grant's initial assault on the defenses around Petersburg in June 1864 led to another bruising engagement, where the Union troops suffered so grievously, despite their overwhelming numbers, that the Union's offensive had to be cut short, General Meade saying "the moral condition of the army" was shattered.[11] Indeed, in the first two months of the siege, the Confederates, somewhat to their surprise, collected 8,000 Union prisoners.

As the siege wore on, the Federal artillery shelling the city, Lee offered his wife a humorous assessment of the situation. "Grant," he wrote, "seems so pleased with his present position that I fear he will never move again."[12] Grant continued to press and probe Lee's army. At its greatest extent, Lee's line of trenches stretched for nearly fifty-five miles.

In the most spectacular incident of the siege, blue-clad Pennsylvania coal miners burrowed beneath the Confederate lines, packed the tunnel with 8,000 pounds of explosives, and on 30 July 1864, detonated it. The blast tore a hole in the Confederate line, the earth collapsing into an enormous crater. The Federals poured into the breach. But the Confederates reformed around the lip of the crater, threw back the Yankees in hand-to-hand combat and opened fire on those who had charged into the pit.

The Battle of the Crater cost the Union another 4,000 casualties to fewer than 1,300 Confederates. Worse than that, from the Union perspective, was the speed with which the Confederates restored their lines. There was no chance to follow up with another attack on the breach. General Grant was appalled. "It was the saddest affair I have witnessed in the war. Such an opportunity for carrying fortifications I have never seen and do not expect again to have."[13]

But Grant kept his men in place, and the siege dragged on through the winter and into the spring of 1865. Lee knew that his army could not hold the line at Petersburg indefinitely. Lee finally convinced President Davis that Petersburg and Richmond had to be abandoned. Lee's army—about 35,000 men, roughly one quarter of Grant's strength—had to be freed to maneuver, to find forage to feed itself, and to attempt to unite with Joseph E. Johnston's fragment of an army in North Carolina.

Lee held the line protecting Petersburg and Richmond as long as he could, keeping the Federals back with occasional offensive maneuvers.

But Grant knew that Lee's lines were paper thin, and on 2 April 1865, the Federals punched through. Lee could only stall him now. Lee dictated a dispatch to the secretary of war. "I see no prospect of doing more than holding our position here till night. I am not certain that I can do that. If I can I shall withdraw north of the Appomattox, and, if possible, it will be better to withdraw the whole line tonight from the James River."[14] Petersburg and Richmond were lost.

The Confederate army—and Lee in his headquarters—were now under continuous bombardment. Lee and his staff mounted their horses, the fire intensifying. As they rode away, their abandoned headquarters exploded under a rain of Union shells, the artillery bursts chasing after them.

The Army of Northern Virginia that left Petersburg numbered no more than 30,000 men. Lee marched them to Amelia Court House, where he expected to find supplies. Instead, they found nothing but inedible cannon balls. The food his men needed was now long marches away. Lee sent a message to Danville, the nearest of the supply dumps on his route to North Carolina, ordering that rations be sent on to the railroad station at Jetersville, Virginia, eight miles south of Amelia Court House. But Federal cavalry under Phil Sheridan were already riding to seize Jetersville; Grant was in pursuit of Lee; and Lee's army, while trying to fight a campaign of maneuver, were caught in occasional bloody engagements, like Sayler's Creek (6 April 1865), that depleted the Confederate forces.

The end was apparent on 9 April 1865. It was then that General John B. Gordon fought the last engagement of the Army of Northern Virginia near Appomattox Court House. "Tell General Lee," Gordon ordered, "I have fought my corps to a frazzle, and I fear I can do nothing unless I am

Books Yankees Don't Want to Read

Gone with the Wind, by Margaret Mitchell (Macmillan, Anniversary Edition, 1975). The continuing popularity of this Pulitzer Prize-winning (and historically accurate) novel must be a constant affront to the politically correct.

heavily supported by General Longstreet's corps."[15] General Longstreet anchored Lee's other flank; he could not be moved short of sacrificing the entire army.

Lee had to surrender.

And so it was done. On Palm Sunday, 9 April 1865, General Robert E. Lee rode to the Appomattox house of Wilmer McLean, where he surrendered to Ulysses S. Grant. After the arrangements were completed, Grant returned to his headquarters and informed his staff: "The war is over. The rebels are our countrymen again."

What You Need to Know:

Lee was noble in defeat (and had dismissed any talk of fighting on in a guerilla campaign), and Grant was magnanimous in victory. Thereafter, Lee allowed no one in his presence to criticize Grant. With four years of savage fighting behind them, nothing so became the combatants—and their respective countries—as the manner in which they ended the war in April 1865.

Part III

★ ★ ★ ★ ★ ★ ★ ★

EMINENT CIVIL WAR GENERALS

Chapter Five

ROBERT E. LEE
(1807-1870)

"Duty, then, is the sublimest word in our language."[1]

Guess What?

- Robert E. Lee considered slavery a political and moral evil

- Lee opposed secession

- After the war, a New York newspaper thought Lee should run for president

Robert E. Lee was *the* general of the war. What George Washington was to the American War of Independence, Lee was to the War for Southern Independence. But Lee had no Admiral de Grasse, no French fleet blasting through the Federal blockade of Virginia's coasts, no general Rochambeau marching at his side with an army of French regulars. He fought no half-hearted English generals who half-sympathized with the enemy and who were kept short of men by a cost-conscious Parliament. His enemy was vastly more powerful, its tenacity beyond compare, its willingness to embrace total war, a shock. And so Lee suffered what George Washington did not: ultimate defeat.

He gave birth not to a new country, but to memories of a Lost Cause. His country—his Virginia, the state of Washington, Jefferson, Madison, Monroe, George Mason, John Marshall, and Patrick Henry—was put under federal military occupation and subjected to martial law that deprived many Virginians of their civil rights; his house, seized by the Federal government, was turned into a national graveyard.

As the epitome of the defeated Confederacy, after a war more sanguinary and bitter than any in American history, one might assume that Lee would be a hated figure: reviled in the North as the slaughterer-in-chief of the boys in blue, repudiated in the South as the man who failed.

But of course, that was not the verdict then or now. In the South, Lee became an icon, a gleaming image of all that was right with the Lost Cause, a man whose deeply rooted love of his state, Christian piety, and chivalrous conduct validated a Southern ideal. In the North, too, Lee was seen as a noble adversary, a hero, in fact, for all Americans. Theodore Roosevelt, son of a Northern father and a Southern mother, said that Lee was "without any exception the very greatest of all the great captains that the English-speaking peoples have brought forth."[2]

The George Washington of the Confederacy

Jefferson Davis might have been the Confederacy's first, and only, president, but it was Lee who was the true father of his country, the Confederate States of America—even though he had wished the day of secession had never come.

Lee's identification with Washington was strong. His father, "Light Horse Harry" Lee had served under Washington and had famously eulogized him in 1799 as "first in war, first in peace, and first in the hearts of his countrymen"—words that were used to introduce Robert E. Lee himself in the Virginia House of Delegates as commander of the state's military forces after secession. One of his first Confederate staff officers was

John A. Washington, a nephew of George Washington. Earlier, at Harpers Ferry, he rescued George Washington's cousin, Lewis W. Washington, from the clutches of John Brown.

Lee had been born a mere eight years after Washington's death and had married into Washington's family. His wife, Mary Anna Randolph Custis, was the daughter of George Washington Parke Custis who had been raised, almost from birth, by George Washington as his own son at Mount Vernon (Custis's grandmother was a Washington, Martha Dandridge Custis Washington). Arlington House, which became Lee's family home, had been the estate of Custis and was filled with mementoes of the first president. Lee's eldest son was named George Washington Custis Lee.

The stoic Washington was Lee's model of what it meant to be a leader, a soldier, an American, and a Virginian. Like Washington, Lee had been born a gentleman, but in circumstances where he quickly learned the necessity of hard work, discipline, and frugality. He shared his class's and his people's Episcopalian convictions, and with that came a belief that, in the fullness of time, slavery would pass away. Washington had freed his slaves upon his death. Custis's will mandated that his slaves would be emancipated five years after his death. And Lee's wife dutifully taught

Lee on Secession

"I wish to live under no other government, and there is no sacrifice I am not ready to make for the preservation of the Union save that of honour. If disruption takes place, I shall go back in sorrow to my people and share the misery of my native state, and save in her defence there will be one soldier less in the world than now. I wish for no other flag than the 'Star spangled banner' and no other air than 'Hail Columbia.' I still hope that the wisdom and patriotism of the nation will yet save it."

Quoted in Douglas Southall Freeman, *Lee* (Charles Scribner's Sons, 1991), 106–7.

the family's slaves how to read and write, and the women how to sew. She wanted to prepare them for their freedom. As Virginians, and as conservatives, they felt that this was the way manumission should be achieved—through the free consent of the masters, and with proper preparation of their slaves; not by force, not at the barrel of a gun, and not by a social or political revolution. For them, the intemperate hectoring of the abolitionists, the agitational propaganda of *Uncle Tom's Cabin* (which bore no relation to their personal experience of slavery), and the threatened insurrection of John Brown was all uninformed and dangerous radicalism.

Lee considered himself a Union man; he deprecated secession as revolution, something no conservative could countenance willingly. "I must say that I am one of those dull creatures that cannot see the good of secession."[3] But he understood that it was an extremity to which abolitionists were forcing the South. Of the northern abolitionists, Lee wrote, "Their object is both unlawful & entirely foreign" and their goal of emancipating the slaves "can only be achieved by *them* through the agency of a civil & servile war."[4] Lee's assessment proved accurate, and it makes one suspect that Lee's other prediction might have been proven right as well: that if the northern abolitionists had only let the South be, Providence would have taken its course and slavery eventually and peaceably would have met its natural end in emancipation. Every other Western, Christian slave-holding society in the nineteenth century followed precisely that path.

Lee had deep roots in Virginia, going back to 1641 on his paternal side and even farther back on this mother's, Ann Hill Carter's, side. Her father, Charles "King" Carter was the largest landholder in the state. Lee's father, "Light Horse Harry" Lee was an adventurer, who, like many adventurers, was less gifted with money and financial acumen than he was with a sword. And just as he had once lopped off the heads of deserters (sending one bleeding specimen to a horrified George Washington), his family found him lopping off the family fortune in a series of bad investments. Nevertheless, he was a man of honor. In 1812, he stood against a mob attacking the newspaper of a friend of his. He and his friend were Federalists; the mob, Jeffersonian Republicans. The mob beat him nearly to death. He never fully recovered, and after a self-imposed exile in the West Indies, he died in 1818.

What this meant for Robert E. Lee was that while he venerated his father, he hardly knew him; while he had been born to moneyed and storied families, his widowed mother had little money and no land of her own. The result was not felt as a tragedy by the young Robert E. Lee, who was by all accounts a happy lad and a conscientious, active, and thoughtful boy.

His character was stamped, from the beginning, by a natural poise. He received a classical education, excelling in mathematics, and had a love of order. From his mother he received a deep and sincere Christian piety practiced within the denominational confines of Virginia's ruling class, the Episcopal Church. He was handsome—indeed, at one point he was considered the handsomest man in the army—and with a powerful physique. But most of all, he seemed gifted with intelligence, dignity, charm, good humor, and a character apparently unstained in thought and deed. He attended West Point and graduated second in his class as a corps adjutant (the highest rank a cadet could receive) without a single demerit.

Action in Mexico

He was commissioned an officer of engineers—the branch of the service that attracted the most talented cadets—and until the age of forty that was the career to which he applied himself. But when Congress declared war on Mexico in 1846, Lee put aside his work in the engineering department—building forts, diverting rivers, and constructing dams—and reported to Texas and then onwards to Mexico. Engineers—aside from their other skills, such as laying roads and erecting bridges—were thought to be particularly well suited to reconnaissance duties.

Lee joined General John E. Wool in San Antonio for the march into Mexico. He collected tools for laying roads and building bridges, but the greatest service he performed was scouting out enemy positions, sometimes covering up to sixty miles a day on horseback. In January 1847, he received orders to join General Winfield Scott for his amphibious operation against Vera Cruz—the largest amphibious invasion before World War II. Once ashore, Lee was set the task of planting Scott's artillery for maximum effect; he sat in on General Scott's councils of war; and he saw his first action, during which his main concern—aside from fulfilling his duty—was that his brother, Smith Lee, a naval officer ashore with the batteries, not be injured. He wasn't. In Lee's words, "He preserved his usual cheerfulness, and I could see his white teeth through all the smoke and din of the fire."[5]

For himself, Lee took the stress of campaigning and combat easily. But he was always troubled by the effect of war on others, especially civilians. He grieved for his dead comrades, "the fine fellows," but even more for the Mexican civilians who had been caught in the city: "My heart bled for the inhabitants . . . it was terrible to think of the women and children."[6]

On the march from Vera Cruz, Lee was quickly winning the notice of General Scott as "the indefatigable Lee." In one striking instance of his indefatigability—a word that often described the dutiful Virginia captain—Lee was on reconnaissance with a scout who fled when Mexican voices came near. Lee dove under a log and there he was stuck most of the day—silent, motionless, impervious to dirt, bugs, and discomfort—while Mexican soldiers sat on his hiding place. His revenge came when he resumed his scouting and blazed a path for the American army to flank the enemy and smash him into flight at Cerro Gordo. In his after-battle dispatch, General Scott wrote, "I am impelled to make special mention of the services of Captain R. E. Lee, engineers. This officer, greatly distinguished in the siege of Vera Cruz, was again indefatigable, during these operations, in reconnaissance as daring as laborious, and of the greatest value. Nor was he less conspicuous in planting batteries, and in conducting columns to their stations under the heavy fire of the enemy."[7]

Lee was eager for the clash of combat. Beneath his calm, gentle exterior, he had a soldier's aggression. He wrote that his horse, Creole, "stepped over the dead men with such care as if she feared to hurt them, but when I started with the dragoons in the pursuit, she was as fierce as possible, and I could barely hold her." Creole sounds much like Lee himself.

Still, however hot-blooded Lee could be in the chase and in a fight, he remained a Christian soldier. He wrote to his son Custis, "You have no idea what a horrible sight a battlefield is." He told him how he had come across a dying Mexican soldier sprawled across a wounded boy—the boy coming to his attention through the crying of a Mexican girl. "Her large black eyes were streaming with tears, her hands crossed over her breast; her hair in one long plait behind reached her waist, her shoulders and arms bare, and without stockings or shoes. Her plaintive tone of '*Millie gracias, Signor*,' as I had the dying man lifted off the boy and both carried to the hospital still lingers in my ear."[8]

Lee's most famous feat in the Mexican War was guiding American troops into action through the *pedregal*, a bed of lava five miles wide, apparently impassable, that blocked the American advance to Mexico City. Roads ran along either side of it, but these were easily and heavily defended. Undaunted, Lee penetrated the volcanic rock field and not only found a passage but led three brigades through it and into action against the enemy's rear, delivering victory at the battle of Contreras. He then retraced his route to Scott's headquarters and guided troops to a flank attack in the battle of Churubusco, chasing the Mexicans from the field. The battles punctuated nearly forty consecutive hours of wakeful action by Lee.

In his after-battle report, General Persifor Smith noted that Lee's "reconnaissances, though carried far beyond the bounds of prudence, were conducted with so much skill that their fruits were of the utmost value, the soundness of his judgment and personal daring being equally conspicuous."[9] General Winfield Scott thought Lee's performance "the greatest feat of physical and moral courage performed by any individual to my knowledge." He referred to the "gallant, indefatigable Captain Lee" who was "as distinguished for felicitous execution as for science and daring."[10] General Scott had by now, in the words of General Erasmus D. Keyes, an "almost idolatrous fancy for Lee, whose military ability he estimated far beyond that of any other officer in the army." Indeed, Scott would later call Lee "the very best soldier I ever saw in the field."[11]

Winfield Scott was the finest military intellect of his time, and Lee's experience on his staff was invaluable. But such was Scott's admiration for Lee that he pushed Lee to the point of collapse. In the assault on Chapultepec, before the occupation of Mexico City, Scott had Lee directing artillery, scouting enemy positions, and bringing him battlefield reports to the point that Lee was in action for nearly sixty straight hours before a flesh wound and sheer exhaustion forced him from his saddle. But after a brief rest, he was well enough the next morning to ride into Mexico City with the conquering heroes of the American army.

Peace at West Point, bandits in Texas, slaves at Arlington

The war was over, and Lee, who had hoped "to perform what little service I can to my country,"[12] had certainly done that. He was soon back to administrative and engineering duties, which were trifling enough compared to war. They had the benefit, however, of freeing him to live at home with his family for long periods of time—a freedom he relished, though adventure lurked if he wanted it. In 1849, Mississippi senator Jefferson Davis met with a group of Cuban rebels and recommended that they consider Robert E. Lee as a possible commander for their army. Lee politely declined the offer.

Lee tried to decline his appointment as Superintendent of West Point in 1852 as well (he had, in 1839, turned down a teaching appointment at the military academy) thinking himself unsuited to the task. Construction, he understood; military tactics, certainly; but shaping young officers—well, that seemed a daunting challenge, especially when one of the young cadets was his own son Custis Lee.

As it was, he acquitted himself dutifully and well (as might be expected), and renewed his own military education by making frequent use of the West Point library, studying the campaigns of Napoleon. He did, however, receive this telling criticism from then secretary of war Jefferson Davis, who wrote that he "was surprised to see so many gray hairs on his head, he confessed that the cadets did exceeding worry him, and then it was perceptible that his sympathy with young people was rather an impediment than a qualification for the superintendency."[13] In 1855, Jefferson Davis won approval for two new cavalry regiments to patrol the West and fight Indians; he chose Lee to serve as lieutenant colonel of the 2nd Cavalry. Lee wrote to his wife's cousin, who lived with the Lees at Arlington House, "The change from my present confined and sedentary life, to one more free and active, will certainly be more agreeable to my feelings and serviceable to my health. But my happiness can never be advanced by my separation from my wife, children and friends."[14]

Instead of fighting the Comanche in Texas, Lee found himself traveling in Louisville and Washington, D.C., going through the bureaucratic

Lee the Emancipator

Robert E. Lee not only freed his inherited slaves before the Emancipation Proclamation took effect, he argued during the war for the South to abolish slavery itself and find ways to encourage blacks to enlist in the Confederate army.

rigamarole of raising the new regiment. This was not the "free and active" service Lee had hoped for, even if it had the unexpected benefit of allowing him to spend December 1855 at Arlington House. His father-in-law put him to work. George Washington Parke Custis was an inattentive and lackadaisical landowner. His estate had run to seed, and confronted with debts he could not pay he turned to Lee, a paragon of responsibility, to set his financial affairs in order. Lee began untangling the paperwork of bills, but then was recalled to military duties in Texas.

His life among the Comanche required more diplomacy than martial prowess, and Lee found the Indians a bore, "the whole race is extremely uninteresting," he remarked in a letter to his wife.[15] Indeed, he spent more of his time traveling to sit on distant courts-martial than he did fighting Indians or pursuing Mexican bandits. In 1857, George Washington Parke Custis died, and the army kindly granted Lee a two-year's leave to put the Arlington House estate back in order. This meant renovating buildings and fields that had fallen into rot, managing the estate's 150 slaves (a task that he found disagreeable), retiring Custis's enormous debts (about $10,000 worth), coming up with the money Custis willed but did not adequately provide for Lee's daughters ($40,000 worth, which Lee achieved through land sales), and freeing all of Custis's slaves within the mandated five-year period, which, as war intervened, meant that Lee's slaves were freed (in 1862) before the Emancipation Proclamation took effect. It was a huge task, which required Lee to request that his leave be extended (it was) through the fall of 1859. What interrupted it was John Brown's raid on Harpers Ferry.

The Crisis

After the election of Lincoln and the secession of the states of the lower South, Lee remained in favor of the Union, but a *voluntary* union, not one held together by swords and bayonets against the will of the Southern states. Though offered command of the Federal armies, he refused to wage war against the South. He believed the American way of resolving political disputes was through discussion, persuasion, and compromise, not through war—a stance that made him an enemy of the Lincoln administration.

For Lee the soldier, paradoxically, the key principle at issue was avoiding the use of force. Lee believed the people of the South should be allowed full liberty of conscience and free will—that was their right as

The Lees of Virginia

Robert E. Lee's decision to resign his commission in the United States Army had been reached with "tears of blood," his wife wrote. But he did not wish to impose his own views on others. Lee wrote his wife to tell his son Custis that "he must consult his own judgment, reason and conscience as to the course he may take. I do not wish him to be guided by my wishes or example. If I have done wrong, let him do better."*

In the event, his sons Custis, Rooney, and Rob all served in Confederate grey. Custis was an engineer, reaching the rank of major general. Rooney (whose given name was William Henry Fitzhugh) became a cavalryman. Though an academic failure (he had to be educated at Harvard rather than West Point), he still managed to reach the rank of major general. Rob enlisted in the artillery, rising to the rank of captain. Lee's brother Smith served as a captain in the Confederate navy. Smith's son Fitzhugh was commissioned into the cavalry, rising to the rank of major general.

* Quoted in Clifford Dowdey, *Lee* (Stan Clark Military Books, 1991), 149. Mrs. Lee's letter is quoted on pages 134–5.

Americans. To that end, he would take up arms only in defense of his native land and its right to determine its own destiny.

It should always be remembered that a civil war, a war of brother against brother, of neighbor against neighbor, is not what the South wanted; it was the Federals who required it in order to bend the South to accept a Union of which it no longer wished to be a part. However painful it was to resign from his service to the United States, Lee believed his ultimate duty was to Virginia and to his people.

Lee's initial service to the cause of the Confederacy was deskbound. He had to raise, train, and equip an army. It was an extraordinary achievement that he did so—and in short order. He found talented officers for command, used cadets from the Virginia Military Institute to train civilians,

He Is an Englishman

Field Marshal Viscount Wolseley, of the British army, on Robert E. Lee:

> He is a strongly built man, about five feet eleven in height, and apparently not more then fifty years of age. His hair and beard are nearly white; but his dark brown eyes still shine with all the brightness of youth, and beam with a most pleasing expression. Indeed, his whole face is kindly and benevolent in the highest degree. In manner, though sufficiently conversible, he is slightly reserved; but he is a person that, wherever seen, whether in a castle or a hovel, alone or in a crowd, must at once attract attention as being a splendid specimen of an English gentleman, with one of the most rarely handsome faces I ever saw.

Field Marshal Viscount Wolseley, *The American Civil War: An English View, The Writings of Field Marshal Viscount Wolseley*, edited by James A. Rawley (Stackpole Books, 2002), 30–31.

and in a matter of about two months had 40,000 troops readied for the defense of Virginia.

Life behind a desk was not what Lee sought, but Jefferson Davis kept him there as his chief military adviser. The few brief forays when he was allowed into the field at the beginning of the war were certainly inglorious. In western Virginia there was a damp squib of a campaign, distinguished more by the bickering of his subordinate (or insubordinate) generals than by any effective action against the enemy. In the Carolinas, he was returned to his training as an engineer, supervising the construction of coastal defenses. His only reward was earning the unflattering nicknames of "Granny Lee" and "the King of Spades" (apparently fonder of the pick and shovel than the bayonet).

Others knew him better. General Winfield Scott told Lincoln that Lee was worth 50,000 men to the Confederacy. Field Marshal Viscount Garnet Wolseley—who ended his career as commander in chief of the British army—noted that "I have met many of the great men of my time, but Lee alone impressed me with the feeling that I was in the presence of a man who was cast in a grander mold, and made of a different and of finer metal than other men."[16] Lee, Wolseley wrote, "knew what an army should be, and how it should be organized, both in a purely military as well as in an administrative sense." [17]

At the Battle of First Manassas, Lee's finer metal, his knowing what an army should be, proved itself, as the army he put into the field brought the Confederates their first major victory (though he remained, to his frustration, in Richmond). He also identified the genius of Stonewall Jackson and guided his star through the Shenandoah Valley.

Then, on 1 June 1862, came the summons: with Joseph E. Johnston wounded at the battle of Seven Pines, Lee, by order of Jefferson Davis, rode onto the battlefield as the commander of the Army of Northern Virginia (the new name Lee gave his army). He remained a battlefield commander until the end of the war.

The one word that best captures Lee's essence as a military commander is audacity—but another would be faith. It was his trust in Providence that left him calm in the most perilous circumstances. Lee was a Christian gentleman who practiced a strict self-control and devotion to duty, who did everything he could to avoid or soothe personal conflicts, but when war was upon him, he was as daring a commander as could be found, repeatedly dividing his already outnumbered and ill-supplied forces and striking with an aggressiveness that chased Federal soldiers from the field.

In a succession of stunning blows, he drove the Federals from Richmond during the Seven Days, forced a second Federal skedaddle from Manassas, eviscerated the Federal Army of the Potomac at Fredericksburg, and routed the Union forces at Chancellorsville. Even at Sharpsburg—where McClellan had captured Lee's plans and outnumbered him better than two to one—the gallant Virginian wrought a tactical victory that ended McClellan's military career.

At Gettysburg, Lee came closer to smashing the Union army than is generally supposed. Lee remained convinced that if Pickett's charge had been supported as he had planned it to be—in other words, if his orders had been properly carried out—the Confederates would have taken Seminary Ridge. Even during the slow dissolution of the Confederacy that followed, it was Lee and his Army of Northern Virginia that remained the rock that Federal waves could erode but not destroy.

During the siege of Petersburg, as Shelby Foote noted, "Lee's veterans fought less... for a cause than they did for a tradition....[A] tradition [now] not so much of victory as of undefeat....Mainly, though, Lee's veterans fought for Lee, or at any rate for the pride they felt when they watched him ride among them."[18]

The pride Lee's veterans felt for Lee was a pride that Americans of the South and the North felt for him after the war. His sterling character shone forth so brightly, even in defeat, that Lee, whose citizenship had never been restored, who could not vote himself, who could in fact have been tried for treason and executed, whose proud Virginia was now under the Reconstruction occupation as Military District Number One with an imposed military governor, was suggested by a Northern newspaper as a possible presidential candidate. The *New York Herald* urged the Democratic Party that if it had any hope of defeating the Republican Ulysses S. Grant, it should "nominate General R. E. Lee . . . making no palaver or apology. He is a better soldier than any of those they have thought upon and a greater man. He is one in whom the military genius of this nation finds its fullest development. Here the inequality will be in favor of the Democrats for this soldier, with a handful of men whom he moulded into an army, baffled our greater Northern armies for four years, and when opposed by Grant was only worn down by that solid strategy of stupidity that accomplishes its object by mere weight."

That was the opinion then and later. At Appomattox, Union Colonel Charles S. Wainwright wrote, "The Army of Northern Virginia under Lee . . . today . . . has surrendered. During three long and hard-fought campaigns it has withstood every effort of the Army of the Potomac; now at the commencement of the fourth, it is obliged to succumb

> ★ ★ ★
> ## An Incident in Richmond
>
> After the war, Lee went to worship at St. Paul's Episcopal Church in Richmond. During the communion service, a black man strode down and knelt to receive communion. There was a silent collective gasp among the congregants and the priest paused not knowing what to do. Lee then rose and knelt beside the black communicant, and in this one act redeemed the time, and the service continued.

without even one great pitched battle. Could the war have been closed with such a battle as Gettysburg, it would have been more glorious for us . . . .As it is, the rebellion has been worn out rather than suppressed."[19]

General Grant was of a somewhat similar mind, later writing, "my own feelings, which had been jubilant on receipt of his letter [Lee's note agreeing to discuss terms of surrender], were sad and depressed. I felt like anything but rejoicing at the downfall of a foe who had fought so long and valiantly, and had suffered so much for a cause, though that cause was, I believe, one of the worst for which a people ever fought."[20]

Though a reluctant secessionist, Lee understood the cause for which he fought, and it was by no means an ignoble one, as witness a letter he wrote to Lord Acton, the great classical liberal statesman, in 1866. Acton had initiated the correspondence, writing to Lee about his admiration for the Confederacy. "I saw in State Rights," Acton wrote, "the only availing check upon the absolutism of the sovereign will, and secession filled me with hope, not as the destruction of but as the redemption of Democracy....Therefore I deemed that you were fighting the battles of our liberty, our progress, and our civilization; and I mourn for the stake which was lost at Richmond more deeply than I rejoice over that which was saved at Waterloo."[21]

Lee replied, "I yet believe that the maintenance of the rights and authority reserved to the states and to the people, not only essential to the adjustment and balance of the general system, but the safeguard to the continuance of a free government . . . whereas the consolidation of the states into one vast republic sure to be aggressive abroad and despotic at home, will be the certain precursor of that ruin which has overwhelmed all those that have preceded it." He outlined his understanding of how the founders had opposed such a consolidation and how secession had been acknowledged as a presumed constitutional right in the past. But, he said, "I will not weary you with such unprofitable discussion. Unprofitable because the judgment of reason has been displaced by the arbitrament of war." During the crisis of 1861, Lee had been on the side of judgment and reason.

He believed his state had done the same: "The South has contended only for the supremacy of the constitution, and the just administration of the laws made in pursuance to it. Virginia to the last made great efforts to save the union, and urged harmony and compromise."

"Who then," he asks, "is responsible for the war?" He does not answer the question, but the implication is clear—and the institution of slavery does not cloud it. "Although the South would have preferred any honourable compromise to the fratricidal war which has taken place, she now accepts in good faith its constitutional results, and receives without reserve the amendment which has already been made to the constitution for the extinction of slavery. That is an event that has been long sought, though in a different way, and by none has it been more earnestly desired than by citizens of Virginia."[22]

Lee's thoughts, at war's end, were on the preservation of order and civilization, on reconciliation and recovery. At Appomattox, Edward Porter Alexander, the young artillery officer who had directed the batteries at Gettysburg, now a thirty-year-old general, was "wound up to a pitch of feeling I could scarcely control" and recommended that the army should "scatter like rabbits and partridges in the woods" and fight a guerilla war. Lee shook his head and replied: "Suppose I should take your suggestion and order the army to disperse and make their way to their homes. The men would have no rations and they would be under no discipline. They are already demoralized by four years of war. They would have to plunder and rob to procure subsistence. The country would be full of lawless bands in every part, and a state of society would ensue from which it would take the country years to recover. Then the enemy's cavalry would pursue in the hopes of catching the principal officers, and wherever they went there would be fresh rapine and destruction."

Somewhat humorously Lee added, "And as for myself, while you young men might afford to go to bushwhacking, the only proper and dignified course for me would be to surrender myself and take the consequences of my actions."

Alexander wrote, in remembrance of this conversation, "I had not a single word to say in reply. He had answered my suggestion from a plane so far above it that I was ashamed of having made it."[23]

Instead of becoming a guerilla leader, Lee counseled Jefferson Davis that a "partisan war may be continued, and hostilities protracted, causing individual suffering and the devastation of the country, but I see no prospect by that means of achieving a separate independence....To save useless effusions of blood, I would recommend measures be taken for suspension of hostilities and the restoration of peace."[24]

Lee devoted himself not only to the restoration of peace, but to the rebuilding of the South, spending the last five years of his life as president of Washington College, in Lexington, Virginia, now Washington and Lee University, where his legacy lives on in the school's honor code, in Lee chapel, and in the young men (and more recently women) who have graduated from the school to become leaders in the South and in the United States.

Lee could have fled, as the Confederate naval officer (and VMI graduate and founder of oceanography) Matthew Fontaine Maury invited him to do, to a Confederate colony in Mexico, but as in 1861, Lee wrote, "The thought of abandoning the country and all that must be left in it is abhorrent to my feelings, and I prefer to struggle for its restoration and share its fate, rather than give up all as lost."[25]

For Lee, all was never lost, because God ultimately decided events. Trusting, then, to conscience, formed by the Episcopal *Book of Common Prayer* as well as "the consciousness of duty faithfully performed," Lee rested his hopes in the Confederate motto, *Deo vindice*. He died a beloved Virginian, Southerner, and American in 1870.

Chapter Six

GEORGE H. THOMAS (1816-1870)

"Gentleman, I know of no better place to die than right here."[1]

Guess What?

✦ Some of the best Union generals—like George Thomas—were Southerners

✦ Though one of the most successful Union generals of the war, Thomas was held suspect because he was a Virginian

✦ Thomas treated his fellow Southerners harshly

George Thomas was fifteen years old when the blood-stained, drunken followers of Nat Turner raided his family's farm. His mother, a widow, had heard they were coming and fled with her two daughters. The renegade slaves left a trail of murder behind them, and it scarred the memories of many people in Virginia and the South.

But Thomas was not among them. Thomas, like many Southern boys, had grown up with black Southern boys for company, and he had an affinity for the slaves on his family's farm. He taught them Sunday school lessons and secular school lessons. Like many Virginians, he looked forward to the day when they might be freemen. Nat Turner's Rebellion did not change that. The adolescent Thomas had no undue fear, no sense that violent upheavals lay in store unless Southern laws kept the slaves down, no concern that educated and freed the slaves would become like the slave rebels of Haiti and plunge Southampton County, Virginia, and the South, into a genocidal race war. George Thomas was always steady as a rock, phlegmatic, deliberate, measured, and sensible.

His virtues and his vices were those of a stolid man. At West Point, the young Virginian was compared to another Virginian—George Washington, to whom he was alleged to bear a striking resemblance. He was also called "Old Tom," a young man mature beyond his years. Later, when he became a cavalry instructor, his troops knew him as "Old Slow Trot"— he was careful not to wear out his horses—and other nicknames he acquired bore a similar bloodline: "Old Reliable," "The Rock of Chickamauga," "The Sledge of Nashville." He was a man of impeccable integrity, and when he was criticized it was almost invariably because impatient superiors thought that "Old Slow Trot" should be moving more quickly; this was a refrain of General Grant, who developed a dislike for Thomas. But in this regard, Thomas, like the Confederate General James Longstreet, might have been slow, but he was a heavy hitter. In fact, he is probably the best Union general you've never heard of.

Part of the reason for his anonymity is that he never wrote his memoirs; more than that, he never sought public attention and was so correct in his character as to turn down promotions he didn't think were merited. His Civil War career was focused on the war in the West, which gets less popular attention than do the dramatic campaigns of the East. But also there is this: Thomas was something of a man without a country. His sisters turned his picture to the wall and refused to acknowledge that they had a brother George. In the South, in his native Virginia, he became a non-person. But in the North, too, he could never evade suspicion of his roots, even though Thomas never showed the slightest faltering to the Union blue and even though other Virginians, including the original general in chief of Union forces, Winfield Scott, had made the same decision Thomas did. Thomas was esteemed by most of his peers—he was one of only thirteen officers to receive an official "Thanks of Congress"—but he has been forgotten or relegated to second rank by posterity.

As a boy, George Thomas was, in the words of his sister Judith, "as all other boys are who are well born and well reared."[2] He had taken over the leadership of the family farm when he was sixteen, worked in a law office, and, at age twenty, was accepted into West Point, where he graduated twelfth (out of forty-two) in the Class of 1840. His first assignments took him to the Seminole Wars of Florida, where his service was uneventful, and then to the War with Mexico, which was rather more so, as he saw action directing artillery at Monterrey and Buena Vista.

In the latter battle, while other batteries retired in the face of charging Mexicans, Thomas kept firing until they were nearly upon him, at which point, serendipitously, other American batteries and infantry came to his aid. As Thomas remarked laconically, "I saved my section of [Brevet-Major Braxton] Bragg's battery at Buena Vista by being a little slow."[3] William Tecumseh Sherman, who was friends with Thomas at West Point, was slightly more effusive: "Lieutenant Thomas more than sustained the reputation he has long enjoyed in his regiment as an accurate and scientific artillerist."[4] It was Thomas's methodical movements— which were so much the character of the man—that helped him to be such an accurate and scientific artillerist, quartermaster, and master of every other task the army assigned him. It was the Thomas way—slow, scientific, and accurate.

After the Mexican War, Thomas returned to West Point as an artillery and cavalry instructor and also managed to marry a New Yorker, which, in the coming crisis, would help solidify his Unionist sympathies. Thomas was then sent west to California, finally ending up in the blazing desert of Fort Yuma, from which he was rescued by the Secretary of War Jefferson Davis. Davis was looking to create an elite cavalry regiment, and Braxton Bragg recommended Thomas. Thomas, Bragg admitted, "is not brilliant, but he is a *solid*, sound man; an honest, high-toned gentleman, above all deception and guile, and I know him to be an excellent and gallant soldier."[5]

The Second Cavalry Regiment had the best of everything, elaborate uniforms, and even color-coordinated horses (each company had horses of the same color). The regiment's job was to patrol—along with the newly raised First Cavalry Regiment and two regiments of infantry—the western frontier. Among the officers serving in these cavalry regiments were Joseph E. Johnston and J. E. B. Stuart (the First Regiment) and Albert Sidney Johnston, Robert E. Lee, and John Bell Hood (the Second Regiment).

His duty in the West was much like Lee's (he actually served under Lee), sitting on courts-martial, keeping the peace between Indians and settlers, and seizing rare chances for action (in one incident, Thomas received a Comanche arrow in his chest).

In the election of 1860, Thomas did the soldierly thing—he opposed the extreme fire-eaters of the South and the rabid abolitionists of the North, and positioned himself with the party of moderation, which was represented by John Bell of the Constitutional Union Party, who carried Kentucky, Tennessee, and Virginia.

Thomas inquired after a position (which had already been filled) at the Virginia Military Institute in January 1861, assuming apparently that his home state would not join South Carolina in secession. But when, in March, Virginia Governor John Letcher asked Thomas whether he would consider resigning his Federal commission and accepting a position as chief ordnance officer of Virginia's military forces, Thomas declined. He did so in terms that, in due course, would cast him in opposition to Lee. After expressing his thanks for the governor's offer, he wrote, "it is not my wish to leave the service of the United States as long as it is honorable for me to remain in it, and therefore as long as my native State remains in the Union it is my purpose to remain in the army unless required to perform duties alike repulsive to honor and humanity."[6]

While Lee considered waging war against his home and native state "repulsive to honor and humanity," Thomas, when the choice came, did not. Like Lee, Thomas opposed slavery, but he was not so opposed as to do without a black cook and a black servant ("Old Phil," who campaigned with him in the coming war), both slaves, whom he eventually sent South, after the war, to be employed by his family.

A humble general

Thomas clearly understood the direction the war would take. In the summer of 1861 he met his old friend William Tecumseh Sherman and the two of them bent over a map and marked out the most important strategic cities of the war: Richmond, Chattanooga, Nashville, and Vicksburg—cities that would soon be much more than mere points on a map, but targets of campaigns in which they would be involved.

Thomas earned his first general's star thanks to Major Robert Anderson, the Kentucky-born West Pointer who was appointed general after his defense of Fort Sumter. Anderson recognized Thomas's talent, but also recognized that as a Virginian Thomas was regarded with suspicion in Washington and had no politicians agitating for his advancement. The Kentuckian Anderson vouched for the skill and loyalty of his fellow Southerner and convinced President Lincoln to make the appointment. And it was to Kentucky and Tennessee that Thomas was dispatched. He was immediately victorious in his first major battle, at Mill Springs, Kentucky, but the stigma of his Southern roots remained, and the War Department paid him no compliments.

Compliments, of course, Thomas didn't need. He was a man of duty and a man who later in the war remarked, "Colonel, I have taken a great deal of pain to educate myself not to feel."[7] He got on with his work, and could remind others to do the same when they unnecessarily sought his advice or filed needless reports, telling one officer who rode up in the midst of battle to report his position, "Damn you, sir, go back to your command and fight it."[8]

But he was a stickler for a certain sort of protocol. His bugbear was civilian interference with military commanders, especially interference with his superior officers, to whom he was faultlessly loyal, even when he doubted them. Thomas was not a politicker; nor would he accept promotions he thought he did not merit. When he was briefly handed command of the Army of the Tennessee, he quickly relinquished it, at his own request, to General Grant (though Grant, for his part, began to develop something of a grudge against Thomas, who had been promoted after the battle of Shiloh without having taken part in it). When Thomas received orders from Washington to take over command of the Army of the Ohio from the laggard General Don Carlos Buell, Thomas refused, thinking this was another instance of civilian interference with a commanding officer. He sent a message to the war office stating that "General Buell's preparations have been completed to move against the enemy and I respectfully ask that he may be retained in command. My position is very embarrassing, not being as well informed as I should be as the commander of this army and in the assumption of such responsibility."[9]

Of this message, Thomas's biographer Freeman Cleaves rightly notes, "Despite the extraordinary lack of self-interest, even though Thomas pleaded unfairness to himself, it was a poor excuse for a man of his caliber. . . . Buell maintained that he even encouraged him to accept the post saying 'nothing remained to be done but to put the army in motion, and that I would cheerfully explain my plans to him and give him all the information I possessed.' Still Thomas would not budge."[10]

The baffled bureaucrats in the War Office accepted Thomas's demurral and thus retained Buell in at least temporary command until after the Battle of Perryville, the following month. Buell's semi-victory there had not been enough to save him. William Starke Rosecrans took his place as commander of what became the Army of the Cumberland. Rosecrans was, however, Thomas's junior in seniority—a problem that President Lincoln dealt with by the expedient of changing the date of his commission. Thomas, who had willingly deferred command to Buell, felt rather differently about being passed over in favor of Rosecrans; it was a violation of protocol. But Rosecrans had always been on good terms with Thomas, and smoothed over the diplomatic niceties.

No better place to die

Rosecrans was an inspiring leader, but like many such he was prone to mood swings himself. Thomas, also popular, was considered his de facto second-in-command and Thomas's unmistakable competence and steadiness under fire soon gained him fame whether he wanted it or not. The first great battle for the team of Rosecrans and Thomas was at Murfreesboro, Tennessee (known to the Federals as the Battle of Stone's River).

On the night of 29 December 1862, Thomas, riding the lines, heard the roar of artillery. An aide asked, "What is the meaning of that, General?" "It means a fight to-morrow on Stone River," Thomas replied.[11] He might have added, "Even if we are facing Braxton Bragg." Bragg, was second only to Joseph E. Johnston in leading Confederate retreats, and Rosecrans, knowing he was facing Bragg, assumed the rebels were retiring. He was wrong, Bragg might have been a miserable officer—an officer so contentious that he was once said to have filed charges against himself—but his ill-served troops were fighters. They had bloodied Buell at Perryville and they would now put up a furious, if mismanaged, fight at Murfreesboro.

The battle began on a rainy New Year's Eve, 1862, and was a bloody affair—Rosecrans rode about issuing orders, his uniform dripping with the blood and brains of an aide whose head was harvested by a Confederate shell. Troops hugged the ground and plugged their ears as cannonades clapped like earth-shattering thunder or bravely tried to charge though blizzards of Minié balls and canister. The Confederates had collapsed the Union lines on the first day of battle, which had the unintended effect of concentrating Federal fire.

That night Rosecrans called a council of war. His losses were tremendous (by the end of the battle nearly a third of his men would be lost as killed, wounded, or missing, more than 13,000 men) and it seemed as though retreat were inevitable. His officers were downcast when he asked their opinions. But an adjutant noted that Thomas, whose opinion Rosecrans had not yet solicited, was, "as always . . . calm, stern, determined, silent and perfectly self-possessed, his hat set squarely on his head. It was a tonic to look at the man." His words were a tonic too. When Rosecrans asked his opinion, Thomas replied, "Gentlemen, I know of no better place to die than right here."[12] Those words rejuvenated Rosecrans who sprang to prepare his army for battle the next day. Union determination—and Bragg's incompetence in the subsequent fighting—brought the Federals victory.

The Rock

An even bigger battle lay ahead at Chickamauga Creek. But first the Army of the Cumberland needed to be replenished with men and supplies. Thomas's way of training replacements was to send them into the field as skirmishers and give them a taste for combat. He, like Rosecrans, was in no hurry to pursue the rebels, remaining cautious, deliberate, and mindful always of the army's lines of communication, which were perpetually threatened and bedeviled by the unmatchable Confederate cavalry. By Washington's standards, the Federal advance was terribly delayed. By Thomas's standards, officers in the field were the only competent judges of campaign reality, and as the army's advance would be an arduous one over mountain passes, haste was a counsel of folly. When the army did advance, it compelled Bragg to retreat.

Then there was a delay. Washington wanted Rosecrans to advance on Chattanooga. Rosecrans agreed, but not before he had secured his lines of communication and supply. He had Thomas's assent, though Thomas was dubious about Rosecrans's plan to divide his forces into three parts and bring them over the mountains to flank Chattanooga. That was a shade too dangerous of an approach for the Virginian who favored a deeper flanking movement that kept the army together. Rosecrans stuck with his plan and was vindicated, as Bragg retreated again—or so it seemed. Bragg was consolidating his force with that of General Simon Boliver Buckner, and was soon to be reinforced by General James Longstreet of the Army of Northern Virginia. Though he remained skittish, Bragg recognized his opportunity to attack the divided Federals.

As it was, on 19 September 1863, Thomas wheeled out a division to attack what he thought was an isolated Confederate brigade on his side of Chickamauga Creek. The Confederates, who had crossed the creek in force, had no idea that Thomas was lodged on the extreme Federal left. A furious battle commenced, first on the Confederate right, and then down a battle line that cut through a forest broken only by occasional farms. The fighting intensified until the dead were piled like cordwood, the Creek was dyed red with blood, and the shrieking of shells, wild-eyed horses, and frenzied fighting men grew deafening. The visuals were harrowing too: "Confederate artillery filled the woods with their shells which in the twilight made the skies seem like a firmament of pestilential stars," wrote a Federal officer. "The 77th Pennsylvania of the first line was lapped up like a drop of oil under a flame."[13] But through the haze of battle, Thomas's men took confidence from their commander's unruffled demeanor. As Stone's River had been a perfectly acceptable place to die, in his opinion, so was his current position as tenable as any. He did, however, advise Rosecrans to pull back the Federal right and reinforce him on the left; advice that Rosecrans followed as best as he thought practicable.

The next morning found Thomas in fighting spirit, and uncharacteristically animated in describing his men: "Wherever I touched upon their [the enemy's] flanks they broke, General, they broke." Thomas spoke "with unusual zest and satisfaction," noted the war correspondent William Shanks. But when Thomas saw Shanks scribbling in his notebook, the forty-seven-year-old general appeared embarrassed at what might be mistaken for boastfulness, "his eyes were bent immediately on the ground and the rest of his remarks were...brief."[14]

Bragg had planned for Thomas to be the focal point of the day's fighting, but the Confederates found more success driving at the center-right of the Union line where they exploited a gap, sweeping away the Federals, sending a flood-tide of butternut and grey uniforms surging forward, and spreading panic and confusion among the bluecoats. Rosecrans, his headquarters in peril, fled with his staff officers. The Union right was dissolved. Rosecrans, cut off from Thomas, fled to Chattanooga in an apparent state of shock.

The Confederates broke off their assault on Thomas's center and left, but the Union general now had Longstreet storming at his right flank. Thomas's men took up position on Horseshoe Ridge, which they reinforced with barricades. Short of ammunition, they searched for unspent cartridges among the dead, as the enemy pressed upon them. Suddenly a dust cloud behind the Federal lines raised hope and fear—fear that beneath it was Confederate cavalry under General Nathan Bedford Forrest, hope that it might be kicked up by blue-clad reinforcements. For once in his life, Thomas appeared nervous until someone thought he saw the fluttering of the Stars and Stripes. Confirmation came as beneath the dust appeared the reserve corps of Union General Gordon Granger.

Thomas now gained his monicker, "the Rock of Chickamauga." When an aide carrying messages asked Thomas where he should find the general on his return ride, Thomas growled, "Here!" He would not be budged from this costly ground.

The fighting became a desperate hand-to-hand affair, with a Confederate lunge matched by a Federal countercharge that brought rifle butts and bayonets—not to mentions fists and rocks—to bear amidst the harsh snapping of the Minié balls. The Confederates were driven back, but they returned again and again, clawing their way towards Thomas's shrinking line. Finally, Granger found Rosecrans and received orders for Thomas to withdraw. Rosecrans had begun writing detailed instructions as to how the retreat should be conducted, but Granger upbraided him: "Oh, that's all stuff and nonsense, general. Send Thomas an order to retire. He knows what to do about as well as you do."[15] Rosecrans was too stunned to protest; it marked the practical ascendancy of Thomas over his Lincoln-appointed superior.

Thomas withdrew his men in excellent order, and from the bloody shambles of Chickamauga he emerged a hero. Again he was compared to Washington. Charles A. Dana, assistant secretary of war, who was present at Chickamauga, said, "I know of no other man whose composition and character are so much like those of Washington; he is at once an elegant gentleman and a heroic soldier."[16] Dana's biographer, General James H. Wilson, who served with Thomas, was of the same opinion, saying that Thomas resembled "the traditional Washington in appearance, manner, and character more than any man I had ever met…and at once inspired me with faith in his steadiness and courage."[17]

Thomas was, as always, popular with the troops who trusted him and knew he looked out for them. They called him "Old Pap." His promotion, however, was stalled once more by Northern politicians loathe to promote a Virginian—and typically, when Thomas discovered that men like Dana were trying to get him promoted over Rosecrans, he interceded on behalf of his commander. Lincoln finally took the matter in hand and replaced Rosecrans with Thomas as commander of the Army of the Cumberland. When Thomas tried to protest to his former commanding officer, Rosecrans stopped him, and told him to do his duty, as directed by the commander in chief. Thomas relented, and was now under the direct command of Ulysses S. Grant who commanded the military division of the Mississippi. Because of Grant's partiality to General Sherman, commander of the Army of the Tennessee (Grant's former command) it would not be a happy partnership.

Dealing with Bragg

It started in fact with what Thomas took to be an insult. Having retreated to Chattanooga after the fierce battle of Chickamauga, his pri-

Black and Blue

After Chattanooga, the Federal army began filling its ranks with black troops. Some officers (like Sherman) disapproved, but Thomas was a strong supporter of the idea:

> The Confederates regard them as property. Therefore the Government can with propriety seize them as property and use them to assist in putting down the Rebellion. But if we have the right to use the property of our enemies, we share the right to them as we would all the individuals of any other civilized nation who may choose to volunteer as soldiers in our Army. I moreover think that in the sudden transition from slavery to freedom it is perhaps better for the negro to become a soldier, and be gradually taught to depend on himself for support, than to be thrown upon the cold charities of the world without sympathy or assistance.[*]

Letter from General Thomas to the War Office

[*] Quoted in Freeman Cleaves, *Rock of Chickamauga: The Life of General George H. Thomas* (University of Oklahoma Press, 1948), 204.

mary goal was to re-supply his men. Grant issued Thomas a peremptory order: "Hold Chattanooga at all hazards." Thomas's return message was laconic: "We will hold the town until we starve."[18] Given Rosecrans's initial wires to Washington after the battle, which referred to Chickamauga as "a serious disaster" and said of Chattanooga, "We have no certainty of holding our position here,"[19] Grant had good reason to worry. But Thomas was made of sterner stuff—and the opposing commander, Braxton Bragg, did not see fit to follow up his victory at Chickamauga with an assault on the half-starved bluecoats in this crucial city.

What awaited Thomas, instead, was a Confederate siege, with Bragg hoping to starve the Federals out rather than roust them out. The Federals, however, established a supply line—"the cracker line"—which effectively thwarted Bragg's strategy (such as it was). Now, under Grant's direction, the Federals began drawing up plans for an offensive to drive Bragg's army away. Thomas disliked Bragg almost as much as Bragg's own generals did (they had tried to have him removed from command) because Bragg had returned a letter of Thomas's with a note insulting Thomas as a traitor to his state. Beneath Thomas's noble countenance burned a desire to avenge himself on his former friend—and he would, as Thomas's troops first seized Orchard Knob, his first objective, on 23 November, and then two days later made their dramatic charge up Missionary Ridge, which broke the Confederate army and put it to flight.

Hammer and Anvil: Sherman and Thomas

After the battle of Chattanooga, Thomas regarded his Army of the Cumberland as the force to defeat Joseph E. Johnston, who had replaced Bragg as the opposition commander. Grant, however, saw Thomas in an auxiliary role, supporting Sherman, and Sherman naturally agreed. While Thomas was one to diligently maintain his lines of communication and supply, Sherman had no qualms about cutting loose in enemy territory, planning to live off—and indeed punish—Southern civilians, and trusting that Thomas could fight any grey-clads in his rear.

This is when Sherman's and Thomas's reputations were made: "Thomas never lost a battle" and "Sherman never won a battle or lost a campaign."[20] The cool-headed Thomas is usually regarded as Sherman's tactical superior while Sherman is given credit for having a more imaginative grasp of campaign-level strategy (Sherman had, of course, the advantage of being Grant's strategic confidant).

Grant and Sherman together held the idea that Thomas—careful, methodical, and not averse to entrenching in the face of the enemy—was slow, though Thomas's defenders would counter that he was not noticeably slower than Grant in his campaign against Lee, that Sherman and Grant routinely left Thomas as the rear guard to mop up after Sherman, and that he had to take care where the reckless Sherman did not.

The contrasting characters of Sherman and Thomas were highlighted at the Battle of Kennesaw Mountain. Thomas had advised a flanking attack on Joseph E. Johnston. Sherman insisted that his own troops would lead a frontal assault on the Confederate positions. Sherman told General John A. Logan that a frontal attack was necessary because "the whole attention of the country was fixed on the Army of the Potomac and that his [Sherman's] army was entirely forgotten." He needed "to show that his men could fight as well as Grant's."[21]

Thomas never felt the need to prove himself in this way—and his men appreciated him for it. After two failed attempts to storm the Confederate lines that cost him 3,000 casualties, Sherman withdrew for a flanking attack, but Johnston had slipped away. Sherman, however, was adamant in self-justification: "Failure as it was...I yet claim it produced good fruits as it demonstrated to General Johnston that I would assault and that boldly." Thomas was more the realist: "One or two more such assaults would use up this army."[22]

After the Federals took Atlanta, Sherman, with Grant's blessing, planned to let Thomas handle the wildcat Confederate army led by Kentuckian-Texan John Bell Hood, the one-legged, one-armed, single-mindedly aggressive general who had been chosen to replace the great tactical retreater Joseph E. Johnston. Rather than tangling with Hood, Sherman would mount a campaign against Southern civilians; his purpose, he said, was to make Georgia "howl"; and to achieve this high purpose he stripped Thomas's army of some of its best units (especially of cavalry).

Thomas's task, then, was to fortify Nashville. This he did, and when both freezing weather and the Confederate army pressed in on the city, he prepared his men for a breakout attack—again too slowly for General Grant, who perhaps did not appreciate the difficulties of launching an offensive on a sheet of ice, in freezing rain, or understand that the weather inhibited the movements of both armies. If Thomas could not move from Nashville, neither could Hood drive far around him.

A General's Call for Prayer

During the battle of Nashville, a group of Confederate prisoners called out to General Thomas complaining about the indignity of their being guarded by black soldiers. They would rather die, they said, than bear the shame of being marched into Nashville this way. Thomas replied: "Well, you may say your prayers and get ready to die, for these are the only soldiers I can spare."*

* Quoted in Richard W. Johnson, *Memoir of Major General George H. Thomas* (J. B. Lippincott, 1881), 196–7.

When Thomas broke out of Nashville on 15 and 16 December 1864, it spelled the end of Hood's command. On 16 December, the Yankees stormed the Confederates' last redoubts in a scene remembered by Union General James T. Rustling: "grape and canister shrieked and whizzed; bullets in a perfect hailstorm....The whole battlefield at times was like the grisly mouth of hell, agape and aflame with fire and smoke, alive with thunder and death-dealing shots. The hills and slopes were strewn with the dead; ravines and gorges crowded with wounded. I saw men with their heads or limbs shot off; others blown to pieces. I rode to a tree behind which a Confederate had dodged for safety, and a Union shell had gone clear through both tree and soldier and exploded among his comrades."

It takes a certain sort of man to see this and remark of the Yankee cheers as the Confederate lines were taken, "the voice of the American people."[23] Thomas was such a man. Just as when Richmond, the capital of his home state, fell to the Federal invader on 3 April 1865 he ordered a 100-gun salute as part of Nashville's enforced celebrations. What sort of man relishes the destruction and defeat of his home state? Of course he had no more regard for the separate states of the North. A chaplain once asked him after a battle whether the dead should be buried in groups by state. Thomas growled, "No, no, no. Mix them up. Mix them up. I am tired of states-rights."[24] Thomas was obviously no respecter of Edmund Burke's dictum that to "love the little platoon we belong to in society, is the first principle (the germ as it were) of public affections." Thomas, who had hardened himself against feeling, had no concern for states or states' rights or little platoons, it was all mix them up, mix them up.

> ## ★ ★ ★ Georgia on My Mind
>
> As Confederate armies surrendered, Thomas threatened one guerilla commander that if he invaded Tennessee, "I will so despoil Georgia that it will be a wilderness fifty years hence."*
>
> The military ethos of William Tecumseh Sherman was apparently contagious.
>
> ---
>
> * Quoted in Freeman Cleaves, *Rock of Chickamauga*, 283.

Punishing rebels

Thomas had no sympathy for his fellow Southerners—he thought Southern women were especially recalcitrant—and endorsed harsh measures during Reconstruction. When the Episcopal bishop of Alabama instructed his priests to omit prayers for the Reconstruction authorities, Thomas retaliated by closing down all the Episcopal churches in Alabama. He was also the military authority in charge of Tennessee, which was coerced into passing the 14th Amendment (a requirement for being readmitted to statehood in the Union) by the expedient of arresting dissident members of the legislature and forcing them to sit in the chamber so that the measure could be passed with a quorum.

Thomas's position, *vis à vis* his fellow Southerners, was expressed in a letter he wrote to the mayor of Rome, Georgia, who merited Thomas's wrath for celebrating Georgia's secession day with Confederate flags:

> The sole cause of this and similar offenses lies in the fact that certain citizens of Rome, and a portion of the people of the States lately in rebellion, do not and have not accepted the situation, and that is, that the late civil war was a rebellion and history will so record it. Those engaged in it are and will be pronounced rebels; rebellion implies treason; and treason is a crime, and a heinous one too, and deserving of punishment; and that traitors have not been punished is owing to the magnanimity of the conquerors. With too many of the people of the South, the late civil war is called a revolution, rebels are called "Confederates," loyalists to the whole country are called d—d Yankees and traitors, and over the whole great crime with its accursed record of slaughtered heroes, patriots murdered because of their true-hearted love of country, widowed wives and orphaned children, and prisoners of war slain amid such horrors as find no parallel in the history of the world, they are trying to throw a gloss of respectability, and are thrusting with contumely and derision from their society the men and women who would not join hands with them in the work of ruining

their country. Everywhere in the States lately in rebellion, treason is respectable and loyalty odious. This, the people of the United States, who ended the Rebellion and saved the country will not permit.[25]

An impassioned missive, but for all its emotion, it rather misses the point. For the bill of particulars that Thomas lays against the South could even more plausibly be laid by King George III against the rebellious American colonists; and the South at least had the precedent of 1776 to draw from as justification for its actions.

Moreover, one cannot say that the South committed treason in establishing its own republic. It did not give aid and comfort to American enemies. It merely separated itself from the United States in order to achieve, to its own satisfaction, a more perfect union of like-minded states. There is, in fact, neither crime nor treachery in that—only the democratic desire of the people of the Southern states to go their own way. The people of the South were loyal to their states and that loyalty in no way endangered the peace of those states that wished to remain part of the United States. Thomas remained loyal not to his state, not to his region, but to the United States government and its forcible subjugation of unwilling members of the Union. Thomas, and Northerners generally, assumed a moral high ground that Southerners—Confederate Southerners, that is—could regard only, at best, as brute humbug.

But it was still no doubt sincerely held. It is therefore all the more ironic that in the remaining five years of his life after the war, he continued to feel maltreated and overlooked by his superiors when it came to promotions. When Confederate general John Bell Hood met with Thomas after the war, he said "Thomas is a grand man. He should have remained with us, where he would have been appreciated and loved"[26]—a remark so true as to deny rebuttal. One can only imagine the result for the Confederacy had Thomas held the command so long abused by Braxton Bragg.

George H. Thomas (1816–1870)

Thomas was above all a soldier. The army defined him. When he died in 1870, it was at his post in California. He was buried in New York, far from his native Virginia, attended by President Ulysses Grant, Generals Sherman, Sheridan, and Meade, and thousands of others (from the governor to a congressional delegation, to former comrades-in-arms). Since his death, he has been largely forgotten. As Grant preferred his fellow Ohioans Sherman and Sheridan, so has history.

Chapter Seven

WILLIAM TECUMSEH SHERMAN (1820-1891)

"He [Grant] stood by me when I was crazy and I stood by him when he was drunk, and now sir, we stand by each other always."[1]

Guess What?

+ Sherman loathed abolitionists

+ He believed that Southerners needed to be exterminated, and their land resettled by Northerners

+ He professed not to know which was "the greater evil": slavery or democracy

The popular image of William Tecumseh Sherman is of a rough-hewn, high-strung (to the point of insanity), ravager of the South. The image is reinforced by photographs of the Federal general. His hair is often unkempt, his look stern, and his countenance apparently reflecting an ill-tempered mind. But the Sherman of reality was a man who loved dancing and parties, was popular with the ladies, and was brutally honest, selfless, and devoted to his duty. He loathed the politicians (his brother was one) who had brought the country to war, despised abolitionists (again, his brother qualified), and embarked on his savage march through Georgia because of his conviction—founded on his own experience in the South—that it was the only way to break such a determined people. One might consider that a compliment. Sherman, however, did not mean it so. As one of his most famous biographers (and admirers) put it in 1929, Sherman believed in the survival of the fittest. The South was not economically fit, and he was in favor of dealing with that unfitness by the "economic sterilization" of the South to the point of driving Southerners from their homes and replacing them with efficient, industrious Northerners.[2] Sherman was the perfect exemplar of the blunt utilitarianism of the North.

Sherman's "religion"

Sherman came from distinguished stock. His father had served on the Ohio supreme court, his grandfather had been a judge, and he was related to Roger Sherman who signed the Declaration of Independence. Sherman, however, was orphaned at the age of nine and taken in by the family of Thomas Ewing, a United States senator, whose daughter Sherman eventually married (President Zachary Taylor and his cabinet attended the wedding). His foster parents were devout Catholics and insisted on Sherman being baptized (which Sherman's Episcopalian/Presbyterian parents had neglected). So it was a priest who gave him the name William, for which Sherman had little use (just as he later had little use for religion). His friends called him "Cump," a shortening of Tecumseh, the name his father gave him in admiration of the famous Indian chieftain.

Though not a churchgoer himself, Sherman allowed his children to be raised as Catholics. He was nevertheless appalled when one of his sons became a Jesuit priest (the priest who would, in fact, preside at Sherman's funeral Mass). Sherman's religious beliefs seem to have traveled from being "not scrupulous in matters of religion"[3] to eventually lodging himself where such people go: in the ranks of the deists. Religious doctrines were not for him, any more than were Southern constitutional doctrines about states' rights. There was, instead, in the practical Northern mind of Sherman, and in that of many of his Union colleagues, a belief in a certain sort of natural law—not the natural law of the Catholic Church, but the natural law of Thucydides who said that the powerful do what they will, and the weak suffer what they must. Or, to put it in the words of one of Sherman's later admirers, the military theorist Basil Liddell-Hart, Sherman's moral compass was a Unionist reading of the United States Constitution, which held that "law, like all law in a democracy, was founded on the natural law that might is right." [4]

Holy Sherman!

The Sherman name was not carried on by his progeny, though he had eight children, four of whom were sons. His eldest, William (Willie), died as a child. His third son, Charles, died as an infant and his fourth, Philemon Tecumseh (Cump) became a bachelor lawyer. His fourth child and second son, Thomas Ewing Sherman, was a graduate of Georgetown (with a degree in English literature), Yale (for graduate studies in English), and George Washington College (for law school). He passed the bar, but chucked the law and became a priest, a Jesuit to be precise. Though his father violently disapproved of his taking the collar, Fr. Sherman not only presided over the general's funeral but followed him into army blue, serving as a chaplain in the Spanish-American War. Fr. Sherman was a popular lecturer, though in his later years he began to show signs of serious depression—which his father believed was a familial trait—and he spent the last quarter of his life in retirement.

Sherman: The young soldier

He was sent to West Point, which he hated—neatness not being a word one associates with Sherman. Still, if he failed on inspections, he made up for it in his studies, graduating sixth in his class. As events would prove, he was a well-educated soldier, however disheveled his appearance.

He was sent to Florida to fight the Seminoles—a project in which he took a healthy enjoyment. "These excursions," he wrote, "possessed to us a peculiar charm, for the fragrance of the air, the abundance of game and fish, and just enough of adventure, gave to life a relish."[5] If only we could all have a period of Indian-fighting.

In Florida he earned quick (which was rare) promotion, which led in due course to his transfer to Charleston, South Carolina. He found he much preferred fighting Indians to the social life of the gallant South. But when the next war came along, with Mexico, he missed it, through sheer bad luck. He tried mightily to get in on the action, but was first diverted to recruiting duties, and when he finally received orders to sail to California with the Third Artillery, he arrived just in time for that theatre of the war to have drawn its curtains. But he was appointed acting adjutant-general to Colonel Richard Barnes Mason, the acting military governor of California. (Mason, a son of Lexington, Virginia, lent his name to the now decommissioned Fort Mason in San Francisco.) Sherman gained a taste for military government, of which he approved: "military law is supreme here and the way we ride down the few lawyers who have ventured to come here is curious... yet a more quiet community could not exist."[6] But he kicked against the fate that kept him in quiet California while his brother officers were gaining fame amidst the roaring artillery, the crackling musketry, and the sabre strokes of battle.

Sherman was seething with self-contempt for having missed his chance: "I really feel ashamed to wear epaulettes after having passed through a war without smelling gun-powder."[7] But General Persifor Frazer Smith, incoming commander of the newly created Department of the Pacific had other ideas for young Sherman, requiring him to stay on as his adjutant-general. From this Sherman graduated to commissariat duty, with assignments in St. Louis and New Orleans.

Since the possibility of war now appeared remote, Sherman, at the age of thirty-three, and with a growing family to support, surrendered his commission and accepted an invitation offered by a friend to return to California as a banker. He had an acute business mind, a steady nerve (necessary in the California bank crisis he had to endure), and an unimpeachable honesty that set him apart from some of his bank's competitors.

Despite his own virtues as a banker, his business career careened from failure to failure. In 1857, Sherman's bank moved from vigilante-governed and economically depressed California to New York, where the credit institutions quickly took a dive. Sherman dutifully made sure his depositors were taken care of (though his personal accounts suffered), and then decided it was time to try his hand at some securer field. He became a lawyer, joining with two of his brothers-in-law, and working largely on keeping the books and surveying property (which tapped some of his military topographical skills).

Yearning to get back in uniform, he eventually ended up as superintendent of a startup military academy in Louisiana (what is now Louisiana State University). Sherman proved himself a resourceful, popular, and effective administrator of the new school, even if it took a while for young Southern gentlemen, used to giving orders rather than taking them, to bend to the discipline. These were the men—the "young bloods," the hard-riding, liberty-loving, young Southern aristocrats—of whom, during the war, when he saw them in the Confederate cavalry, Sherman would say, "War suits them, and the rascals are fine, brave riders, bold to rashness and dangerous subjects in every sense."[8]

Sherman had always despised abolitionists, whom he thought ignorant idealists, rabble-rousers driving the country to war. But he was equally contemptuous of Southern fire-eaters, of the sort who now surrounded him, who spoke pridefully of secession and Southern independence, and deprecated the danger of war. As for Southern unionists, he scoffed at how easily they allowed themselves to be intimidated.

Sherman was, if nothing else, a forthright and honest man and he never altered his own strongly anti-secession views to suit his employers, the cadets, or their families; and it is a tribute to him and to the gentlefolk of the South that he was tolerated and respected as a pro-Union man.

When Louisiana withdrew from the Union, the governor of the state, who had officially appointed Sherman to his position, did not ask for him to resign. Indeed, the administration was keen to keep him on, but Sherman would have no part of it. He tendered his resignation, moved to St. Louis, became president of a streetcar company, and then in May 1861, one month after General Beauregard—a former colleague and friend of Sherman's—fired on Fort Sumter, he accepted a commission to fight for the Union.

Sherman: Free trade equals war, and so does Democracy

Sherman did not see the abolition of slavery as an appropriate Union war aim. When his brother John Sherman—who won the unflattering political nickname "the Ohio Icicle"—was elected to Congress in 1854 (as a Republican, a member of the newly formed anti-slavery party), Sherman wrote to him, saying: "Having lived a good deal in the South, I think I know practically more of slavery than you do . . . .There are certain lands in the South that cannot be inhabited in the summer by whites, and yet the negro thrives in it—this I know. Negroes free won't work tasks of course, and rice, sugar, and certain kinds of cotton cannot be produced except by forced negro labour. Slavery being a fact is chargeable on the past, it cannot, by our system, be abolished except by force and consequent breaking up of our present government."[9] His counsel, then, was to leave the South alone, for the North to use its increasing political predominance prudently, to trust that Missouri and Kentucky would eventually, of their own volition, abolish slavery, and that the other states of the South would in due course follow as they watched the rapid-growing prosperity of the North compared to the South's own economic stasis.

Death and Taxes

The first federal income tax in American history was enacted in August 1861 (and went into effect the following year) by the United States Congress. Two years later, even the anti-tax Confederacy followed with a national income tax of its own.

It's worth thinking about what life was like before a national income tax. For one thing, it emphasized the authority of the states. As the *New York Herald* noted on 1 September 1862, (the day the income tax came into effect): "To-day begins a new era of this country. Beyond a few local and state taxes, which were felt by none but owners of real estate, this country has never been taxed before. We have jogged along quietly and comfortably, and have amused ourselves greatly by laughing at the over taxed people of England, where a man is taxed from the cradle to the grave; where light, heat and water are taxed, and where not only every rich man, but even the poorest peasant, is obliged to pay largely to the privilege of bad government...."

The *Herald* went on to praise the innovation of the income tax: "The effect of the tax will be to deepen public sentiment. The people will be less ready to excuse the mistakes of our government and our generals....The war will be better conducted, for every man, having to pay his money towards carrying on the war, will insist and assist that it shall be properly prosecuted and speedily and gloriously conducted."*

In fact, it is not at all clear that the income tax has made people more public-spirited. All that is clear is that it has massively shifted power to the Federal government, added a large financial burden on taxpayers, and radically increased the American people's dependence on the Federal government's largesse.

* Quoted in the *Washington Times*, "Lincoln's Odd Ways with Finances," D3, 22 December 2007.

But war having now come, he believed that "the question of the national integrity and slavery should be kept distinct, for otherwise it will become a war of extermination—a war without end." He did not want to spend the rest of his life trampling out the vintage where the grapes of wrath are stored. Indeed, he wished the war had never come and said that he would "recoil from a war, when the negro is the only question."[10]

In Sherman's mind the idea of simply letting the South go—without binding it to the Union by armed force—was an impossibility, because free trade (such as the Southern Confederacy professed) meant war. The North relied on money from tariffs, so "even if the Southern States be allowed to depart in peace, the first question will be revenue. Now if the South have free trade, how can you collect revenues in eastern cities. Freight from New Orleans to St. Louis, Chicago, Louisville, Cincinnati, and even Pittsburgh, would be about the same as by rail from New York, and importers at New Orleans, having no duties to pay, would undersell the East if they had to pay duties. Therefore, if the South make good their confederation and their plan, the Northern Confederacy must do likewise or blockade. Then comes the question of foreign nations. So, look on it in any view, I see no result but war and consequent change in the form of government."[11]

It was a war that he thought could last thirty years, with casualties in the hundreds of thousands. Beside the economic issue, which made war inevitable, Sherman saw as the great crusade not the "side issues of niggers, state rights, conciliation, outrages, cruelty, barbarity, bankruptcy, subjugations, etc.," which were all "idle and nonsensical"[12] but for the preservation of the Federal union in such a way that would forever destroy the power of the separate states, those "ridiculous pretences of government, liable to explode at the call of any mob," and put an end to the "the tendency to anarchy. . . . I have seen it all over America, and our only hope is Uncle Sam."[13]

For Sherman, loyalty to the Federal government, the Constitution, and the Union meant crushing the democratic spirit of such as Southerners who thought they had a right to determine their own form of government, their own confederation. As Sherman wrote to his brother, "A government resting on the caprice of the people is too unstable to last....[A]ll *must* obey. Government, that is, the executive, having no discretion but to execute the law must be to that extent despotic." So Sherman did not fight to free the slaves (whom he thought freed and armed would become another tribe, or tribes, of marauding Indians); he did not fight for a Constitution that envisioned a limited Federal government with real sovereignty lying with the states; nor by any stretch did he fight for democracy. He explicitly fought against it. "We have for years been drifting towards an unadulterated democracy or demagogism. Therefore our government should become a machine, self-regulating, independent of the man."[14]

Sherman, then, fought for order; ideally perhaps for martial law as the proper government model, which would ensure that government was run like a self-regulating machine where "popular opinion" would not interfere with the execution of the "law." Certainly in California he saw martial law as preferable to its apparent alternative, vigilantism, and it seems that he came to apply that prescription to the nation as a whole. And this being the case, it is not hard to understand why he came to desire the exaction of a Carthaginian peace upon the proud, aristocratic, and liberty-loving South.

Early campaigns

Sherman returned to the colors as a colonel. He fought at First Manassas, receiving minor wounds to his knee and shoulder, but felt thoroughly disgraced by the way his troops and the rest of the Federal army were routed. He blamed the defeat on having to lead an army of volunteers who "brag but don't perform" and did whatever they pleased. "I doubt," he wrote, "if our Democratic form of government admits of that organization and discipline without which an army is a mob." And "a mob," he thought, was a precise description of the men he led: "No curse could be greater than an invasion by a volunteer army. No Goths or Vandals ever had less respect for the lives and property of friends and foes, and henceforth we ought never to hope for any friends in Virginia."[15] Luckily, "Our adversaries have the weakness of slavery in their midst to offset our democracy," he said, "and it's beyond human wisdom to say which is the greater evil."[16]

Still, depressing as First Manassas had been, Sherman emerged from the scrap promoted to brigadier general. Sherman was, of course, pleased by his promotion and devoted to his duty, but also interested in keeping a low-profile at the outset of the war, for he expected not only a long and costly war, but a war full of early reverses, which would lead the mob to demand the heads of generals. He wanted to emerge after the politicians had bollixed things up and the fickle public had executed its scapegoats.

Lest Sherman be regarded as having overly saturnine views, it should be remembered that he was serving in close proximity to Washington, and the sight of the elected government in action did not breed confidence. Nor was there much good to be found in volunteer regiments, which conducted sit-down strikes—mutiny, in military terms—refusing to take orders or form ranks, and insisting that their short-term enlistments were up. Sherman retained his confidence in the regular army; it was the rest of the country about which he had doubts.

He was sent to Kentucky, a vital border state of divided loyalties and the birth place of the presidents of both the Union and the Confederacy. Sherman welcomed the new assignment. He considered himself a man of the West, thought the vital point in the war was control of the Mississippi River, and that the lynchpin that could hold and restore the Union, or without which it would disintegrate, was Kentucky. Not long after he arrived General Robert Anderson, a native Kentuckian, and like Sherman a pro-slavery Unionist, asked that Sherman replace him as commander of the Department of the Cumberland, (Anderson, the hero of Fort

Sumter, felt obliged to retire because of ill health). Sherman was duly appointed. He had emerged, perhaps sooner than he hoped, to a leading position in the war.

Sherman thought the situation in Kentucky was dire. His assessment that he needed 200,000 more men, his wildly inflated view of the number of Confederates confronting him, his frustration at the lack of weapons and supplies, his contempt for the volunteer regiments at his disposal, and his worry that the Federals were surrounded by Confederate sympathizers, all kept him in a constant state of active turmoil that left little time for rest or meals, to the point where he seemed overwhelmed by his duties and some doubted his sanity. Was Sherman a gloomy, ill-tempered martinet—a gruff professional whose pessimism reflected a military reality beyond the grasp of amateur officers and ignorant politicians—or was he insane? That Sherman felt the burden of command was obvious—he asked McClellan to relieve him, and McClellan obliged, sending General Don Carlos Buell to take his place.

Sherman was then assigned to Missouri, under the command of General Henry Halleck, who quickly became concerned about Sherman's alarums about a presumed Confederate threat—so concerned that he had a doctor examine Sherman. The doctor declared him of "such nervousness that he was unfit for command,"[17] which corresponded with Halleck's own opinion. Halleck, who was well disposed to Sherman, sent him on three-week's leave to recover himself.

Sherman's recovery was speeded by an article he read in the *Cincinnati Commercial*. It carried the quaint headline: "Gen. William T. Sherman Insane" and was quickly picked up and discussed in newspapers across the country. Its chief evidence was that Sherman had frequently been panicked and grossly exaggerated the dangers posed by the Confederate forces in Kentucky and Missouri.

But if misconstruing the size of the enemy is a sign of insanity, General George B. McClellan, commander of all the Union forces, was as insane as anyone. McClellan, however, had the advantage of a polished manner and a hauteur that rested on his reputation for excellence (though he too would give way to panicked messages in action).

Sherman detested reporters, had a harsh and abrasive manner, and could indeed be impulsive in his orders. This was both Sherman's gift and his flaw. His mind, for all its claims to hard practicality, was intuitive. One of his professors in Louisiana said of Sherman that "his mind went like lightning to his conclusions, and he had the utmost faith in his inspirations and convictions." Sherman once told him, "Never give rea-

Gen. William T. Sherman Insane

The painful intelligence reaches us in such form that we are not at liberty to discredit it, that Gen. W. T. SHERMAN, late commander of the Department of the Cumberland is *insane*. It appears that he was at times when commanding in Kentucky, stark mad. We learn that he at one time telegraphed to the War Department three times in one day for permission to evacuate Kentucky, and retreat into Indiana. He also, on several occasions, frightened the leading Union men of Louisville almost out of their wits, by the most astounding representations of the overwhelming force of BUCKNER, and the assertion that Louisville could not be defended. The retreat from Cumberland Gap was one of his mad freaks. When relieved of the command in Kentucky, he was sent to Missouri and placed at the head of a brigade at Sedalia, where the shocking fact that he was a madman, was developed, by orders that his subordinates knew to be preposterous and refused to obey. He has, of course, been relieved altogether from command. The harsh criticisms which have been lavished upon this gentleman, provoked by his strange conduct, will now give way to feelings of the deepest sympathy for him in his great calamity. It seems Providential that the country has not to mourn the loss of an army through the loss of the mind of a general into whose hands were committed the vast responsibility of the command of Kentucky.

The Cincinnati Commercial, 11 December 1861

sons for what you think or do until you must. Maybe, after a while, a better reason will pop into your head."[18] This revealing comment of Sherman's, was, of course, to one way of thinking, the height of practicality. Reasoning after all was too abstract, too Thomistic perhaps, to be the chief tool of the practical man. Better by far to provide rationalizations after the fact.

Recovery in battle

Sherman's first assignment was a quiet one, training troops, but he yearned for an opportunity to reclaim his reputation, and Halleck looked to give him his chance, eventually sending him up the Tennessee River to engage the enemy. His early attempts to strike a reputation-recovering blow fizzled. But fate was awaiting him and his troops at Pittsburgh Landing. Serving now under General Grant, Sherman established his headquarters at the Shiloh Methodist Meeting House. Sherman's men took the brunt of the Confederate assault, and the general who had been turfed out on leave for a nervous breakdown now showed himself a capable commander under fire. He was wounded through the hand, which he wrapped up himself while leading his troops on horseback. Several horses were shot and killed beneath him, as was one of his aides riding alongside him. But Sherman kept his command presence.

The great controversy of Sherman's part in the battle of Shiloh is whether the Confederates had caught him napping. Sherman denied it, pointing out that Federals and rebels had been skirmishing for days before—and if nothing else, Sherman was an honest man. Still, it appears the Confederates had the jump on him.

But Sherman's troops held up better than other Union troops, who turned tail and fled (they certainly seemed surprised), and many journalists this time found Grant a more inviting target for criticism. Sherman hated journalists, regarded them as the nearest thing to traitors (because they betrayed important information to the enemy), and held them within the same contempt that he held democracy. Journalists could never tell the truth about the cowardly, indisciplined mob of volunteer soldiers in blue; in a democracy, Sherman reflected bitterly, ignorant and malicious reporters flattered the rabble at the expense of the professionals who knew what they were doing. Sherman, however, felt no such restraint on his truth-telling. He sought out units that he thought had performed poorly and gave them detailed tongue-lashings about their shortcomings; and he cooperated with Grant in weeding out officers who had failed. But for Sherman personally, the greatest result of Shiloh was that he had been engaged in the biggest battle in American history. He had handled himself creditably, and after the initial shock of battle, his men had mounted a stubborn defense that turned into a counterattack and drove the rebels from the field.

Advice from General Sherman

In a letter to a Miss Elbit of Columbus, Ohio, who wrote protesting Sherman's imprecations against cowards who fled from the battle of Shiloh, the good general noted,

> "I did not say the absent soldiers were all cowards, but I did say what is true, that the bulk of the cowards did escape from Pittsburgh Landing under the pretense of being sick. They are not confined to Ohio....Don't distress yourself about 'the men of Ohio,' but get you a good husband and mind your own business."*

* Quoted in Lee Kennett, *Sherman: A Soldier's Life* (HarperCollins, 2001), 168–9.

Military governor of Memphis

On 20 July 1862 Sherman took over the occupation of Memphis. He kept his troops busy—he didn't want them getting fat and lazy in barracks. Sherman told the people, according to a newspaper reporter, that "he thought Memphis was a conquered city....He had not heard that there had been any terms at the capitulation." His army, he added, "didn't come here to visit their friends. The people of the city were prisoners of war. They may be Union, and they may not. He knew nothing about that. One thing was certain: they had not fought for the Union so far as he had heard....He had nothing to do with social, moral, or political questions; he was a soldier and obeyed orders and expected his orders to be obeyed."[19]

So far, so Sherman, but in fact he relaxed the previous strict administration of the city, granting the people considerably more freedom of movement, returned to them the right to buy and consume alcohol, deprecated Northern speculators and merchants who came to the city and put trade before the war effort, and tried to crack down on Federal soldiers who were disgracing their cause by pillaging civilians. Sherman confessed in a letter to one of his daughters that "I feel that we are fighting our own people, many of whom I knew in earlier years."[20]

Sherman's brother John, now a United States senator, advocated that Confederates be treated "as bitter enemies to be subdued—conquered—by confiscation—by the employment of their slaves—by terror...rather than by conciliation." Sherman, at this point, thought differently, and especially disagreed with his brother's abolitionist sentiments. He wrote his brother telling him that he was "wrong in saying that Negroes are free & entitled to be treated accordingly by simple declaration of Congress.... Not one Nigger in ten wants to run off. There are 25,000 in 20 miles of Memphis—All could escape & receive protection here, but we have only about 2,000 of whom about half are hanging about camps as officers servants."[21] He believed that freeing slaves was pointless unless alternative work was provided for them—and if it had been up to him, he made clear, slavery would not be disturbed.

Vicksburg

After four months of governing Memphis according to "the law," which was actually his whim—and all the better for it—Sherman gained an assignment that he could relish: he would be joining Grant on the campaign to take Vicksburg, the "Gibraltar of the South." In this campaign Sherman showed less interest in conciliating the enemy. His troops traveled by boat down the Mississippi. Sherman gave orders that if the boats took fire from the shoreline, the troops were to disembark and lay waste the nearest town in retaliation. If any journalists found their way on board his boats, they were to be conscripted immediately or arrested as spies. But Sherman's first attempt at the Southern citadel was admirably summarized in his Caesarean official report: "I reached Vicksburg at the time appointed, landed, assaulted, and failed."[22]

He failed again in his attempt to take the Confederate defenses at Chickasaw Bluffs in a landward assault. He had attempted this after overruling Admiral David Porter's proposal of a joint naval-army attack on Haynes' Bluff. Fighting in difficult, swampy terrain, Sherman's men attributed their failures to more than bad luck, there were rumors again about Sherman's sanity, and even Admiral Porter, who got on well with Sherman, thought the general was a burnt-out case—a commander who shared too many of the physical hardships of the men. These, combined with the already arduous physical, mental, and emotional strains of command, had broken him down. Porter helped buck up Sherman's spirits by telling him that the loss of 1,700 men at Chickasaw Bluffs was as nothing in a war like this. Such minimizing of the butcher's bill seemed to cheer Sherman immensely.

Serving now under John A. McClernand, a politician appointed as a general, whom Sherman despised as a vainglorious idiot (Admiral Porter seconded that view), the Federal troops withdrew for easier pickings, starting with Fort Hindman on the Arkansas River. Though Fort Hindman fell to Union hands, it was a minor engagement and Sherman had to share the credit (though he was loath to do so) with McClernand. That in itself was, as McClernand put it, more "gall and wormwood to the clique of West Pointers."[23]

Sherman took out his gall and wormwood by calling for the execution of a reporter who had criticized him and by ferreting out how officers who didn't like him (like McClernand) were using the press to play up their own achievements while disparaging his. Things improved when Sherman became a corps commander under Grant. Though Sherman thought Grant had let him down in not supporting his assault on Vicksburg, Grant was a man he respected and liked: the two Ohioans trusted each other and mistrusted the press and self-promoting officers like McClernand.

In Grant's conquest of Vicksburg, Sherman played a supporting role, preventing Joseph E. Johnston from relieving the besieged Southern fortress, and then occupying Mississippi's capital of Jackson, after Johnston retreated from it. At Grant's request, Sherman was promoted from a brigadier general of volunteers to a brigadier general in the regular army. When Grant became commander of the Military Division of the Mississippi he rewarded Sherman with command of the Army of the Tennessee. Sherman's first assignment was to join the Federal breakout from Chattanooga; and here his preparations came in for as much criticism for slowness and delay as were usually leveled at General Thomas (though Sherman had the added burden of grieving over the death of his favorite son, Willie, who had contracted a deadly fever while visiting his father in Mississippi). When Sherman sent his troops against the Confederate right at Missionary Ridge, they were stymied; it was Thomas's men who eventually swept the rebels off the high ground. But Grant gave Sherman credit for tying down the Confederate right and guaranteeing Thomas's success.

The following year, 1864, was the year that would truly make Sherman's name. It was also the year he finally gave up trying to enforce his previously strict opposition to pillaging and plunder. It was a utilitarian decision driven in part by his noticing that when the Federal army lived off the land (that is, Southern farmers) it effectively stripped that area of provisions for the enemy. The idea formed in Sherman's mind of creating a "belt of devastation."[24] The South, he reckoned was united against the Union, and every Southern male was a potential guerilla, such as fired on Federal boats, harassed Federal supply lines, or broke up Federal rails. While Sherman respected most Confederate commanders, especially those who were fellow West Pointers, he had no truck with guerilla leaders and believed them simply outlaws—outlaws supported by Southern civilians, who were therefore accessories to their crimes.

Sherman also declared, as a matter of law, that "by rebelling against the only earthly power that insured them the possession of such property"—the United States government—Southerners had lost their right to own slaves, and "*ex necessitate* the United States succeeds by act of war to the former lost title of the master."[25] So Sherman's legal training was put to good use, apparently.

When Lincoln promoted Grant to command of all Federal armies, Grant appointed Sherman as his successor to the Military Division of the Mississippi. Grant would take on Lee in the East, and Sherman would face Joseph E. Johnston in the West, with the objective of seizing Atlanta. The outcome of Sherman v. Johnston was inevitable: Johnston was outnumbered, entrenched, was outmaneuvered, and retreated. Johnston's entire career in the war rested on brilliant tactical retreats. The one time Sherman assaulted Johnston directly, at Kennesaw Mountain, it was another defeat for Sherman, though he brushed if off with Admiral Porter's earlier rationalization that losses were as nothing in this war. Or, in Sherman's own words, "I begin to regard the death and mangling of a couple of thousand men as a small affair, a kind of morning dash—and it may be well that we become so hardened."[26] Compare this to Lee's famous line that "It is well that war is so terrible—we should grow too fond of it."[27]

The gallant Confederate General John Bell Hood replaced Joseph E. Johnston and if his tactics were different—frenzied, hopeless assaults rather than clever retreats—the results were the same. Atlanta fell into Sherman's hands, and the conqueror of the city promptly, on 5 September 1864, ordered expelled its entire civilian population. Sherman had not innovated this strategy. Grant was already trying to drive Virginians out of the Shenandoah Valley; and in Missouri, some 20,000 suspected Confederates had been driven from their homes (which were burned). To Sherman it was another matter of practicality: the city was on his supply lines and he was not about to take on the responsibility of feeding Southern civilians. In the North, Sherman was now a hero.

He was also the ultimate military commander of a region stretching from the Mississippi River to the Appalachian Mountains. He had a plan, of which Secretary of War Edwin Stanton approved, of expelling Confederates outside the United States (any location would do, though among his suggestions were Madagascar and French Guiana). This was preliminary to his grander scheme of repopulating the South with Northerners: "The whole population of Iowa & Wisconsin," he wrote his brother the senator, "should be transferred at once to west Kentucky, Tennessee & Mississippi."[28] Though like many grand schemes, this bore little fruit at first. The repopulating of the South had to wait for the great rust belt migrations of the last quarter of the twentieth century.

Meanwhile, Hood's army still existed and was looking for a fight. Sherman was content to leave that fighting to Thomas. His great plan was for a march to the sea in which he could wreak a path of destruction on the South, destroying railroads, burning cities, and of course eating any comestible in sight. The idea of restraining the destruction of civilian property was gone with the wind—Sherman's men even burned houses as a signaling system between units—and his attitude to such destruction had come to resemble his attitude to casualties: *che sera sera*. It couldn't be helped, and in any event the South needed to be taught a lesson. Certainly there were orders limiting the wreckage (and Sherman could be kindly when his personal attention was engaged), but these orders were more honored in the breach than in the observance. When justice was meted out, it could be delivered as roughly to soldiers as civilians. During the burning of Columbia, South Carolina, Federal officers simply shot out of hand riotous drunken soldiers in blue.

Such forces as the Confederacy had were largely arrayed on the South's northern borders. For all his fuming about "partisans," Sherman met with little resistance as his army burned its way through Georgia and the Carolinas, the only battle of consequence being Bentonville, on 19–21 March 1865, when Joseph E. Johnston made his last stand in North Carolina before the end of the war. Besides that, and the occasional skirmish with Joe Wheeler's Confederate cavalry, Sherman's march was not a running battle, but the plowing of a desolate trench that obliterated (with a few exceptions, like the city of Savannah) anything in its way.

When the end was finally near, Sherman wrote his wife that Jefferson Davis and "at least 100,000 men in the South must die or be banished before we can think of peace. I know them like a book. They can't help it any more than the Indians can their wild nature."[29] Since cutting his swath through the South, Sherman had won an avalanche of Northern accolades, and it clearly went to his head. When he met with Joseph E. Johnston to discuss an armistice (the duo later joined by Confederate General and Secretary of War John C. Breckinridge), Johnston convinced Sherman to go beyond the terms Grant had offered Lee in order to achieve a general peace. Sherman seized the opportunity, thinking that by it he could tamp down any possible remaining Southern insurrections and guarantee "peace from the Potomac to the Rio Grande."

Though Sherman counseled Breckinridge to leave the country, the terms agreed were remarkably lenient, leaving the South's state governments intact (where pro-Union and pro-Confederate governments jostled for recognition in the same state, the Supreme Court would decide). Confederate troops, in order to maintain civil order, would retain their arms until they reached their state capitals. In exchange for pledges of loyalty to the Union, a general amnesty and all Constitutional rights would be granted to Southern citizens, including property rights. The terms were forwarded to Washington for President Andrew Johnson's approval. Instead of plaudits, Sherman was showered with abuse and subject to accusations of treachery and insanity (again) by the press. General Grant came to see Sherman, breaking the news of the disaster and telling him that his agreement with Lee had to be the model for Sherman's agreement with Johnston, and so it was done.

After the war, Sherman was made a lieutenant general and given command of the Military Division of the Missouri, a region that stretched from New Mexico north to Montana, east across the Dakotas through Minnesota and as far south as Arkansas and Oklahoma. He made his home in St. Louis, where he'd lived before, and maintained an active social schedule, without his wife whom he considered suitable for raising his children and listening to his complaints but little else. As for his work, he disdained the southwestern territories under his command (as well as Texas, which was not) and thought they should be returned to Mexico as wasteland. He had a certain sympathy for the Indians, thinking, at times, that he would have liked to have been one—his wife agreed with him; she thought he might be more at home with a squaw than a white woman—while regarding them as a primitive race that, realistically, did not have much of a future. They either had to be tamed and kept on their reservations or exterminated.

As for the South, he returned to his prewar views that the region should be left alone and not be goaded, trampled upon, and reconstructed by Radical Republicans. He opposed giving voting rights to blacks, supported the idea of segregation (and enacted it when he occupied Savannah during the war), and preferred that political power in the South be returned to the planter and professional classes, the only ones capable of wielding it intelligently.

With Grant's election as president in 1868, Sherman was promoted to full general and became commander of the entire United States Army. It meant moving from St. Louis to Washington, a transfer he did not relish, and in 1874 he managed, with Grant's approval, to become a telecommuter, working out of St. Louis and relying on the telegraph lines to keep him in touch with Washington. Sherman always loathed everything about politics—something that, as a soldier, he thought he was above—and his sense of honor did not allow him to do the sort of lobbying, currying favor, and politicking that Washington's ways required. He did, however, return to Washington in 1876.

Sherman's vision was for a large professional army. Congress's was for a small frontier force supplemented by militia. Congress won. He had more successful influence over West Point where, while he was a jealous guardian of tradition, he oversaw the transformation of the academy from a de facto school for engineers to a school truly for soldiers. He was also not a traditionalist when it came to uniforms and weaponry, where he was always on the side of practicality and firepower.

On 8 February 1884, Sherman retired, and famously repudiated any talk that he might run for president: "I will not accept if nominated and will not serve if elected."[30] He returned to St. Louis, and in 1891 he died, repeating what he had prepared to be his last words: "Faithful and honorable. Faithful and honorable." By his own lights, he was.

Chapter Eight

JAMES LONGSTREET
(1821-1904)

"Ah! Here is Longstreet; here is my old war-horse!"[1]

- Longstreet fought the battle of Sharpsburg while wearing carpet slippers

- After the war, Longstreet led black militia in battle against former Confederates

- Longstreet endorsed Ulysses Grant for president

A t the beginning of the war a cavalry officer, Moxley Sorrel, joined the staff of Brigadier General James Longstreet. Sorrel described Longstreet as "a most striking figure, about forty years of age, a soldier every inch, and very handsome, tall and well proportioned, strong and active, a superb horseman and with an unsurpassed soldierly bearing, his features and expression fairly matched; a full brown beard, head well shaped and poised. The worst feature was the mouth, rather coarse; it was partly hidden, however, by his ample beard."[2]

Longstreet was, indeed, "a soldier every inch," which was why General Robert E. Lee made him his senior corps commander and regarded "Old Pete" as his "old war-horse." Second only to Stonewall Jackson, he was Lee's most trusted subordinate. But after the war, he also became the most controversial of the Confederate generals, with many Southerners blaming Longstreet for the South's defeat because of his conduct at Gettysburg.

A Dutchman among Cavaliers

Born in South Carolina, though raised in Georgia (which he considered his true home state), and sent to West Point by Alabama, James Longstreet was, like most of the leading officers of the war, the product of an American lineage that went back to colonial times. He was the son of a small-scale planter, and grew up as a tall, vigorous youth—a man of few words (and not much book learning), but a hardy, rough, dependable, confident, and independent soul. He was also stubborn as a Dutchman, and it was Dutch blood that ran in his veins.

Not a Virginia Cavalier

Longstreet felt he was different from the Virginians with whom he fought. Indeed, according to one of Longstreet's aides, there was "a good deal of the roughness of the old soldier about him,"* more so than one found in other officers in the army. At the end of the Seven Days campaign, for instance, one of Lee's aides presented a flask of whiskey—a gift from a captured Union general. The flask was passed around. The Virginians Lee, Jackson, and Stuart abstained. President Jefferson Davis took a polite sip. But Longstreet, the campaigner, took "a good soldierly swig."* And it wasn't just for Dutch courage.

* Quoted in Jeffrey D. Wert, *General James Longstreet: The Confederacy's Most Controversial Soldier* (Simon & Schuster, 1993), 94, 150.

One of the most famous early twentieth century biographies of Longstreet noted that "there was something curiously unSouthern about him. He was serious and stolid, not romantic as proper Southerners of that age were, more materialistic than idealistic."[3] He also, as it happened, was a great friend of U. S. Grant both at West Point and as young officers. Longstreet in fact introduced Grant to one of his cousins, Julia Dent, whom Grant subsequently married. After the war, Longstreet and Grant not only renewed their friendship but became political allies, with Longstreet famously (or infamously) turning Republican politician during Reconstruction in Louisiana.

Longstreet was the only non-Virginian of Robert E. Lee's early corps commanders—Stonewall Jackson, A. P. Hill, Richard Ewell, and J. E. B. Stuart—a singularity that Longstreet noted with disapproval, thinking there was a prejudice in favor of Virginians. Longstreet had no lack of *amour propre*, and though Lee was too high-minded to notice it, Longstreet was a bit of a mulish lieutenant, forever thinking that he should be in charge. While Lee sometimes characterized Longstreet as slow—which he was, because he was a very careful soldier—he never recognized that part of that slowness was a repeated reluctance to follow Lee's ideas when they disagreed with his own.

Though he had performed admirably as a combat soldier in the Mexican War, he found that as a family man, for he married in 1848, he needed more pay than he could earn as a line officer. So he became a military accountant, a major in the paymaster department of the United States Army. Had the War not intervened, Longstreet would have lived out his life contentedly settling accounts and spending his free time as a bluff, vigorous outdoorsman.

After Fort Sumter was fired upon, Longstreet made a simple calculation—and it was one not guided by narrow self-interest. While many of his brother officers urged him to stay loyal to the Union, he countered with the argument: "I asked him what course he would pursue if his State should pass ordinances of secession and call him to its defence. He confessed that he would obey the call."[4] Longstreet decided that he belonged to Alabama, the state that had not only sponsored his military education but from which he was the senior West Point graduate (and thus likely to attain a higher rank).

Before he departed Fort Fillmore, New Mexico, he was asked by a young officer how long he thought the war would last. Longstreet replied, "At least three years, and if it holds for five you may begin to look for a dictator," at which, as Longstreet relates in his autobiography, the lieutenant responded, "If we are to have a dictator, I hope that you may be that man."[5] Longstreet's lack of comment seems a nod of assent.

From Manassas to Manassas

In the short term, Longstreet's goal was not to be a dictator, and not even to be a line officer, it was to be a paymaster of the Confederate armies—but West Pointers were too valuable for that. Longstreet had left the United States Army as a major, was commissioned a lieutenant colonel in the Army of the Confederate States of America, and was promptly promoted to brigadier general. He was sent to the frontlines of Northern Virginia to serve under the command of General P. G. T. Beauregard, and saw action at First Manassas. Though the bulk of the fighting was away from him, his troops fought well at Blackburn's Ford and withstood a long Federal bombardment. Longstreet, who had drilled his men to a fine pitch (for that stage of the war), showed his usual calm courage and tactical acumen.

But he was infuriated when, at the end of the battle, with the bluecoats on the run, he was ordered to make no pursuit. Moxley Sorrel recounts that he "saw Longstreet in a fine rage. He dashed his hat furiously on the ground, stamped, and bitter words escaped him."[6] Those bitter words were recorded as: "Retreat! Hell, the Federal army has broken to pieces."[7]

Longstreet was not alone in his assessment. Stonewall Jackson shared it, as did Edward Porter Alexander, a young staff officer who would become a brigadier general of artillery. Alexander noted that "in fact the battle was treated as over as soon as the Federals retreated across Bull Run. It should have been considered as just beginning."[8] As it was, Longstreet's men cheered him—they recognized him as a sturdy, talented, professional soldier, scrupulous with the lives of his men, and fearless under fire.

Roll, Alabama, Roll

Longstreet was not the only adoptive Alabaman to win fame in the War. Raphael Semmes, a Catholic and Marylander by birth, lived most of his adult life in Alabama and commanded the famed rebel raider, the CSS *Alabama*. He served in the United States Navy for fourteen years, seeing action in the Mexican War, but also, enjoying extended shore leave, practiced law from offices in Mobile, Alabama. For the Confederacy, he was the only officer to serve as both a rear admiral and as a brigadier general (towards the end of the war when he commanded sailors turned infantry). But the bulk of his fame rests on his command of the CSS *Alabama*. For twenty-two months, he and the *Alabama* were almost always at sea. He sank the warship, the USS *Hatteras*, captured more than sixty-five merchant ships, and took 2,000 prisoners, while suffering no casualties—not even to sickness or accident. In a gallant engagement, the CSS *Alabama* was finally sunk on 19 June 1864, off the coast of France. Most of the crew survived, and Semmes was rescued by a British yacht. After the war he again took up the law in Mobile (he also taught at the school that Sherman helped found, LSU). The town of Semmes, Alabama, a suburb of Mobile, is named after him.

Though Stonewall Jackson won fame from Manassas, Longstreet won the race for promotion, rising to major general. The autumn was spent in inactivity, but the winter was marked by personal tragedy when three of Longstreet's young children, ages one, four, and six died of scarlet fever, and the previously convivial, if laconic, Longstreet became tighter-lipped and more devoted to his Episcopal faith, the church in which, later in the war, perhaps under Lee's influence, he was confirmed.

The Viking General

"Six feet tall, broad as a door, hairy as a goat, there was something about Longstreet that would have inspired confidence even if his dogmatic utterances on all subjects had not done so....It was hard to resist that Viking, with his immense Lombard beard, his rugged power, and his invincible certainty."

H. J. Eckenrode and Bryan Conrad, *James Longstreet: Lee's War Horse* (University of North Carolina Press, 1986), 55.

In the spring and summer of 1862, Longstreet turned in creditable performances overall—enough to make Lee regard him as "the staff in my right hand."[9] Though a taciturn man, Longstreet was, at his best, an inspiring presence on the battlefield. As Lee's senior corps commander, Longstreet was considered the best administrator among his top generals. Longstreet certainly agreed, and estimated himself highly as a strategist and tactician. He saw his duty as bringing his men to the right place at the right time; and if he disagreed with the commanding general on what was the right place and the right time, he tried to impose his will on him, often successfully.

Longstreet had command presence. Not one for blustery words and speeches, Longstreet motivated his men to face danger and win by acting as though a battle were no more dangerous for a brave man than sitting on a porch and drinking iced tea. Or in the words of Moxley Sorrel, Longstreet was "that undismayed warrior. He was like a rock in steadiness when sometimes in battle the world seemed to be flying to pieces."[10]

Though he commanded with certainty, conviction, and a reassuring calm, he was, of course, not always right. At Malvern Hill, during the Seven Days' battles in front of Richmond, Jackson counseled Lee to flank the entrenched Federal position. Longstreet, however, argued for a frontal assault and even joshed the dyspeptic General D. H. Hill who was full of dire warnings, "Don't get scared, now that we have got him licked."[11] What makes his exchange particularly interesting is its contrast with Longstreet's later playing the role of D. H. Hill to the aggressive Lee at Gettysburg. And as at Gettysburg (where Longstreet was late in his attempt to take Little Round Top) there are those who wonder why Longstreet did not take Malvern Hill himself, before that high ground was occupied by the Federals.

At Second Manassas, Longstreet turned in a characteristic performance, both in the way it frustrated Lee's desire to get at the enemy but also rewarded him with victory. Longstreet left Jackson's men holding the Union front in desperate battle, while he thoroughly surveyed the ground and put his troops in order. His delaying of his attack, despite three direct orders from Lee and the obvious pressure on Jackson, in favor of an unhurried reconnaissance, was "surely a characteristic Longstreetian touch." But just as Longstreetian was the crashing blow that landed when he finally did make his assault, giving the Confederates a tremendous victory.

"I will kill them all before they reach my line"

At Sharpsburg, in the Maryland campaign, the Confederate army fought on the defensive—Longstreet's sort of battle. It was an epic of courage and endurance, the bloodiest day of the war, and as one pair of historians put it, "There are few things finer than the stand of the Southerners at Sharpsburg. It ranks with Thermopylae."[12]

Longstreet's mastery of military tactics, learned from experience, and calmly applied in the heat of combat showed themselves here. Moxley

Sorrel wrote that Longstreet's tactician's "eyes were everywhere,"[13] adding that his "conduct on this great day of battle was magnificent. He seemed everywhere along his extended lines, and his tenacity and deep-set resolution, his inmost courage, which appeared to swell with the growing peril to the army, undoubtedly stimulated troops to great action, and held them in place despite all weakness."[14]

Sharpsburg also highlighted Longstreet's mordant, soldierly humor. At one point in the battle, Longstreet called out to D. H. Hill, who was riding up a crest while he and Lee walked. "If you insist on riding up there and drawing the fire," Longstreet said, "give us a little interval so that we may not be in the line of fire when they open up on you."[15] Longstreet pointed to a puff of cannon smoke and joked that Hill was its target. Unfortunately, he was right. The artillery shell plowed into the front legs of Hill's horse, severing them. Hill was stuck, unable to dismount as his

★ ★ ★ ★ ★

The Commander in Carpet Slippers

Longstreet fought the battle of Sharpsburg wearing carpet slippers because of a painful blister on his heel. But however ludicrous Longstreet's footwear, Lee cherished Old Pete's stubborn defense. Staff officers painted the scene for Moxley Sorrel, "Longstreet, big, heavy, and red, grimly stern after the long day's work, that called for all we could stomach, rolled in on his clumsy carpet slippers. Lee immediately welcomed him with unconcealed joy. 'Here comes my war horse just from the field he has done so much to save!'"* Some war horse; some horseshoes.

---

* General G. Moxley Sorrel, *At the Right Hand of Longstreet: Recollections of a Confederate Staff Officer*, (Bison Books, 1999), 116.

rearing, screeching horse stumbled, lurched, and rolled on its bloody stumps. Longstreet had stomach enough, as a leathery old trooper, to laugh and make fun of his colleague's predicament.

In the same battle, one of Longstreet's staff officers—John Fairfax, a wealthy, fierce-eyed Virginia aristocrat never to be separated from his Bible, his portable bathtub, his supply of whisky, or his horses—blurted to Longstreet: "General, General, my horse is killed! Saltron is shot; shot right in the back!"

Longstreet gave Fairfax a "queer look," amidst this slaughter of men in the bloodiest day of the War and counseled, "Never mind, Major. You ought to be glad *you* are not shot in the back!"[16]

Lee so valued Longstreet's performance at the battle of Sharpsburg that he was promoted to lieutenant general—making him Lee's senior corps commander (ahead of Stonewall Jackson and J. E. B. Stuart). At Fredericksburg in December 1862, Longstreet's men, behind the stonewall at Marye's heights, spent all day mowing down the charging Federals, with Longstreet assuring Lee: "General, if you put every man now on the other side of the Potomac on that field to approach me over the same line, and give me plenty of ammunition, I will kill them all before they reach my line."[17] Union losses at the battle were more than 12,500 men. Longstreet's casualties were only about 500 of the 5,300 Confederate casualties.

Through his cool presence on the battlefield, Longstreet was able to transmit his own stubborn streak to his troops, making them resolute defenders and, when circumstances called for it, unstoppable chargers. Longstreet's greatest insight as a battlefield leader was that in every battle, somebody is bound to run, and if the troops "will only stand their ground long enough like men, the enemy will certainly run."[18] That insight made him tenacious—especially tenacious at digging in and holding ground as he did at Fredericksburg were he not only had the protection of the stonewall, but had set his troops to building defensive fieldworks.

For Old Pete the lesson of Fredericksburg and previous battles was obvious: for the Confederacy the advantage—indeed the necessity—was to fight on the tactical defensive. It was the only way the South could make up for its relative lack of manpower. Southern troops—and their officers—might be hot-blooded, but a strong defensive line was far more likely to deliver victory, in Longstreet's view, than gallant charges.

It wasn't, then, just a lack of sentimentality about horses that separated Longstreet from the Virginians. As a leader and as a soldier, Longstreet was far removed from lightning bolt Stonewall Jackson, the impetuous A. P. Hill, or the swashbuckling J. E. B. Stuart. While Lee accepted the strength of his defensive position at Fredericksburg, he was not as tied to the tactical defensive as Longstreet was—and indeed, Lee and Jackson regretted they could not capitalize on the Federals' defeat, given the nature of the ground, with an offensive counterstroke to destroy the Union army. At both Sharpsburg and Fredericksburg, Jackson and Lee accepted the necessity of a tactical defensive posture, but were always probing and hoping for a chance to shift to the attack, while Longstreet was content to repel and annihilate the attacking Federals.

Longstreet analyzed the South's disadvantages in manpower, money, and materiel as clearly as did Lee, Jackson, Stuart, and A. P. Hill. But Longstreet came up with a different solution from that of the Virginians. The Virginians sought audacious offensive maneuvers to shock, surprise, and crush the enemy as quickly as possible, hoping to stun the Federals into thinking the cost of the war was too great. Longstreet believed a more important goal was sparing the Confederacy casualties it couldn't afford by adopting the comparative safety of the tactical defensive. But if the South could not afford a long war, it could not afford Longstreet's strategy.

Whatever their differing opinions on strategy and tactics, Lee and Longstreet had a cordial and respectful relationship during the war. The British officer and observer Lieutenant Colonel Arthur Fremantle noted that "it is impossible to please Longstreet more than by praising Lee" and that Longstreet "is never far from General Lee, who relies very much on his judgment. By the soldiers he is invariably spoken of as 'the best fighter in the whole army.'"[19] But it is equally true that Longstreet wanted an independent command. He asked to be detached from Lee's forces and sent to Kentucky. Lee dismissed that idea, but did accept detaching him as departmental commander of Southern Virginia and North Carolina to help guard the coastline and bring in supplies for the Army of Northern Virginia.

Though Longstreet did eventually return with supplies, he was unable to bring his troops back in time to join Lee for the great battle at Chancellorsville, where Lee, with 60,000 men, bested 130,000 Federals. Writing in 1936, historians H. J. Eckenrode and Bryan Conrad commented, "In his extremity Lee had fully exercised his genius and audacity and had won the greatest victory in American history,"[20] and unfortunately, Lee's old war horse, dispatched to foraging rather than fighting (though he did lay siege to the Federals in Suffolk, Virginia), wasn't there.

But with Jackson's death, Lee relied more than ever on his senior corps commander, "the staff in my right hand." In reorganizing his army, he created an additional corps. Lee retained Longstreet as commander of the First Corps and Stuart as his commander of cavalry. The Second Corps went to Richard Ewell who had exchanged a leg of flesh for a leg of wood at Groveton during the Second Manassas campaign. The newly created Third Corps went to A. P. Hill. Lee called Ewell "an honest brave soldier who has always done his duty well" and A. P. Hill as "the best soldier of his grade with me." Both were West Pointers and professional soldiers, but neither had Longstreet's accomplishments nor his stamina.

Ewell had always been high-strung and Hill had always been impetuous. But there were already signs that Hill's health was faltering and that Ewell was not the fighter he once was. Ewell was brave, but also a champion eccentric, in an army with no shortage of these. Short, with a "bald and bomb-shaped head" and "bulging eyes" protruding "above a prominent nose" many thought he looked like a bird, "especially when he let his head droop toward one shoulder, as he often did, and uttered strange speeches in his shrill, twittering lisp." He could also be "spectacularly profane."[21] If he was popular with his men, he certainly lacked the solidity of Longstreet. No one would have called Ewell an old war horse. Instead, they called him "old baldy."

Longstreet had no objection to Lee's initial strategy of invading Pennsylvania, because he did not shy away from *strategic* offensives. In fact, he continually recommended an invasion of Kentucky in the western theatre. But once an offensive was launched, he preferred to switch back to the *tactical* defensive, entrenching and waiting for the enemy to attack. He was happy enough following Lee on daring campaigns—as long as he felt the army would eventually hunker down. As he exclaimed to Lee during the Maryland campaign, "General, I wish we could stand still and let the damned Yankees come to us."[22]

He wanted the damned Yankees to come against a strong Confederate line in Pennsylvania too, by putting Lee's army between the Federal army and Washington. But once the two armies became entangled, virtually by accident, at Gettysburg, Lee felt compelled to beat the Federals where they were. For all the second-guessing of Longstreet, and later historians, Lee's accepting of the need to attack the Federals was rational. He wanted to deliver a quick, crushing defeat to the Federal army when the Confederacy needed it most. Yes, he was outnumbered, and the odds were against him, but his army had triumphed over such odds before. Striking the Union center on the third day of battle at Gettysburg was certainly no more impracticable and certainly no less likely to deliver victory than what Longstreet recommended: trying to disengage from a battle already started, maneuvering in enemy territory, and potentially risking the defeat of the entire army, whose lines of retreat could have been sundered. Had Lee been able to entrust Stonewall Jackson with responsibility for flanking the Union left on the second day of Gettysburg or leading Pickett's charge on the Third Day, the battle might have had a very different outcome. Jackson's lightning obedience was what Lee needed, not Longstreet's endless delays and stubborn reluctance to obey his orders.

Fredericksburg, where behind the stone wall at Marye's Heights his soldiers mowed down wave after wave of Union troops, was Longstreet's model battle, but those circumstances could not be recreated in Pennsylvania. Longstreet's caution—and his ego—occasionally caused him to stumble, as he did at Gettysburg, where his half-hearted execution of Lee's plans guaranteed their failure. But once the charge was shattered, Longstreet, conscience stricken, in his own words, "rode back to the line of batteries, expecting an immediate counterstroke, the shot and shell ploughed up the ground around my horse, and an involuntary appeal went up that one of them would remove me from scenes of such awful responsibility."[23] Longstreet, the responsible soldier, was back in action.

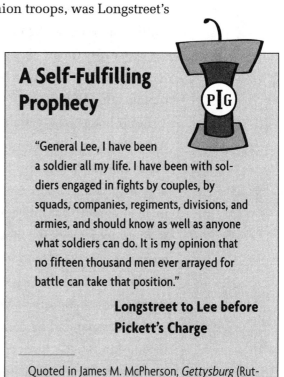

A Self-Fulfilling Prophecy

"General Lee, I have been a soldier all my life. I have been with soldiers engaged in fights by couples, by squads, companies, regiments, divisions, and armies, and should know as well as anyone what soldiers can do. It is my opinion that no fifteen thousand men ever arrayed for battle can take that position."

Longstreet to Lee before Pickett's Charge

Quoted in James M. McPherson, *Gettysburg* (Rutledge Hill Press, 1993), 83.

"Longstreet is the man!"

After Gettysburg, Longstreet was eager to try his own hand, out from under Lee's shadow, in the western theatre of the war. At Chickamauga, his first great engagement, he met with success, filing his troops into the right position at the right time for maximum effect. Chickamauga made him a hero in the West, where good news had been scarce. General John Breckinridge led the chorus of praise, proclaiming, "Longstreet is the man, boys, Longstreet is the man."

Cigar between his bearded lips, Longstreet was again an imperturbable figure in combat. One officer in Tennessee called Longstreet "the boldest and bravest looking man I ever saw. I don't think he would dodge if a shell were to burst under his chin."

When another officer ducked as a shell passed overhead, Longstreet smiled and remarked, "I see you salute them."

"Yes, every time."

"If there is a shell or a bullet over there destined for us," Longstreet replied, "It will find us."[24]

But if Longstreet was a hero at Chickamauga, his fall was precipitate. After Chickamauga, he performed poorly at Lookout Mountain, acting oddly disengaged from his duties and (understandably) chafing at the authority of his superior officer, General Braxton Bragg. He even joined in an attempt to get Bragg removed from command.

Bragg was one of the most difficult officers in the Confederate service, and so prone to contention that he reputedly even argued with himself. But he was also a favorite of Jefferson Davis, to whom Longstreet and Bragg's other subordinate generals appealed.

Davis responded by coming to Tennessee. Gathering Bragg's generals together in Bragg's presence, he asked them, individually, to state their case against their commander. After all the generals, however reluctantly, had confessed their belief that Bragg was unfit to command, Davis reaffirmed his confidence in Bragg and returned to Richmond, leaving in his wake a commanding officer poisoned with personal animosity against every one of his subordinate generals.

Bragg, at Davis's suggestion, detached Longstreet for a quasi-independent command. His assignment was to recapture East Tennessee from the occupying Federals. If this fulfilled Longstreet's desire for autonomy, he soon wished he was back under Lee's sheltering wing. Longstreet's Knoxville campaign was a fiasco, plagued by delays, and ending in abysmal, costly failure and in ugly recriminations when he tried to pass off blame for the defeat to his former friend General Lafayette McLaws.

In a mere three months, Longstreet's star fell so drastically that he went from being "Longstreet the man" to "Peter the slow." One well-placed observer in Richmond, Mary Chestnut, whose husband served on Jefferson Davis's military staff, wrote: "Detached from General Lee, what a horrible failure, what a slow old humbug is Longstreet."[25]

Even Longstreet might have been inclined to accept Mrs. Chestnut's verdict. The fact was, he was an excellent corps commander for Lee, but he was not Lee's rival, or even Jackson's, when it came to independent operations.

But back under Lee's command, Longstreet was brilliant at the battle of the Wilderness, where he lived up to the postwar praise of Confederate General John Bell Hood who paid Longstreet the ultimate fighter's compliment when he said, "Of all men living, not excepting our incomparable Lee himself, I would rather follow James Longstreet in a forlorn hope

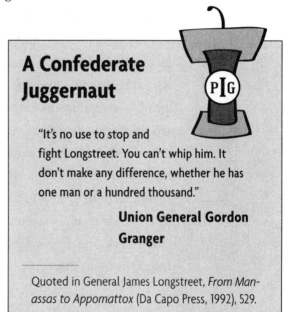

A Confederate Juggernaut

"It's no use to stop and fight Longstreet. You can't whip him. It don't make any difference, whether he has one man or a hundred thousand."

Union General Gordon Granger

Quoted in General James Longstreet, *From Manassas to Appomattox* (Da Capo Press, 1992), 529.

or desperate encounter against heavy odds. He was our hardest hitter."[26]

Longstreet was a hard hitter for many reasons. One was simple competence. Robert E. Lee considered Longstreet his most reliable corps commander. As such, Longstreet had more troops under his command than any other officer, and when he committed men to combat, it was with carefully positioned skill, the ground surveyed, the troops at full strength. As one Virginia soldier put it: "Like a fine lady at a party, Longstreet was often late in arrival at the ball. But he always made a sensation when he got in, with the grand old First Corps sweeping behind him as his train."[27]

At the Battle of the Wilderness, however, Longstreet was wounded by his own men while scouting ahead of his lines—shot through the neck and shoulder. With Longstreet down, the planned Confederate counter-stroke faltered and was cancelled. The Wilderness was still a Confederate victory, but the opportunity to make it an overwhelming one was lost.

Longstreet survived his wounds (though he would never regain full use of his right arm), and after recuperating in Georgia, he rejoined Lee for the final defensive struggle. Fighting the kind of war he preferred he was sturdy and immovable against Federal assaults, remaining stubbornly devoted to the cause until the end. It was unshakable Longstreet who at Appomattox disdained Union General George Armstrong Custer's demand that he surrender to General Phil Sheridan. "I am not the commander of this army," Longstreet said, glaring, "and if I were, I would not surrender it to General Sheridan." A little later, Longstreet advised Lee, as Lee rode to meet Grant, "General, if he does not give us good terms, come back and let us fight it out."[28] For as long as the South fought, Longstreet was there.

Longstreet the scalawag

But after the war, he was swiftly traduced and regarded as a scalawag. As a soldier, Longstreet was a cautious and clever tactician. As a politician and controversialist, he was not. The "old bull of the woods," a nickname he earned at Chickamauga, became the old bull of the china shop.

It was not that Longstreet accepted Reconstruction, counseled in favor of cooperation, and repudiated any ideas of rebellion against the Federal government's authority—many leading Confederates did that. It was that Longstreet took the additional step of allying himself with the Republican Party that was in charge of the Reconstruction program. He even commanded mostly black police and militia units in defense of the Republican governor of Louisiana—after a contested election in which the Republican and Democrat claimed victory, though the Republican was recognized by the Grant administration as the legitimate winner—and fought a battle in the streets against the Democrats' Crescent City White League, many of whom were Confederates.

Longstreet believed that "Since the negro has been given the privilege of voting, it is all important that we should exercise such influence over that vote, as to prevent its being injurious to us, & we can only do that as Republicans....Congress requires reconstruction upon the Republican basis. If the whites won't do this, the thing will be done by the blacks, and we shall be set aside, if not expatriated."[29]

For Longstreet, it was a simple matter of pragmatism, but for other Southerners, joining the "Black Republicans" amounted to a betrayal. Still, he was not alone in taking this course. In Virginia, the "Grey Ghost," John Singleton Mosby, joined the Republican Party for much the same reason that Longstreet did. Both men were friends of Ulysses Grant, whom Longstreet endorsed for president, and won appointment to a variety of political posts.

But if becoming a Black Republican was shock enough, a further shock to Southern sensibilities came when Longstreet entered the battle of the books over who was to blame for the South's defeat. He had the reasonable excuse of needing to defend himself from Lee's partisans who, after Lee's death, blamed Longstreet's performance at Gettysburg for the loss of the war. But Longstreet's ill-tempered counterattack did not become a man who had enjoyed such an enduring and cordial relationship with Lee, and who had a son, born during the bitter Tennessee winter of 1863, who bore the name Robert Lee Longstreet.

Longstreet miscalculated how he should defend his reputation. The "old bull of the woods" simply charged a red cape. He had done the same when he became a Republican, judging that "we are a conquered people.

Recognizing this fact, fairly and squarely, there is but one course left for wise men to pursue, and that is to accept the terms that are now offered by the conquerors."[30] He did not realize that the conquering party's control would soon be replaced by the "solid" Democratic South.

Longstreet outlived most of his colleagues, and despite the controversy that surrounded him he was an active and eager participant in Confederate veterans' activities, memorial associations, and reunions. He did not moulder in retirement, but received jobs from every Republican administration, starting with Grant's successor Rutherford B. Hayes, until his death at age eighty-two. He also tried his hand at farming, which he enjoyed; remarried (he was a widower), finding a bride forty-two years his junior (she lived until 1962); and became a Roman Catholic.

But however many civilian jobs he held, Longstreet died like an old soldier, with his last words to his wife being, "Helen, we shall be happier in this post."

Chapter Nine

NATHAN BEDFORD FORREST
(1821-1877)

"Git Thar Fustest with the Mostest"[1]

When asked to name the greatest soldier of the war, Robert E. Lee replied, "A man I have never seen, sir. His name is Forrest."[2] Nathan Bedford Forrest was certainly an extraordinary man, a Herculean hero of the American wilderness who has blotted his copybook amongst the politically correct because of allegations stemming from his capture of Fort Pillow and his part in the original Ku Klux Klan. But there is more to the story than that.

During the war, Forrest killed thirty men in hand-to-hand combat, had twenty-nine horses shot from beneath him, and proved himself a very "wizard of the saddle." William Tecumseh Sherman said, "Forrest is the devil....I will order them [two of his officers] to make up a force and go out to follow Forrest to the death, if it costs ten thousand lives and breaks

Guess What?

- Even before the war, Forrest had been in a frontier-style gunfight

- Forrest, though a slave trader, freed his own slaves

- Though allegedly a commander of the Ku Klux Klan, he wanted more free blacks—and Chinese—in the South

the Treasury. *There will never be peace in Tennessee until Forrest is dead!*"[3]

To the Federals he might have been the "that devil Forrest," as Sherman called him in a 6 November 1864 message to Grant, but to Confederates in Tennessee and Mississippi, he was a hero, the very embodiment of all the virtues of the Southern frontiersman: fearless, enterprising, honor-bound, unstoppable. Confederate General Richard Taylor (President Zachary Taylor's son) said of Forrest that "I doubt if any commander since the days of lion-hearted Richard has killed as many enemies with his own hand as Forrest,"[4] who was not only a strong-right arm in battle but an intuitive genius of a general.

The gunfighter

Forrest was born the son of a blacksmith in Bedford County, Tennessee. The family hunted and farmed for its food, and made their own clothes. Forrest had little formal schooling (less than a year, and his headmaster remembered him as being more interested in wrestling than reading). But he had plenty of good sense, worked hard for his family (especially after his father died), and killed varmints (including, like a young Hercules, beating a snake to death and hunting down a panther that had attacked his mother).

When it was rumored that Mexico would invade Texas, Forrest went off to fight. Unfortunately, there was no fighting to be had, so he worked his way back home, and set out to make his own fortune. That took him to Hernando, Mississippi, where an uncle had invited him to join his business, which included buying and selling horses and cattle.

On 10 March 1845, in a scene out of the old West, or the frontier South, four men—a planter named Matlock, two Matlock brothers, and an overseer—came to settle a dispute with Forrest's uncle. Forrest saw their ill intent and intervened. He had no interest in the quarrel, he told them, except to even the odds: four against one wasn't fair. One of the brothers drew on Forrest, missing him, but his uncle was struck and killed. Bedford fired back with his two-shot pocket pistol, each shot striking one of the Matlocks, leaving them wounded in the mud. Out of ammunition, he accepted a Barlow knife from a bystander, slashed the last Matlock into submission, and watched the overseer flee.

Though wounded himself by a pistol ball, Forrest was no easy man to take down. Six-foot-two, broad-shouldered, muscular, his dark wavy hair combed back from his unwavering iridescent blue eyes, he was, as John Allan Wyeth, who rode with him, remembered, "born a leader of men, not a follower of man."[5]

In that, too, he was a Southerner, for civilization in the old South was based on honor; and honor meant that Forrest was punctilious about dressing immaculately, about treating women with deference, and making sure that folks minded their manners (or paid the price). It meant that he worked hard, aiming not only to make money, but to earn a reputation as a respectable man. When he became a millionaire (largely through slave-trading), it was as a means to become a landed gentleman and leader—not to pursue the life of a sybarite.

He was soft spoken, except when angry. Then his face would flare and his tone would menace. He had a furious, animal temper, and could swear a blue-streak, but abhorred obscene language and never used it himself. Nor would he tolerate dirty stories. He didn't drink, saying "My staff does all my drinking,"[6] and didn't smoke. His amusements were horse-racing and gambling. He refused to tolerate disorder, to the point where if his headquarters wasn't swept he'd do it himself. When it came to romance, he was a buckskin knight. He might not have read *Ivanhoe*, the most influential book in the Old South after the Bible, but chivalry was ingrained in him.

He met the woman who would be his wife when she and her mother were in a wagon stuck in a mud hole. Bedford rode up and rescued the women, carrying them across the mud, and then pushing the wheel free. Two men on horseback sat by watching. Bedford, in the words of Andrew Nelson Lytle, "told them they were ungallant and unfit to be in the presence of ladies, that if they didn't ride away immediately, he would give them the worst whipping of their lives."[7] They took his word for it and skedaddled. After returning the ladies to their wagon, he asked permission to call on the younger, Miss Mary Montgomery. Permission granted, he turned up the next day, found the same two ungallants in the parlor, scattered them like hares, and told Miss Mary he wanted to marry her. Her father Cowan Montgomery, a Presbyterian minister, disapproved. "Why, Bedford, I couldn't consent. You cuss and gamble and Mary is a Christian girl." Forrest replied, "I know it, and that's just why I want her."[8] In a battle of wills, Forrest was not the sort who would ever relent; Cowan did.

The slave trader

Forrest's growing business interests led him to Memphis and slave-trading, at which he grew so adept that he became one of the leading slave dealers of the Middle South. To read about the slave trade of the 1850s is to enter a world where brokers advertise that they have "constantly at hand the best selected assortment of Field Hands, House Servants & Mechanics, at their Negro Mart." The firm welcomes customers to "examine their stock before purchasing elsewhere" and volunteers to sell slaves on commission, promising that they will always acquire "the highest market price . . . for good stock."[9]

It sounds a bit like something out of the casbah. But it should also remind us of something else: slavery was an accepted commercial transaction in the South. One inspected a prospective slave the way one inspected a horse one was hankering on buying (or perhaps today a car). The slave dealer—or the slave's previous owner—had a large financial stake in ensuring that the slave was strong, healthy, and unmarked by a whip or beating. Slaves were expensive, and a slave who bore scars not only reflected badly on the previous owner (the way a mistreated horse might) but was no more attractive to purchase than a car full of dings and dents and whose warning lights flash on the dashboard: either the slave was of bad character or the owner was—and planters prided themselves on their honor as much as any Southerner did.

As an aspiring planter, Forrest strove to be an impeccably honest and well-meaning slave trader. There is, of course, no getting around the fact that he was buying and selling human beings, and working to make a profit. But within that sadly confined moral circle, he acted as well as he could. According to his biographer Andrew Nelson Lytle, "He never separated a family, and he always did his best to find and buy the husband and wife, when either one was missing. He treated his slaves so well that he was burdened with appeals from them to be bought [by him]."[10]

Not like Wal-Mart

In the Old South slave marts were open, unlike today where slavery, except in some Islamic countries (or de facto, in Communist countries) is underground, and confined mostly to Africa and the Indian subcontinent. Nevertheless, slave traders had the social status of used car salesmen. Though many defenses—political, social, cultural, and theological—were made of slavery, any redeeming quality that could, in the antebellum South, be attached to slavery, could only be attached to a feudalistic, *noblesse oblige* relationship of a gentleman planter to his slaves. No honor could be attached to the slave trader, and certainly no honor could be attached to the equivalent of a Simon Legree (who was, in any event, an irreligious Yankee).

If cynics doubt the honesty of this portrayal, they should read Forrest's advertisements, which take a similarly paternalistic line, promising that "cleanliness, neatness and comfort" were "strictly observed and enforced" in his slave mart. Moreover, "Persons wishing to dispose of a servant may rest assured that, if left with us, a good home will be secured."[11] It was this paternalism that allowed Southerners to tell themselves that while heartless Yankee capitalists treated their workers with callous inhumanity, Southerners treated their black "property" as real people, people to be clothed, fed, housed, and found "a good home," and that could never be cast away into the streets.

By the time of Lincoln's election, Forrest's business interests—from real estate to his slave mart—had made him a millionaire. He was now what he had aspired to be, a planter and a respected member of the community. Since the day he had faced down the Matlock brothers, he had always been marked as a leader. In Hernando, Mississippi, he was a constable, in Memphis an alderman. In every position of authority he held, he was rigorously honest, and an enemy of corruption and cowardice. In one incident in Memphis, he single-handedly rescued a man from a lynch mob's noose, fighting through the crowd to put the untried man in jail. When the mob surged around the jail threatening to break in, Forrest strode out, a six shooter in each hand, a big knife tucked visibly in his belt, and said matter of factly: "If you come by ones, or by tens, or by hundreds, I'll kill any man who tries to get in this jail." That put paid to the mob's ardor.[12]

When war came, Forrest, as a wealthy man, had much to lose and opposed secession. He, like most men in the upper South and many in the lower South, hoped for a regional compromise. But it is characteristic of the man that when Tennessee seceded, he followed his native state and enlisted as a private (as did his youngest brother and fifteen-year-old son) in Captain Josiah White's Tennessee Mounted Rifles.

Confederate cavalryman

But Forrest was not long for the enlisted ranks. Local notables petitioned the governor and soon Forrest was a lieutenant colonel charged with raising his own regiment of mounted rangers. Troopers were asked to bring their own horses, equipment, and arms (shotguns and pistols preferred), but for those without he bought 500 Colt navy pistols, 100 saddles, and other cavalry impedimenta, which he cleverly smuggled (along with recruits) out of officially neutral Kentucky and past the noses Federal forces.

His first major engagement was at Sacramento, Kentucky. His men, riding through the town of Rumsey on the way to Sacramento, were cheered by the Kentucky belles who urged the men forward. Among them, according to Forrest's report, was "a beautiful young lady, smiling, with untied

Not an Illiterate Hick

Forrest once said that "I never see a pen but what I think of a snake."[*] Nevertheless his lack of formal education did not handicap him as an officer. He was literate—as a businessman, he had to be, and he was an avid reader of newspapers—and though, as one of his officers remembered, he "was indisposed to the use of the pen himself, he had clear and exact ideas of what he had written, and few were more exacting in requiring a precise statement of the ideas furnished."[†] Left to his own devices he was a bad speller but he had an instinctive feel for grammar and would correct ungrammatical draft reports and say of an awkward sentence, "That won't do, it hasn't the right pitch."[‡] As a commander, he was pitch perfect. Or as one of his troopers recalled, Forrest's later commission as a general "was signed not only by Mr. Jefferson Davis, but by the Almighty as well."[¥]

[*] John Allan Wyeth, *That Devil Forrest: A Life of General Nathan Bedford Forrest* (Louisiana State University Press, 1989), 554.
[†] Quoted in Jack Hurst, *Nathan Bedford Forrest: A Biography* (Alfred A. Knopf, 1993), 76.
[‡] Wyeth, 555.
[¥] Quoted in Brian Steel Wills, *A Battle from the Start* (HarperCollins, 1992), 1.

tresses floating in the breeze, on horseback, [who] met the column just before our advance guard came up with the rear of the enemy, infusing nerve into my arm and kindling knightly chivalry within my heart."[13] More than kindling knightly chivalry within his heart, she told Forrest what she knew of the Federal dispositions at Sacramento.

Forrest's men raced to the attack of the enemy, engaging first in skirmish fire, and then, with flankers on the left and right, a head-on charge that broke the Federals, sending them reeling through the town. One trooper reported that at the outset of the battle, "there were at least fifty shots fired" at Forrest "in five minutes" and that Forrest, in turn, must have "killed 9 of the enemy."[14] Forrest led the charge after the retreating Federals, and fighting with pistol and saber brought down at least two more Federals and disabled another officer in blue who became his prisoner.

In action, he was a berserker, or in the words of Major David C. Kelley, this was "the first time I had seen the Colonel in the face of the enemy, and, when he rode up to me in the thick of the action, I could scarcely believe him to be the man I had known for several months." Forrest's face was flushed red so that "it bore a striking resemblance to a painted Indian warrior's, and his eyes, usually mild in their expression, were blazing with the intense glare of a panther's springing upon its prey. In fact, he looked as little like the Forrest of our mess-table as the storm of December resembles the quiet of June."[15]

"I am going out of this place or bust hell wide open"

His troopers' next assignment was at Fort Donelson where Forrest immediately distinguished himself by picking off a Federal sniper. But the bigger problem was the tightening Federal grip around the besieged fort, which fronted the Cumberland River. The first plan agreed to by Confederate generals Gideon Pillow, John B. Floyd, and Simon B. Buckner was to force a passage through the Union right. In fierce fighting, in which two horses were killed beneath him, one by an artillery shell, Forrest and his men blazed a trail that would have allowed the Confederate army to escape to Nashville, but General Pillow recalled the Confederates to their original lines.

That night the generals resolved to surrender the fort. Forrest, disgusted, told the generals that the men had a lot more fight left in them and won their permission to bring out his own command if he could. Forrest told his men, "Boys, these people are talking about surrendering, and I am going out of this place or bust hell wide open." He told one soldier who decided to remain behind with his comrades, "All right; I admire your loyalty, but damn your judgment!"[16] Most of his command shared his judgment and rode out into the frosty night, and into freedom, on 16 February 1862.

Forrest and his men saw duty at Shiloh, where Forrest was disconcerted to hear that his son had gone missing, only to find the fifteen-year-old trooper shepherding Union prisoners. When Beauregard decided to retreat, Forrest was assigned to the rear guard, where he battled William Tecumseh Sherman at Fallen Timbers. In an engagement of typical Bedfordian fury, the fiery Tennessean charged the Federals, broke through their ranks—and suddenly found himself cut off and surrounded by bluecoats yelling "Kill him! Kill him!" One of the Federals planted a rifle barrel in his side and pulled the trigger, shooting a ball of lead near Forrest's spine. But Forrest merely grimaced, hurled a bluecoat up behind him as a shield, and spurred and shot his way through the Federals, dropping the bullet-ridden Yankee once he was safe. Forrest's right leg was numb, and the doctors, probing bloodily, couldn't find the ball in the small of his back.

He was given two month's leave to recover. He only allowed himself three weeks, and spent that time advertising for new recruits with this winning tagline: "Come on, boys, if you want a heap of fun and to kill some Yankees."[17] As it was, Forrest took command of a new unit of cavalry made up of Georgians and Texans, which he led on raids into Tennessee, where they learned his tactics of charge—"Mix with 'em, boys!"—and bluff.

After shocking a Federal position by his sudden appearance or with a brief, bold attack, he would demand its unconditional surrender. Failing that, he threatened, he could not be held accountable for the consequences, given that his men's blood was up. While the Federals considered his demand, Forrest would make a show of his riders and artillery—the same riders and artillery repeatedly pulling in and trotting out, but fooling the Federals into thinking they were ever expanding numbers of grey cavalrymen and rebel cannon.

Switch-hitter

At the battle of Parker's Crossroads, Forrest was flanked by Federals front and rear. He responded with the innovative order: "Charge them both ways!" (Some of his biographers doubt he actually said this, but it certainly captures Forrest's spirit.)

He performed this theme of fierce charges and gambler's bluff with variations throughout the entire war, and it was crucial to his success because his troops were usually ill-equipped. To gain an adequate supply of guns and ammunition his men had to take them from the Federals. Surrendering Federal officers became the inadvertent quartermasters of Forrest's "critter company."

"Ah, Colonel, all is fair in love and war"

Though an accomplished raider, Forrest was also a brigadier general (as of late July 1862). But Confederate General Braxton Bragg tended to think that raiding and recruiting were Forrest's forte, and so rather than incorporate him into a regular body of cavalry, Bragg repeatedly chose to take Forrest's troopers for the army, and send Forrest out to raise more men and engage in more raids. Forrest didn't mind the call to action, but he did come to resent Bragg's limitation of his role.

That Forrest was aggressive cannot be doubted, but he was also a real-ist and advocated against an attack on the Federal position at Dover, near Fort Donelson, in February 1863, though he was ordered to do so by General Joseph Wheeler, a Georgia-born West Pointer and cavalry officer. The attack itself was a failure—in part because of Forrest's aggression leading him to charge the Federals when he thought they were retreating; they weren't. Forrest's horse, as was common, was blown from beneath his legs, though Forrest, as ever, survived. His temper, however, didn't. After the battle he told Wheeler, "I mean no disrespect to you; you know my feelings of personal friendship for you; you can have my sword if you demand it; but there is one thing I do want you to put into your report to General Bragg—tell him that I will be in my coffin before I will fight again under your command."[18] Wheeler reassured him of his esteem, the moment passed, and Forrest would serve under Wheeler again.

In April 1863, Forrest's men, usually the chased (after their raids), became the chasers, pursuing a unit of Federal raiders under the command of Colonel Abel D. Streight who charged across northern Alabama. Forrest kept his men at Streight's heels, but at one point it looked like the Federal colonel had bested Forrest, escaping over Black Creek and burn-ing the bridge behind them. As at Sacramento, however, help came from the fairer sex. A young girl at a nearby farmhouse called out to Forrest and told him she knew another crossing. He pulled her up behind him on the saddle (reassuring her mother that he'd bring her back safe) and had her guide him to the ford, where his men crossed to continue their harassment of the Federals. Forrest left the girl (named Emma Sansom) a note—an official commendation of her service.

When Forrest finally called upon the Federal commander to surrender his exhausted troops, his men employed the old Forrest bluff strategy, moving around artillery pieces until Streight said: "Name of God! How many guns have you got? There's fifteen I've counted already!" Forrest replied, "I reckon that's all that has kept up." After a little more bluff and

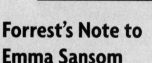

Forrest's Note to Emma Sansom

Hed Quaters in Sadle

May 2, 1863

My highest Regardes to miss Emma Sansom for hir Gallant conduct while my posse was skirmishing with the Federals across Black Creek near Gadsden Alabama

N. B. Forrest

Brig Genl
Comding N. Ala—-

The actual handwritten note is reproduced by Captain Eric William Sheppard, O.B.E. (M. Div.), M.C., Royal Tanks Corps, in *Bedford Forrest: The Confederacy's Greatest Cavalryman* (Morningside, 1992), 110-111.

Handwritten, in haste, and with no staff officers to make a corrected copy, one supposes that Emma Sansom didn't mind.

threat, Streight tossed in his hand—1,466 blue-coated soldiers. When he saw that Forrest had only 400 to 600 men, he protested, to Forrest's laughing rebuke: "Ah, Colonel, all is fair in love and war."[19]

"No damned man shall kill me and live"

Forrest was feared and hated by Northern commanders, but his fame also gained him respect. Once, seeing a white flag over a Union fortification, he rode up, only to be told by a chivalrous Federal officer, "General Forrest! This isn't a flag of truce. It's a signal flag. Go back, sir, go back!"[20] Forrest saluted and galloped back to his lines.

He was less fortunate in a misunderstanding with one of his own officers, Lieutenant A. W. Gould, whom Forrest had rashly and wrongly accused of cowardice, and ordered transferred to another unit. Gould met with Forrest at the Masonic hall (commandeered by the quartermaster) in Columbia, Tennessee, to personally protest the order. Forrest took it personally, too. When Forrest refused to reconsider, Gould allegedly pulled a gun on Forrest. The gun misfired, wounding Forrest, who struck back with a pen knife (which he used as folks today use dental floss), slamming it into Gould's ribs while he simultaneously deflected Gould's gun hand upwards.

Gould fled and was taken in by two doctors who tried to stanch the bleeding; Forrest was assisted by another doctor who told him that the gunshot in his side might be fatal. Forrest pushed him aside and stumbled out into the street swearing "No damned man shall kill me and live."[21] One man tried to stop him, saying Gould was mortally wounded. That didn't matter. Having picked up a revolver, Forrest burst in on Gould and his doctors. Gould had life enough still in him, to make a break for it, running down an alley before collapsing in a pile of weeds. Forrest strode over to him, rolled him over with his boot, and, seemingly satisfied, stalked off.

Forrest's wound was, miraculously, not fatal as the ball hit no vital organs. Gould was not so lucky, and now that the mortal balances had shifted in Forrest's favor, Forrest was filled with remorse. He told his doctors to go away, "It's nothing but a damn little pistol ball; leave it alone!" And he demanded that Gould be given every consideration of treatment, which Forrest would pay for. Gould died, but not before he and Forrest were reconciled, according to some accounts.[22]

Forrest versus Bragg

Within a fortnight Forrest was back in action, covering the retreat of Bragg's army and being barracked by a woman as he sped through her town: "You great big cowardly rascal; why don't you fight like a man, instead of running like a cur? I wish old Forrest was here. He'd make you fight."[23]

Forrest fought again, and was wounded again, at Chickamauga, with another ball lodged near his spine. But while he broke his rule of abstention and accepted a swig of whiskey for the pain, he stayed in action at the battle—indeed he stayed in the battle more than the commanding general Braxton Bragg did. With the Federals in retreat, Forrest sent a dispatch through General Leonidas Polk for Bragg, laying out what he saw of the Federal evacuation and offering the admonition, "I think we ought to press forward as rapidly as possible." He followed this up with another dispatch, urging haste because "every hour is worth 10,000 men." His reports were seconded by a Confederate soldier who had escaped the Federals and was sent to Bragg to relay information on the Union retreat. The skeptical Bragg asked the trooper if he knew what a retreat looked like. "I ought to General, I've been with you during your entire campaign." Forrest likewise grumbled about Bragg: "What does he fight battles for?" [24]

Bragg's advance on the Federals was not only, in Forrest's view, lackluster at best, but he redoubled the crime by sending an order to Forrest—now fighting off Union cavalry—that his command was being transferred

Bedford Forrest on Leadership

If Forrest could be an outspoken subordinate, he was equally tough with the enlisted men, once physically smashing one of his scouts into a tree because he had brought back a rumor of Federal troops rather than seeing them for himself; once hurling a reluctant trooper into icy water; and once catching a fleeing conscript soldier and thrashing him with a splintered branch, telling him to "go back to the front and fight; you might as well be killed there as here, for if you ever run away again you'll not get off so easy."* Likewise, any officer who claimed he shouldn't have to engage in physical labor (which Forrest always readily did) could suddenly find the general's saber under his nose along with threat, "I'll officer you!"*

* Quoted in Brian Steel Wills, *A Battle from the Start* (HarperCollins, 1992), 161.

to Wheeler. This set the stage for the greatest verbal showdown of Forrest's career. He spurred into Bragg's camp, burst into his tent, and let fly with a speech of damnation that ended with these words:

> I have stood your meanness as long as I intend to. You have
> played the part of a damned scoundrel, and are a coward, and
> if you were any part of a man I would slap your face jaws and
> force you to resent it.
>
> You may as well not issue any more orders to me, for I will
> not obey them. And as I hold you personally responsible for
> any further indignities you try to inflict on me.
>
> You have threatened to arrest me for not obeying your
> orders promptly. I dare you to do it, and I say to you that if you
> ever again try to interfere with me or cross my path, it will be
> at the peril of your life.[25]

Bragg decided to grant Forrest a transfer.

Controversy at Fort Pillow

In early 1864, Forrest's youngest brother was killed in action—and Forrest, to avenge his death, personally charged the enemy in such fierce hand-to-hand fighting that his own men thought he was engaged in suicidal combat. By March 1864, Forrest was seeking to avenge more than his brother, he was seeking redress for outrages against pro-Confederate Tennesseans at the hands of Union troops or pro-Union militia. The alleged crimes included murder (one such being an officer of Forrest's command who was captured while looking for deserters, and then, allegedly, tortured, killed, and mutilated), detention without charge, and extortion (bilking Southern townsmen out of thousands of dollars to spare their towns being burnt). Forrest sent a note of protest to the Union commander at Memphis and a dispatch to Confederate General Leonidas

Polk. But he also prepared for action. In April 1864 he fought the most controversial battle of his career, at Fort Pillow, Tennessee.

Forrest hoped to capture the fort in order to supply his men; he did not expect much resistance. The Federal force defending the fort was made up of black troops (mostly freed slaves) and pro-Union Tennesseans. Forrest thought little of them as soldiers, and thought of the latter as traitors and the sort of renegades who abused their pro-Confederate neighbors. His approach against the fort was well-conducted, seizing forward buildings and surrounding the fort which, however, backed onto the Mississippi River, where the Federals had a gunboat.

Forrest's men outnumbered the Fort's defenders (not including the gunboat) by about three to one. As per his usual procedure, he tried to convince the bluecoats to surrender and threatened that if they did not he could not be responsible for the fate of the Federal command. But the Yankees refused—apparently doubting that they were really dealing with the fearsome Forrest—and the defenders behind their parapet even goaded the attackers to come and get them. Forrest was willing to oblige. Forrest set his Missourians, Mississippians, and Tennesseans the contest of seeing who could breech the Federal lines first. Forrest, uncharacteristically, did not lead the charge himself. He had already had one horse shot beneath him that day (two more would follow) and it appears he might have been a nursing a sore hip.

The Confederates swarmed through the fort's outer defenses (a ditch and parapet followed by earthworks) and then charged into the fort. The resulting melee, with Confederates firing into the Federals at point-blank range degenerated into a massacre as bluecoats fled to the river in vain hope of joining the gunboat, which Confederate fire kept driven back. In the frenzy and chaos of the blood-dimmed tide, bluecoats threw down their guns and were cut down after them. Men attempting to surrender were shown no quarter. But what happened was no organized atrocity, though Federal propaganda later tried to make it so, especially playing the race card, accusing the Confederates of murdering the black troops who suffered disproportionate casualties. (Fifty-eight of the 262 black defenders were made prisoners, as were 168 of the 295 whites.)

But any disinterested view of the battle and sober assessment of the evidence leads one to an opposite conclusion. Though he had no love for "Damn Nigger Regiments" and "Damn Tennessee Yankees," Forrest and his officers tried to rein in their men as quickly as they could, once they realized that what had started as a battle had degenerated into a rampage.[26] That Forrest had hoped to take the fort without bloodshed was obvious from his demand for its surrender. That men on the sharp-end (rather than the propaganda end) of battle understood the Fort Pillow "massacre" for what it was can be demonstrated by the fact that Sherman, who investigated the incident, declined to seek retaliation, though he had been authorized to do so by Grant, if the facts justified it.

Bluff and Bluster

Forrest once scouted his way through a Union camp. When a Federal sentry challenged him, Forrest chastised the trooper so thoroughly for insulting his commanding officer that the Yankee made his apologies and let Forrest pass.

Fighting to the end

On 10 June 1864, Forrest fought his greatest independent pitched battle, ambushing Federal forces under Union General Samuel D. Sturgis at the Battle of Brice's Crossroads, and sending Sturgis's much larger force—8,500 Federals to 3,500 Confederates—in harried retreat, with Sturgis pleading, "For God's sake, if Mr. Forrest will let me alone, I will let him alone."[27] Forrest not only defeated the Federals but relieved them of 16 pieces of artillery, 176 wagons, and a huge amount of ammunition and arms. Sherman was appalled at Sturgis's defeat but noted that "Forrest is the devil, and I think he has got some of our troops under cower. . . . I will order them [two Federal officers] to make up a force and go out to follow Forrest to the death, if it costs ten thousand lives and breaks the Treasury. *There will never be peace in Tennessee until Forrest is dead!*"[28]

Unfortunately for the Confederacy, Forrest was not sent to harry Sherman's rear in Tennessee and Georgia; he was kept in the sideshow war of Mississippi, where he remained audacious even as his years of hard campaigning were starting to take their toll on his health. He was shot again, this time in the foot, at the Battle of Harrisburg, near Tupelo, Mississippi—a bloody repulse for the Confederates, and one that shattered Forrest's command, but not badly enough for Sherman's liking, because despite rumors to the contrary, Forrest survived. His presence, riding back from the hospital, reinvigorated the Confederate cavalry.

Indeed, this seemed to be Forrest's role in the last year of the war: to reinvigorate Confederate morale with daring raids, such as he made into Memphis in August 1864, while the country's borders withered under the torches of the advancing Federals. General Richard Taylor more or less gave him this duty, telling Forrest to do what he would, and report only to him. Forrest, operating now in Alabama, captured the Federal garrison (1,900 men) at Athens in September 1864, destroyed the heavily guarded trestle at Sulphur Springs, and caused such trouble that Sherman had 30,000 men converging on the Confederate commander to "press Forrest to death." But Sherman confessed that Forrest's "cavalry will cover one hundred miles in less time than ours will ten."[29]

Forrest followed up his Alabama-Tennessee raids with a long-held plan to harass the Federals' river-borne supplies. His men captured Federal supply boats and turned them into impromptu gunboats for Forrest's new-styled "Hoss Marines." They shelled Federal transports on the river and obliterated supply dumps. At Johnsonville, Tennessee, on the Tennessee River, they inflicted millions of dollars worth of damage on Federal stores on 3 November 1864. He did this, while Federal intelligence reports had him roaming about up North, in disguise, preparing, according to a Union provost-marshal, to "seize telegraph and rail at Chicago, release prisoners there, arm them, sack the city, shoot down all Federal soldiers, and urge concert of action with Southern sympathizers."[30] Forrest had no plans of fomenting an insurrection in Chicago. His plans were closer to home, as he wistfully remarked to his artillery officer John Morton, "John, if they'd give you enough guns and me enough men, we could whip old Sherman off the face of the earth!"[31]

Instead, Forrest was recalled to join in the bloody futility of John Bell Hood's invasion of Tennessee in which the Confederate army of the West smashed itself to pieces, and then retreated, covered by Forrest, through bloodied ice and snow. Forrest finished the war as a lieutenant general, and to the end, he continued to fight the enemy hand-to-hand. In battle at Bogler's Creek, he was attacked and pursued by Federal cavalrymen whom he held off and parried with his revolver, while battered by saber blows.

When it came time to surrender, he declined thoughts to lead his men to Mexico (though he entertained the idea later, after the war, as a possible mercenary adventure) or to go farther west and continue the struggle. He knew the game was up, though defeat was as bitter for him as for any who wore the rebel grey. In early May 1865, about a month after Lee's surrender, he told a die-hard politician, "Any man who is in favor of a further prosecution of this war is a fit subject for a lunatic asylum, and ought to be sent there immediately."[32]

He also did something that his detractors might not expect. Before the war was over, he freed his slaves. In later congressional testimony, Forrest said that at the beginning of the war he called his slaves together and

A Laconic Confederate

Woman: "General, why is it the hair on your head is gray and your beard is black?"

Forrest: "I don't know, ma'am, unless it's because I work my head more'n I do my jaws."

Quoted in Andrew Nelson Lytle, *Bedford Forrest and His Critter Company* (J. S. Sanders & Company, 1992), 329.

told them that if they stuck with him to the end of the war, he would set them free. He was as good as his word.

Reconstruction's foe

By his own confession, the war had "pretty well wrecked him." He felt "completely used up—shot to pieces, crippled up."[33] His finances were equally shattered. He relinquished some of his land, which he could no longer afford, and set about trying to farm some of the rest and return his saw mill to operation. He employed newly free blacks—at higher than standard wages, according to the Freedman's Bureau—and brought into partnership several Union officers. The gentlemen in blue got a rude welcome when the general's surviving war horse, King Philip, always

Forrest's Farewell Address to His Troops

Like Lee, Forrest advocated a path of conciliation. His final words to his soldiers included these admonitions:

> Civil war such as you have just passed through naturally engenders feelings of animosity, hatred, and revenge. It is our duty to divest ourselves of all such feelings and so far as in our power to do so, cultivate friendly feelings towards those with whom we have so long contested....
>
> I have never on the field of battle sent you where I was unwilling to go myself, nor would I now advise you to a course which I felt myself unwilling to pursue. You have been good soldiers, you can be good citizens. Obey the laws, preserve your honour, and the Government to which you have surrendered can afford to be, and will be, magnanimous.
>
> N. B. FORREST,
> Lieutenant-General.

You can find the entire farewell address in Captain Eric William Sheppard, *Bedford Forrest: The Confederacy's Greatest Cavalryman* (Morningside, 1992), 280–2.

enraged at the sight of blue uniforms, tried to attack them. One of the Union officers remarked it was no wonder that Forrest had built up a reputation as the very devil of a general, "Your negroes fight for you, and your horses fight for you."[34]

Still, Forrest faced the prospect of being tried for treason (he was indicted but never brought to trial) and for murder. The murder trial did happen, and Forrest was found innocent on the grounds of self-defense. He had intervened when he heard a black field hand named Thomas Edwards assaulting his wife. Edwards was notorious as a wife beater and for having a foul temper. Forrest burst into Edwards's cabin and told him his days as a wife-beater were over. Edwards swore and said that no one would stop him from thrashing his wife. Edwards grasped a knife. Forrest whacked him with a broom handle—and when that only incited Edwards to attack, the general reached for an axe and struck Edwards dead.

According to one Union officer working for the Freedman's Bureau, Forrest exhibited a dangerous leniency with his freedmen that encouraged affairs like that of Thomas Edwards. It was one thing, and a just thing, to treat the freedmen well—which he said, Forrest did to an unparalleled degree—but it was quite another to make liberal loans to the freedmen and allow them to buy and carry arms. And indeed, while Forrest waited for the authorities to arrive after his fight with Edwards, a group of armed freedmen had apparently surrounded Forrest's house, though no further incidents of violence occurred.

Violence, however, was endemic in the tensions of Reconstruction, with disgruntled Confederate soldiers feeling stripped of their rights, freedmen heady with their new freedom, and Federal troops sitting in occupation on the South, executing the laws passed by the Radical Republicans who controlled the U. S. Congress.

Forrest tried to live by the advice he had given his troops—to obey the law. He applied for a pardon from President Johnson, and put his energies to work at a variety of business interests hoping one of them would bring his family financial security. He also apparently joined the newly formed Ku Klux Klan to, in his own mind, return order to the South.

The Klansman

What Forrest did within the Klan is ambiguous if for no other reason than that he denied having been a member of it or having anything more than a general knowledge of it, though he is often considered to have been elected its first commander in chief, or "Grand Wizard." By his own testimony he was not a member, but was "in sympathy" with the Klan and would have cooperated with them in a stand-off against Reconstruction radicals.

Forrest openly thought of the Klan as a defender of Southern rights against the depredations of the Radical Republicans. He publicly discounted reports of its crimes as mostly untrue. He believed that it was led by former Confederate officers who were honorable and disciplined, whose purpose was not the spread of anarchy or insurgency, but the preservation of order and peace. If Longstreet believed in accommodating the new order by being a Republican, Forrest, characteristically, called for peace and obedience, *unless* the Radical Republican authorities were to press things too far. If, Forrest told a reporter, the governor of Tennessee ordered out the militia against the people of the state and committed "outrages," it would be the equivalent of a declaration of war; and if the governor declared war against the people of Tennessee, he would fight against him. It is in this light that Forrest viewed the Ku Klux Klan.

The view that the Radical Republicans did not have the interests of the South, or the Constitution, at heart, was widespread among former Confederates. The Radical Republicans, they believed, were using their power in Congress to grind the faces of former Confederates in the mud, denying them their political and civil rights and setting up newly freed blacks as chattel voters to enforce the Republicans' will. So sober a figure as Robert E. Lee, who like Forrest had made the case for submission and obedience, told a U.S. senator: "a policy which will continue the prostration of one-half the country, [and] alienate the affections of its inhabitants from the Government... appears to me so manifestly injudicious that I do not see how those responsible can tolerate it."[35] Tolerating insults was not Forrest's strong suit.

Forrest said that he would defend the people of Tennessee against any radical

Neglecting Its History

Forrest told a reporter that the Ku Klux Klan was originally "a protective, political, military organization," and one "sworn to recognize the Government of the United States". It was now "a political organization, giving its support, of course, to the democratic party"—something the Democratic Party scarcely ever mentions these days.

depredations, but he wanted to make it clear: "I have no powder to burn killing negroes. I intend to kill the radicals [Radical Republicans]....I have told them that they were trying to create a disturbance and then slip out and leave the consequences to fall upon the negro; but they can't do it."

In Forrest's mind and public professions, the Klan was not an anti-black organization—except in its origins, which were, it was said, to defend white women and children from hungry, armed, newly freed blacks looking for food on Southern farms—it was an anti-Radical Republican organization. Though the Klan was notorious for plying its trading of frightening, intimidating, and threatening freedmen, when not whipping and lynching them, Forrest maintained that such terrorism was not its purpose. It was organized to protect Southerners from pro-Reconstruction groups who were "killing and murdering our people." He confessed, "There were some foolish young men who put masks on their faces and rode over the countryside frightening negroes; but orders have been issued to stop that, and it has ceased."[36]

Whether or not Forrest led the Ku Klux Klan, its "General Order" dated 17 July 1867, said much the same: "We are not the enemy of the blacks, as long as they behave themselves, make no threats upon us, and do not attack or interfere with us." It also denied that the Klan had authorized any of the acts of unprovoked violence that had been carried out in its name; and in fact repudiated these as "wrong! wrong! wrong!" The Klan, it pronounced, "is prohibited from doing these things, and they are requested to prohibit others from doing them, and to protect all good, peaceful, well disposed and law abiding men, whether white or black."[37] When the Klan could no longer be controlled as a force for order, or according to some views, once Forrest thought he could no longer control it, it was dissolved as a unified organization in 1869. Forrest himself testified that he had helped dismantle it. And it is certainly true that he was later a public opponent of white vigilantism and a proponent of racial amity.

Damn Yankees and Scalawags

"I am not an enemy of the negro....We want him here among us; he is the only laboring class we have, and more than that, I would sooner trust him than the white scalawag or carpetbagger."

Nathan Bedford Forrest

Quoted in Brian Steel Wills, *A Battle from the Start* (HarperCollins, 1992).

Forrest actually wanted more blacks to come to the South (in one cockamamie scheme, he thought perhaps the United States could ransom the prisoners of African chiefs and bring them to the South as free laborers). He also testified on behalf of importing Chinese coolies. When it was protested that black laborers would disapprove, he countered that the railroad project he was promoting had support both in financial subscriptions and in a stockholders' vote among black Southerners (and he had the numbers to prove it).

Forrest died in 1877. Only two years before he had declared himself a Christian and became a member of the Presbyterian church. He had always supported Christianity in principle and shown an interest in it and believed in its moral teachings, but it was only at the end of his life, when he was pretty well used up, that the gambler locked up his cards and the man of violent temper and words tried to keep both shackled. He confessed he felt the better for it, and as he said, "I have seen too much of violence, and I want to close my days at peace with all the world, as I am now at peace with my Maker."[38] And so he did.

Chapter Ten

ULYSSES S. GRANT
(1822-1885)

"I propose to fight it out on this line if it takes all summer."[1]

"My family is American, and has been for generations, in all its branches, direct and collateral."[2] So begin Ulysses S. Grant's memoirs, and from that beginning, one already gets a good impression of the man, a man who is a prototypical American type: direct, unassuming, sturdy, independent, and practical. There is no preening on aristocratic European origins. No pretense of somehow being related to Richard the Lionhearted. No Southern sense of medieval chivalry and feudalism transported to the landed estates of the cotton kingdom. Grant was an American; and he, more than anyone else, prevented there being two Americas. It was his implacable will, his stubborn devotion to the cause, his unceasing determination to fight, no matter what the cost, to ultimate victory—and his magnanimity in

Guess What?

✦ Grant (and Lincoln) thought the Mexican War was morally wrong, but had no qualms waging a far bloodier war to deny the South its independence

✦ Grant's wife owned slaves

✦ Grant rated Joseph E. Johnston higher than Robert E. Lee, though Johnston never inflicted the casualties on Grant that Lee did

that victory—that ensured the cause of the Union. Before the war, he was an unlikely hero. But his heroism is a very American story—an Horatio Alger story in Union blue. No less a man than William Tecumseh Sherman thought so: "Each epoch creates its own agents, and General Grant more nearly than any other man impersonated the American character of 1861–5. He will stand, therefore, as the typical hero of the Great Civil War."[3]

A horse-loving boy

He was born Hiram Ulysses Grant in Ohio, a son of a tanner and farmer. While his father tanned hides, his son preferred them on living beasts, on horses, and he became an adept horseman. He hated the stench and blood of the tannery—so much so that in later life his meat had to be blackened free of blood.

Avoiding the tannery, he preferred working on his father's farm, applying himself to practical, solitary tasks, and leading the plough horses. By the age of fourteen, he was running a livery business, driving horse-drawn wagons and carriages for families needing a ride out of town. Getting out of town, and away from the tannery, was a constant desire of his boyhood. In fact, like many boys, he seemed happiest wandering alone outdoors, daydreaming under the sun, lost in his own thoughts (which were not entirely unproductive: he taught himself algebra).

His father, perhaps recognizing that Ulysses would not a tanner be, ensured him a good education and won him a nomination to West Point. For a man like Grant's father, successful, self-taught, and with interests in social standing and politics (he was a Whig and opposed slavery), the military academy offered his son a heady combination: prestige, a fine education, a career, and had the added benefit of being free. In his memoirs, Grant records his father's announcement:

"Ulysses, I believe you are going to receive the appointment."
"What appointment?" I inquired. "To West Point; I have
applied for it." "But I won't go," I said. He said he thought I
would, *and I thought so too, if he did.* I really had no objection
to going to West Point, except that I had a very exalted idea of
the acquirements necessary to get through. I did not believe I
possessed them, and could not bear the idea of failing.[4]

Grant, then, was not a rebellious teenager in the usual sense. He was
honest, modest, quiet, and self-contained, and if his humility made him
fearful of West Point, there was one more immediate and important gift
the military academy gave him: it was his ticket out of Georgetown, Ohio.
"I had always a great desire to travel. I was already the best traveled boy
in Georgetown, except for the sons of one man, John Walker, who had
emigrated to Texas with his family, and immigrated back as soon as he
could get the means to do so."[5]

West Point gave him another gift: his adult name. Gone, because his
nominating congressman had made a mistake, was Hiram. Ulysses (the
name he had always used) became his official Christian name, and Simpson (his mother's maiden name) was suddenly inserted as his middle
name. Characteristically, it was an error Grant never bothered to correct—
too shy, and perhaps too pleased at the practical improvement, to do so.
It also won him a new nickname—"Sam" from his new initials U. S.,
"Uncle Sam" Grant.

He felt no military calling and by his own account was not a studious
cadet. He enjoyed mathematics, but otherwise preferred reading novels
from the school's library rather than studying. "I read all of Bulwer's
[Edward Bulwer-Lytton's novels] then published, [James Fenimore]
Cooper's, [Captain] Marryat's, [Sir Walter] Scott's, Washington Irving's
works . . . and many others." He even hoped that the military academy

might be abolished while he was a student (such a motion was being debated before Congress). Nevertheless, he was a quick study and managed to graduate in the middle of his class (and was also known as West Point's best horseman) in 1843. His shyness, or what his friend and fellow West Pointer James Longstreet called Grant's "girlish modesty,"[6] is the reason for Grant's famous indifference to military dress. Initially, like most young officers, he was eager to display his new uniform. But when a ragged young boy and a dissipated stable hand mocked his appearance, Grant confesses, he gained "a distaste for military uniform that I never recovered from."[7]

He was sent to Jefferson Barracks, St. Louis, as a lieutenant of infantry where one of his fellow lieutenants (and fellow West Pointers) was Richard S. Ewell, his senior, who, as he states, "later acquired considerable reputation as a Confederate general during the rebellion. He was a man much esteemed, and deservedly so, in the old army, and proved himself a gallant and efficient officer in two wars—both in my estimation unholy."[8]

Those two "unholy" wars were the Mexican War and the War for Southern Independence—indeed the two were related. "The occupation,

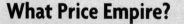

What Price Empire?

Grant's View of the Mexican War

"It is to the credit of the American nation, however, that after conquering Mexico, and while practically holding the country in our possession, so that we could have retained the whole of it, or made any terms we chose, we paid a round sum for the additional territory taken; more than it was worth, or was likely to be, to Mexico. To us it was an empire of incalculable value; but it might have been obtained by other means."

Ulysses S. Grant, *Personal Memoirs* (The Modern Library, 1999), 24.

separation, and annexation of Texas," which set the stage for the Mexican War, was, in Grant's view, "a conspiracy to acquire territory out of which slave states might be formed for the American Union." Moreover, the "Southern rebellion was largely the outgrowth of the Mexican war. Nations, like individuals are punished for their transgressions. We got our punishment in the most sanguinary and expensive war in modern times."[9]

It is telling, of course, that Grant thought Southern independence was an "unholy" cause, but its suppression a righteous one—just punishment for the sin of acquiring America's Western empire. Grant nevertheless participated in the "unholy" war against Mexico because "Experience proves that the man who obstructs a war in which his nation is engaged, no matter whether right or wrong, occupies no enviable place in life or history."[10]

At war in Mexico

Grant served under "Old Rough and Ready," General Zachary Taylor, and got his first taste of combat on 8 May 1846 at Palo Alto. As "a young second-lieutenant who had never heard a hostile gun before," Grant remembered, "I felt sorry that I had enlisted."[11] Nevertheless, he acquitted himself well, and no one ever accused Grant of quivering under fire—precisely the opposite; he showed no emotion at all.

Grant learned more than the blunt task of soldiering through cannon balls and bullets; he learned generalship. Taylor shared Grant's disdain for the pomp, refinery, and spit and polish of military etiquette, but, as Grant saw, he knew how to get things done. Among other things, "General Taylor was not an officer to trouble the administration much with his demands, but was inclined to do the best he could with the means given him." If he thought a directive was impossible to achieve he would say so. "If the judgment [of the authorities] was against him he would have gone on and done the best he could with the means at hand without parading his grievance before the public. No soldier could face either danger or responsibility more calmly than he." What Grant admired in Taylor were the very traits that shone through Grant himself in the Civil War.

Grant's coolness under fire was manifest from the start. "There is no great sport in having bullets flying about one in every direction but I find they have less horror when among them than when in anticipation," he wrote. He had seen violent death, decapitation from a cannon ball, and an officer horribly maimed with his lower jaw torn off. Yet he could still say, "War seems much less horrible to persons engaged in it than to those who read of battles."[12] Grant knew that fear comes from the imagination; courage comes from a relentless focus on the duty at hand—even in a hail of musketry and cannon.

In August 1846, Grant was assigned as quartermaster to the Fourth Infantry—a vast job, but one he didn't want; not because of the pressure of its responsibilities but because it took him out of the firing line. "I respectfully protest against being assigned to a duty which removes me from sharing in the dangers and honors of service with my company at the front..." His protest was rejected on the grounds that it was his meritorious conduct and skill that merited him this promotion. Grant was not appeased, venting his frustration by writing on the back of the rejection he had received from Lieutenant Colonel John Garland: "I should be permitted to resign the position of Quartermaster and Commissary.... I *must* and *will* accompany my regiment in battle."[13]

Grant, however, did his duty. General Zachary Taylor needed an energetic young officer to keep his army supplied on its march through Mexico. In "Sam" Grant, he had found his man. Grant had a logistician's mind. He was methodical, but quick in acquiring and sifting information, and he was diligent. He was also creative: when former Congressman Thomas L. Hamer joined his staff (serendipitously he was the congressman who had appointed Grant to West Point), Grant used the terrain they rode past to pose tactical problems for Hamer, war-gaming their way through the Mexican countryside.

At the battle of Monterrey (21–23 September 1846) Grant capitalized on his Indian way with horses. As regimental quartermaster he should have had no role in the action, but, "My curiosity got the better of my judgment, and I mounted a horse and rode to the front to see what was going on. I had been there but a short time when an order to charge was given, and lacking the moral courage to return to camp—where I had been ordered to stay—I charged with the regiment. . . . I was, I believe, the only person in the 4th infantry in the charge who was on horseback."[14] The charge was fruitless and costly, with one-third of the men going down as casualties. But though he was mounted, and therefore an easy target, Grant emerged without a scratch. This was only the beginning. Once engaged in battle in the city Grant volunteered to ride through the streets of Mon-

Champing at the Bit

"You could not keep Grant out of a battle."

James Longstreet on Ulysses S. Grant in the Mexican War

Quoted in Geoffrey Perret, *Ulysses S. Grant: Soldier and President* (Random House, 1997), 67.

terrey, through enemy fire, to reach the division commander and acquire more ammunition for his hard-pressed brigade. He rode like a circus rider, flipping his body to the horse's side away from the enemy, then throwing himself full in the saddle and dashing to safety.

After Monterrey the American thrust against Mexico shifted from Zachary Taylor to "Old Fuss and Fathers" General Winfield Scott, a military genius who plotted a course from Vera Cruz to Mexico City, following the path of Cortez. On the march and in battle, Grant did as he did at Monterrey, performing his quartermaster duties, but joining the action whenever he could. As ever, he was stalwart, brave, and enterprising—including, during the fight for Mexico City, talking his way into a church, identifying its belfry as a perfect site from which to strike, rushing off in search of howitzer, finding one, disassembling it, bringing it up to the church belfry, and then reassembling it there to pound the enemy.

Peace but not prosperity

With the war won, Grant's thoughts turned from battle to the only thought that continually interrupted his concentration on his duty: marriage to his sweetheart Julia Dent. It was a mixed marriage. Grant the Ohioan, whose family had abolitionist sentiments, had conjoined himself to a family of Missouri slave owners. The fathers-in-law of the happy couple despised each other.

Nevertheless, the Grant-Dent marriage was a success. Grant relished time with his family, and military assignments that separated him from his wife and their children (of whom there would be four) left him depressed. The peacetime army, with its long, unpredictable postings in remote locations, low pay, and inevitable boredom (Grant went from combat to clerical work) was distasteful to the brave, young West Pointer who had never considered the military his career. The best thing about a West Point education—besides its being free—was that it set one up for remunerative employment as an engineer or a business manager after one's obligatory service.

Grant stayed in the army for six years after the Mexican War. They were years of frustration—tedious work punctuated by loneliness—that took him to Detroit, New York, a perilous passage through cholera-ridden Panama, the Oregon Territory, and California. He filled the unforgiving minutes with drinking, moonlighting business ventures (which failed), and reading (Grant was an unusually well-read man who never advertised the fact). When he resigned his commission, he found he could not even afford his passage home to Missouri. In New York, a brother West Pointer and a Southerner (most of Grant's friends in the army were Southerners), Simon Bolivar Buckner, loaned him the money he needed.

Grant turned down a position in his father's leather goods shop in order to become a farmer on sixty acres that had been given Grant by his wife's father, "Colonel" Frederick Dent, a colonel of the Southern honorific type. Farming suited Grant, and his enterprising nature—necessary given the depressed agricultural market of the time—kept him busy with other businesses as well, among them, supervising slaves on the Dent plantation. He also built a house for his family. He called it Hardscrabble.

As the country slid into an economic depression, Grant's circumstances became increasingly precarious; he floundered trying to find work that would keep him solvent. At one point, in an incident that

Ulysses S. Grant: Slave Owner *and* Abolitionist

Grant only ever owned one slave, whom he set free shortly after he acquired him (which probably cost him, at a time when he was hard-up for cash, a good $1,000 to $1,500), but his wife owned four, and his father-in-law was an outspoken proponent of "the peculiar institution." When Grant needed workers, he preferred hiring black freeman to slaves, and was notorious for paying them more than the going rate. He was also notorious among his neighbors for his soft-heartedness, one of them saying that Grant was "tyrannized over by the Negroes given to his wife."* Though wedded to a slave-owning family, Grant never budged from his own belief that slavery was wrong. He would not tolerate cruelty to slaves, once stopping a neighbor from whipping a slave. Interestingly, Grant's father had been a business partner of John Brown's father, and Grant himself knew Taylor Blow, the owner of Dred Scott.

* Quoted in Geoffrey Perret, *Ulysses S. Grant: Soldier and President* (Random House, 1997), 57.

could have come straight from an O. Henry short story, he pawned his watch to buy Christmas presents. In 1860, Grant's father again offered him a position in his leather goods store, and this time, in desperation, Grant accepted. He moved his family to Galena, Illinois.

He was again a clerk, a job that hadn't suited him in the army and that suited him no better in peacetime. But if his duties did not engage him, the newspapers did, and so did political talk in the shop. He felt the country dividing, the fault lines separating. He said, "It made my blood run cold to hear friends of mine, Southern men ... discuss dissolution of the Union as though it were a tariff bill."[15]

In 1856, he had voted for the Democrat James Buchanan over the Republican John C. Frémont, because, as he said, "I knew Frémont," but also because, though opposed to slavery, he saw Buchanan as a moderate candidate who could keep the country together. He could not vote in the election of 1860, because he had not been resident long enough in Illinois, but if he could have voted, he would have cast a ballot for the Democrat Stephen Douglas, perhaps on the same grounds. While Grant's brother celebrated Lincoln's victory, Grant himself, having seen war, was gloomy, telling one reveling Republican, "The South will fight." Later, when another doubted the Southern states' willingness to secede, arguing that "There's a great deal of bluster about Southerners, but I don't think there's much fight in them," Grant demurred. "There *is* a good deal of bluster; that's a product of their education; but once they get at it they will make a strong fight. You are a great deal like them in one respect—each side under-estimates the other and over-estimates itself,"[16] which was right enough.

Return to the colors

When the South seceded, Grant's course was clear. He wrote his father, "We are now in the midst of trying times when every one must be for or against his country.... Having been educated for such an emergency, at the expense of the Government, I feel that it has upon me superior claims, such claims as no ordinary motives of self-interest can surmount."[17] His father had given him financial security. But the country was at war, and Grant took up the responsibility of drilling volunteer troops, then working for the governor as mustering officer (though still a civilian), while waiting for an appropriate commission, which the governor finally handed him, making Grant a colonel of Illinois volunteers.

Grant was not an imposing figure. In fact, he took care not to appear as one, disdaining bluster, pomp, and hard language. (He believed he had never sworn in his life.) But without raising his voice he carried a certitude about him. If Grant gave an order—and his orders were always very clear—he expected it to be done quickly and well. His quiet authority was such that even such an undisciplined mob as the Twenty-first Regiment of Illinois Volunteers felt it would be wrong and foolish not to obey.

Grant's volunteers (Grant was, ironically, put under the command of John C. Frémont) were sent to subdue rebels in Missouri. It was here that Grant had an epiphany about the nature of combat. His men were moving against a Confederate unit commanded by Colonel Thomas Harris. As they approached the site of Harris's camp,

> . . . my heart kept getting higher and higher until it felt to me as though it was in my throat. I would have given anything then to have been back in Illinois, but I had not the moral courage to halt and consider what to do; I kept right on. . . . The place where Harris had been encamped a few days before was still there and the marks of a recent encampment were plainly visible, but the troops were gone. My heart resumed its place. It occurred to me at once that Harris had been as much afraid of me as I had been of him. This was a view of the question I had never taken before; but it was one I never forgot afterwards.

> From that event to the close of the war, I never experienced
> trepidation upon confronting an enemy. . . . [18]

Grant was promoted to brigadier general. When Confederate forces invaded neutral Kentucky, Grant moved swiftly, proclaiming that he was acting in Kentucky's defense, taking the city of Paducah. Grant once said, "The only way to whip an army is to go straight out and fight it."[19] That was his *modus operandi*, inhibited only when he had cautious or conspiring superiors working against him. There was something else too. Grant confessed in his memoirs that "One of my superstitions had always been when I started to go any where, or to do anything, not to turn back, or stop until the thing intended was accomplished."[20] That superstition—or tenacity—was put at the service of the Union with devastating effect.

On 5 November 1861, Grant moved with boats and troops to Belmont, Missouri, on the Mississippi River, where in a short, sharp battle, he scattered a Confederate detachment—only to find the Confederates reforming to cut him off from his transports. The boys in blue—whose victory celebrations had been premature—had a sweaty time of it, but Grant reminded them: "We cut our way in and we can cut our way out,"[21] and so they did. If Grant was still learning generalship, he displayed all the right moral virtues: mounted on his horse he was the last man up the gang plank to safety. He was also lucky. "When I first went on deck I entered the captain's room . . . and threw myself on a sofa. I did not keep that position a moment, but rose to go out on deck. . . . I had scarcely left when a musket ball entered the room, struck the head of the sofa"—right where his head had been.[22]

States like Kentucky, Missouri, and Union-occupied Tennessee confronted the army with what to do with runaway slaves and what position to take with slave-owning families (some of which were pro-Confederate and others pro-Union). Grant confessed, "My inclination is to whip the rebellion into submission, preserving all constitutional rights [including the right to slavery]. If it cannot be whipped in any other way than through a war against slavery, let it come to that legitimately." John C. Frémont had tried to abolish slavery in Missouri and had been rebuked, indeed relieved of his command, by the president.

In the West, the eventually settled policy was to leave slave-owning Union families alone, but to enforce penalties on slave-owning Confederate families. For instance, in southeast Missouri, where Grant said, "there is not a sufficiency of Union sentiment left in this portion of the state to save Sodom,"[23] pro-Southern households could be subject to additional taxes (in order, it was said, to support pro-Union refugees). In Memphis, a very pro-Confederate city, Grant appropriated the grand house of one Confederate sympathizer for his own use and that of his family and sent

Drinking with the Enemy

Before and after the Battle of Belmont, Grant met with Confederate General Leonidas Polk, known as "The Fighting Bishop," because he was also an Episcopalian bishop. When Grant referred to Belmont as a "skirmish," Polk blurted out: "Skirmish! Hell and damnation! I'd like to know what he calls a *battle*." (Episcopalian bishops were made of sterner stuff in those days.)

At one meeting, Polk raised a toast to George Washington. As Grant brought the tumbler to his lips, Polk added, "...the first rebel."

At their next meeting, Grant proposed the toast, "Equal rights to all." As Polk raised his glass, Grant added, "White and black."[*]

* Quoted in Brooks Simpson, *Ulysses S. Grant: Triumph Over Adversity, 1822-1865* (Houghton Mifflin Company, 2000), 105.

the owner to a Federal prison. As for fugitive slaves, the army was entitled to employ them rather than return them to their masters.

"Unconditional Surrender" Grant

Before Belmont, Grant had said, "What I want is to advance."[24] That desire was constant. But equally constant were the impediments put in his way, chiefly by Henry "Old Brains" Halleck who had replaced Frémont as regional commander. General George McClellan memorably said of Halleck: "Of all the men whom I have encountered in high position, Halleck was the most hopelessly stupid. It was more difficult to get an idea through his head than can be conceived by anyone who never made the attempt. I do not think he ever had a correct military idea from beginning to end."[25] Halleck was a jealous, short-sighted, bureaucrat of a general, and as long as he was under Halleck's command Grant suffered (and had to endure constant rumors about his drinking) until President Lincoln promoted Grant above his restrainers.

Grant's next desired target was Fort Henry on the Tennessee River, followed by Fort Donelson on the Cumberland. Halleck restrained him at first, but Flag Officer Andrew Foote of the United States Navy came to

Grant on the Butcher's Bill

At the Battle of Fort Donelson, the scene of the wounded and dead so moved Grant that he spontaneously muttered lines from Robert Burns:

Man's inhumanity to man
Makes countless thousands mourn.

The lines are from the poem "Man Was Made to Mourn."

Grant's aid, saying that with Grant operating by land and Foote by river, they could capture the forts. Halleck's permission in hand, Fort Henry was quickly subdued. Fort Donelson was more challenging, because it had been reinforced. But Donelson not only fell, it fell in such a way as to gain Grant national fame.

Left holding the fort after generals Gideon Pillow and John Floyd had abandoned it, was General Grant's old friend and benefactor General Simon Bolivar Buckner. Buckner sent a message to Grant to negotiate a surrender. Grant wrote back, saying, "No terms except an unconditional and immediate surrender can be accepted. I propose to move immediately upon your works."

Buckner, clearly taken aback, confessed that he had no choice but "to accept the ungenerous and unchivalrous terms you propose."[26] Ungenerous and unchivalrous, they might have been, but for folks up North they made U. S. Grant "Unconditional Surrender" Grant.

Grant's success (he had even, without orders, helped force the surrender of Nashville) put him further afoul of Halleck who tried to get him dismissed. General George B. McClellan, for a short while yet the commander of all Union forces, told Halleck that if he had to arrest Grant for the good of the service than so be it. But when Lincoln stripped McClellan of his title of general in chief and Grant himself threatened to resign over Halleck's incessant complaints, "Old Brains" Halleck had enough political grey matter to realize that he needed to give Grant some rein. Grant's men went back on the move, gathering at Pittsburgh Landing on the Tennessee River.

Grant was an aggressive commander and strong on strategy, but like a chess player so consumed with his plan to force a checkmate in four moves, he neglected to think about what his opponent would do. After Grant's initial thrust at Belmont, his men had been surrounded. At Fort Donelson, the Confederates almost forced a breakout. Now, at Pittsburgh Landing, three miles from Shiloh Church, Grant plotted his attack on Corinth. He did not suspect that the Confederates might attack him.

The Battle of Shiloh began badly, the Federals driven back in scenes of carnage more horrendous than ever before witnessed on this continent. At the end of the first day's fighting, Grant sat beneath a tree, rain soddening his uniform and dripping from his hat (he'd decided that he'd rather rest here than among the wounded). He smoked a cigar and nursed a badly bruised ankle, injured when his horse had slipped and fallen. Sherman came up to him, wondering if they should retreat, and said, "Well, Grant, we've had the devil's own day, haven't we?" Grant replied: "Yes. Lick 'em tomorrow, though."[27] Grant's determination—as well as a massive infusion of Federal reinforcements and the tentative generalship of Confederate commander P. G. T. Beauregard—ensured the Federals' success.

Though Grant could claim a victory at Shiloh, in popular opinion it was an almost unbearable one. More then 13,000 boys in blue had been killed, wounded, or gone missing in a single battle. The shock was so profound, and some of the newspaper reports so misleading and slanted against Grant, that the hero of Fort Donelson was made to look an insensible brute, and his reputed falls from sobriety became a matter of public debate.

Grant's enemies, including Halleck, sprang. Halleck reorganized the armies of the Department of the Mississippi and left Grant without a command, kicking him into an office as Halleck's purported deputy, without any substantial duties. Grant, however, had a more important friend than Halleck, namely the president of the United States. When President Lincoln was told he must sack General Grant in order to appease public outrage over the losses at Shiloh, Lincoln was adamant, "I can't spare this man. *He fights.*"[28] Lincoln's solution was to promote Halleck to general in chief. Grant became commander of the Army of the Tennessee, and immediately set his sites on capturing Vicksburg.

Vicksburg was the Gibraltar of the Confederacy. Take that, and the Mississippi River, from New Orleans to Chicago, would be in Federal hands, a major tributary of Confederate supplies and men would be shut off, and Texas, Louisiana, and Arkansas, would be severed from the rest of the Confederate States of America by a curtain of Union blue. It took two campaigns to seize Vicksburg. But while the first petered out in the dank winter of 1862–1863, the second brought Grant not only plaudits, but, following on Lee's defeat at Gettysburg seemed to augur the end of the Confederacy. Grant certainly thought so. In his memoirs, he wrote, "The fate of the Confederacy was sealed when Vicksburg fell"[29] on 4 July 1863.

Grant's qualities as a commander, no matter what the rumors against him, were now unmistakable to all but the most benighted. In October 1863, he was promoted to command the Military Division of the Mississippi, a stretch of territory extending from the Mississippi River to the Appalachian Mountains. In his new role he broke the Confederate siege of Chattanooga on 25 November 1863, and then sent Sherman to break Longstreet's siege of Knoxville, which Longstreet abandoned on 4 December 1863. Grant—still an unassuming man of quiet, disinterested devotion to duty—reached a pinnacle of military recognition when he was promoted to Lieutenant General on 2 March 1864. No man since George Washington had held that rank. The promotion was great, but also meant coming to Washington and the sort of political and diplomatic flummery that Grant disdained.

The road to Appomattox

Less than a fortnight after his appointment, Grant was back in the field, traveling with George Meade, commander of the Army of the Potomac. The final great pincer movement of the war—a war that would last another year—now began, with Sherman handling one end, Grant the other, and Phil Sheridan driving a dagger down the middle. Sherman's blue-coats torched their way through Georgia and the Carolinas. Phil Sheridan burned out the breadbasket of the Confederacy in the Shenandoah

Valley. Federal troops were also active in southeastern Virginia and along the Gulf Coast. Everywhere the Confederacy was under assault. But the focal point was with Grant and Meade and the great slugging campaign against Lee. It was yet another on to Richmond campaign, but this time directed by a man who never turned back once he set himself a goal, and whose grim resolution would not be swayed by masses of casualties. Many in the North called him a "butcher," but Lincoln stuck by his butcher; he trusted he would serve up victory.

The campaign was one of the Federals swinging left hooks at the Confederates, then pivoting left toward Richmond, trying to find an opening to land a knockout punch on the Southern capital. Lee, however, proved a masterful counterpuncher, deflecting Union blows and so punishing the Federal forces that a lesser man (or a man with fewer moral and material resources) than Grant might have broken down in defeat.

As commander of all Union forces, Grant had half a million men under his command, and traveled with an Army of the Potomac that was itself 120,000 men strong (more than twice the strength of Lee). There was no swift Union victory to be found in the Battle of the Wilderness on 5 and 6 May 1864, only 18,000 Federal casualties; or at Spotsylvania Court House, from 8 May to 21 May 1864, only another 18,000 Federal losses; or at North Anna River, from 23 May to 26 May 1864 or at Cold Harbor from 31 May to 3 June 1864, though nearly another 13,000 more dead, wounded, and missing were added in combined totals from those two battles. In short, in one month, Grant and Meade had lost nearly 50,000 men to Lee's army that numbered barely 60,000. It was in light of this that Grant said at Spotsylvania Court House, "I propose to fight it out on this line if it takes all summer." Some of his men were less impressed, with one officer writing of the failed Union assault on Cold Harbor that it was "not war but murder."[30]

Grant, though undaunted in his pursuit of victory, confessed that he had erred in his frontal attack on the Confederate positions at Cold Harbor, telling his staff, after more than 7,000 men had fallen, "I regret this assault more than any I have ever ordered. I regarded it as a stern necessity, and believed that it would bring compensating results; but no advantages have been gained sufficient to justify the heavy losses suffered." Meade wrote to his wife that "I think Grant had his eyes opened [after Cold Harbor], and is willing to admit that Virginia and Lee's army is not Tennessee and Bragg's army."[31]

Grant, in the words of Major General J. F. C. Fuller, who wrote two book-length studies of him, was "one of those rare and strange men who are fortified by disaster instead of being depressed."[32] Perhaps so; it is certainly the case that he remained immovable from his objective. He showed little emotion to his subordinates, remained apparently indifferent to danger, and continued issuing orders that showed a clear and unruffled mind. He refused to give Lee the almost mythic quality that Lee's own men and many Federal commanders did. Lee was a commander of quality, Grant would

Cool as an Unlit Cigar

"Ulysses don't scare worth a damn."

A Federal soldier after watching Grant calmly writing orders under fire

acknowledge that, but he was not invincible. Grant said, "I never ranked Lee as high as some others in the army. . . . I never had as much anxiety in my front as when Joe Johnston was in front."[33] Given Lee's and Johnston's respective records, this comparison rather beggars belief, and one can't help but wonder whether Grant was in some ways defensive about the status given to Lee both during and after the war.

Still, it was Grant's refusal to acknowledge the possibility of defeat that kept him going. The thing—victory—simply must be done, and he had the resources to ensure that ultimately it would be done. Lee remained in front of him, so Grant would continue to attack him. He did so now by investing Petersburg.

The siege of Petersburg lasted ten months, but the outcome was inevitable. Lee was finally forced to abandon Petersburg, and with it

Richmond, in a desperate attempt to join forces with Joseph E. Johnston in North Carolina. Grant made this reunion—a quixotic hope in any event—impossible. The drama of the war climaxed at Appomattox Court House, where Grant, in his mud-spattered uniform accepted the surrender of the immaculately dressed aristocrat from Virginia. As Grant said, "In my rough traveling suit, the uniform of a private with the straps of a lieutenant-general, I must have contrasted very strangely with a man so

The Infamous Jew Order

In December 1862, Grant issued his soon to be notorious General Order No. 11, which stated that "The Jews, as a class, violating every regulation of trade established by the Treasury Department, and also Department [of the Tennessee] orders are hereby expelled from the Department [of the Tennessee]."* Jews who did not leave could be, and were, arrested.

Now as pogroms go, this was relatively mild, and the order was quickly rescinded after it reached Washington and caused a flutter of protests. It would be wrong, however, to conclude that Grant was an anti-Semite (something he always denied) save in this regard: Grant loathed greed, he loathed people who put commerce before country, he loathed in fact people like his father who were always looking for a sharp angle to make a buck, and it does seem that he attributed these qualities not only to his Christian father, but to Jews in general. Perhaps not all Jews, but his prejudices here are in direct contrast to his sympathy for blacks and Indians.

Still it might be worth comparing Grant's "Jew order" with the fact that Judah P. Benjamin, a Jew, served in the Confederate cabinet (the first Jewish cabinet member in North America). Benjamin and David Yulee, the first two Jewish U. S. senators—representing Louisiana and Florida—were both Confederates.

---

* The order is quoted in Brooks Simpson, *Ulysses S. Grant: Triumph over Adversity, 1822–1865* (Houghton Mifflin Company, 2000), 164.

handsomely dressed, six feet high and of faultless form. But it was not a matter that I thought of until afterwards."[34]

Grant was fully aware of the poignancy of the moment. While he had rejoiced at the knowledge that Lee was meeting with him to surrender, now, face to face with the noble Confederate general, Grant felt "sad and depressed. I felt like anything rather than rejoicing at the downfall of a foe who had fought so long and valiantly, and had suffered so much for a cause, though that cause was, I believe, one of the worst for which a people ever fought, and one for which there was the least excuse."[35]

Their meeting, however, was cordial. Lee, correct and polite, Grant so happy to reminiscence about the old army that he claimed he almost forgot the subject of their meeting. Lee made sure he didn't. Grant called for a pen and paper and then wrote out his terms. In his memoirs he remembered that "When I put pen to the paper I did not know the first word that I should make use of in writing the terms. I only knew what was in my mind, and I wished to express it clearly, so that there would be no mistaking it."[36] There was no mistaking it, or Grant's generosity, which Lee held so highly that he refused to hear a harsh word said against Grant thereafter. Indeed, according to one source, Lee said, "I have carefully searched the military records of both ancient and modern history, and have never found Grant's superior as a general." But this sounds so little like Lee in style and temper as to be dismissed as apocryphal, though it is still quoted approvingly by some of Grant's admirers.[37]

From lieutenant general to commander in chief

If Grant was an unlikely lieutenant general of the United States Army, he was an even less likely president of the United States. But so it came to pass, and not once but twice: Grant, elected in 1868, became the first president since another fighting general, Andrew Jackson, to serve two full terms as president.

Grant said, "I am a Republican because I am an American, and because I believe the first duty of an American—the paramount duty—is to save the results of the war, and save our credit."[38] His priorities were clear: ensure the newly won rights of black Americans, destroy the Ku Klux Klan, and, as far as it could be done while achieving his first two objectives, conciliate the South. He also intended to govern frugally.

Grant is generally regarded lowly as a president, largely because his administration was rife with corruption (though he himself was honest; his downfall was his trusting nature) and because the country endured an economic depression under his watch. But scandals are the stuff of little minds, and economic cycles are not always malleable to politics. The more important truth is that Grant succeeded in upholding the legacy of the Union victory.

In foreign policy, his record was mixed. He kept the United States out of a war with Spain over Cuba (that, of course, would come later) and he achieved the Washington Treaty with Great Britain, which settled damages on the British for their role in building Confederate raiders (chiefly the CSS *Alabama*). Where he failed—as in his attempt to annex Santo Domingo, which its president had offered to the United States—he still was undoubtedly in the right. He saw the island as a potential refuge for black Americans and

The Perils of a Military Education

Grant once remarked "Some of our generals failed because they worked out everything by rule. They knew what Frederick [the Great] did at what one place, what Napoleon at another. They were always thinking about what Napoleon would do. Unfortunately for their plans, the rebels would be thinking of something else."*

Grant's point was not to deprecate military knowledge—even as a civilian he eagerly read dispatches of European wars and plotted strategy on a map—only "slavish" adherence to rules that neglected practical facts.

* Quoted in William S. McFeely, *Ulysses S. Grant: An Album* (W. W. Norton & Company, 2003), 79.

as a strategic asset for the Republic. But his congressional nemesis, the Radical Republican Charles Sumner of Massachusetts (the one whom South Carolina Congressman Preston Brooks had tried to beat some sense into before the war), scuppered the attempt.

In domestic policy, it was during Grant's administration that Congress created the Department of Justice (largely to prosecute Klansmen), Reconstruction officially ended, all the former Confederate states were allowed to elect members to Congress, and restrictions on former Confederates holding public office were quietly dropped. Grant looked forward to the day when the black man was treated "as a citizen and a voter, as he is and must remain, and soon parties will be divided not on the color line [blacks voting Republican, and white southerners voting Democrat], but on principle."[39]

When Grant left the White House he took a celebrated tour of the world. That might have been the pleasurable part of retirement. Far less so was his being swindled out of all his money by Ferdinand Ward who had formed an investment partnership with Grant's son Ulysses Jr., and in which Grant had sunk his savings. He was diagnosed at the same time with throat cancer. Bankrupt, he sat down to write his memoirs, hoping to provide for his family. He finished the manuscript just days before he died, penning an American classic. It was Grant's final victory.

Chapter Eleven

THOMAS JONATHAN "STONEWALL" JACKSON(1824-1863)

"You can be whatever you resolve to be."[1]

Guess What?

✦ Jackson founded a Sunday school for slaves and taught them how to read

✦ Jackson was a Unionist, even, initially, after the election of Abraham Lincoln

✦ The devout Christian Jackson thought the South should attack Northern cities

Thomas Jonathan Jackson was an orphan. His father died when he was two, after having frittered away his money on cards and failed investments, which forced the family to sell their home. Jackson's mother, known for her good looks and high character, died when he was seven. She left a lasting imprint on the boy, even though Jackson had already been sent to board with his uncle Cummins Jackson at Jackson's Mill in northwestern Virginia.

Jackson read from an early age. He read the Bible and heroic tales of military history, especially the history of the American War of Independence. But his formal education was necessarily spotty, because he had to work. He nevertheless still found plenty of time for fishing, hunting, and riding.

He also taught a young slave to read. There weren't many slaves in mountainous northwestern Virginia, but Jackson, like everyone else, took slavery for granted and was friendly with such slaves as worked at the Mill. They certainly weren't "property" to Jackson in the sense of a saddle or a mare; they were people and weren't to be subjected to the whip or a beating. Indeed, they were friends with young master Jackson. Some of Jackson's own people had come to colonial America as indentured servants. The slaves were in more extended bondage, their class was different in kind and degree from the Scotch-Irish Jacksons, but he felt there was plenty of commonality too.

As a boy he was handsome, quiet, honest, and a trifle awkward. He knew he was lacking in the refinements that make a great man and he was determined to change that. Jackson was driven, all his life, by the idea of self-improvement, of overcoming circumstances through sheer focus, concentration, and will. There was no school at Jackson's Mill, but Jackson convinced his uncle to create one, and when that didn't last, he enrolled in another school in nearby Weston for impoverished boys. Finally, Colonel Alexander Withers took him in and agreed to be his tutor. The Colonel was impressed by young Jackson, his transparently good character and his dogged determination to learn. Jackson was also sincerely religious and that rare sort of boy who sat up tall to listen to sermons.

Reliability and durability shown out of Jackson; he was only seventeen years old when he was appointed as a constable of Lewis County, which had him tracking down deadbeat debtors. He also stood in well enough stead that he was one of two county finalists for an appointment at West Point. He lost, but when the winner turned back home after one day at the Point, Jackson worked hard to be nominated as his replacement. When the obvious was pointed out to him—that his schooling was hardly such as would make him likely to pass West Point's entrance examination, let alone survive the demanding curriculum—Jackson replied: "I know that I shall have the application necessary to succeed. I hope that I have the capacity. At least I am determined to try."[2]

Carrying a packet of recommendations, Jackson traveled hard to reach Washington and win the nomination from his Congressman Samuel Hays. He arrived, mud-spattered, in the congressman's office without an appointment (Hays was not even aware his previous nominee to West Point had resigned until Jackson presented him with the letter). A quick interview convinced Congressman Hays of Jackson's fitness and he recommended him for his "manly appearance...good moral character... [and, ahem,] improvable mind."[3] The eighteen-year-old Jackson had won his appointment to West Point—assuming he could pass the entrance examination; and for that he crammed, as only a man of Jackson's tenacity could. He had failed his examinations at home; he passed them at the Point—barely, but he had done it.

From West Point to Mexico

Jackson was determined to succeed. While other cadets slept, he continued studying by the light of coal-fire in the grate. He was already renowned as an eccentric, a young man tormented by dyspepsia, socially and physically awkward (though he kept a notebook of self-improving maxims). He confided in few, was quiet but courteous, and no one worked harder or from higher principles of conduct. Fellow cadet Ulysses Grant recalled that "He had so much courage and energy, worked so hard, and governed his life by a discipline so stern."[4] An artillery officer losing patience with Jackson's ungainliness at a cannon, rebuked him, cursing, only to be cut short when he saw Jackson's face, dripping sweat. It "revealed," he wrote, "the soul-touching patience and suffering of the 'Ecce Homo.' No anger, no impatience, only sorrow and suffering."[5] It was hard not to give Jackson his due.

Jackson struggled through the academic rigors of West Point, but kept advancing relentlessly up the ranks of cadets. Every final examination was a torture for him as he went sweating up to the blackboard, a smile creasing his face when his power of concentration paid off, he chalked the answer down and could relax, at least momentarily. He was gaining confidence too. He told a cousin back home: "I tell you I had to work hard.... I am going to make a man of myself if I live. I can do anything I will to do."[6] He graduated seventeenth in his class, and the joke was, if they'd had another year, Jackson would have driven his way to number one.

Jackson's class, the class of 1846, graduated directly into the Mexican War; and Jackson, the newly commissioned lieutenant was now an erect six-footer, handsome, stalwart, with unwavering grey-blue eyes. After arriving in Mexico, he met Second Lieutenant D. H. Hill, West Point class of 1842. Hill had already seen combat. Jackson told him, "I really envy you men who have been in action.... I should like to be in one battle." As Hill recalled, "His face lighted up and his eyes sparkled when he spoke, and the shy, hesitating manner gave way to the frank enthusiasm of a soldier."[7]

A professional soldier is not what Jackson had aspired to become. His West Point education was a means to an end, the end of helping him become a better man, a respected professional. But the training and opportunity bit into him. In Mexico, he distinguished himself from his first taste of combat at Vera Cruz. Manning a battery of artillery, one observer noted that Jackson "was as calm in the midst of a hurricane of bullets as though he were on dress parade at West Point."[8]

Later, as an artillery officer under Captain John Magruder, Jackson fought his batteries on the approaches to Mexico City. Repeatedly under fire, he again never showed a hint of fear, whether men toppled beside him, caissons were smashed before him, or even as a cannon ball plowed directly between his legs. At one point during the assault on Chapultepec, Jackson walked calmly in front of his batteries, enemy lead bursting all around him, reassuring his men, "See, there is no danger. I am not hit!" As Jackson later confessed, it was the only lie he could remember telling— but at least it was in the line of duty and in the service of his men.

In a letter to his sister, six weeks later, he noted, "I have been exposed to many dangers in the battles of this valley but have escaped unhurt. I was once reported killed and nothing but the strong and powerful hand of Almighty God could have brought me through unhurt. Imagine, for instance, my situation at Chapultepec, within full range, and in a road which was swept with grape and canister, and at the same time thousands

The Slaughterer of Mexicans

At a reception at the National Palace in Mexico City, "Old Fuss and Feathers," General Winfield Scott, six-feet-five-inches of military genius, strategic daring, and love of pomp, was introduced to the shy Lieutenant Jackson. The perfect stage actor, the general thrust his hands behind his back, stiffened his shoulders, and left Jackson's proffered hand hanging and the poor lieutenant reddening in embarrassment. "I don't know that I shall shake hands with Mr. Jackson," he bellowed, so that all eyes turned to him. "If you can forgive yourself for the way in which you slaughtered those poor Mexicans with your guns, I am not sure that I can."[*]

Then he clasped Jackson's hand in approbation. It was perhaps the most harrowing compliment Jackson ever received.

---

[*] Quoted in Frank E. Vandiver, *Mighty Stonewall* (Texas A&M University Press, 1992), 40.

of muskets from the castle itself above pouring down like hail upon you."[9] A hot time, indeed, but Jackson had not wavered.

Though he had labored at French at West Point, Jackson taught himself Spanish to a fair degree of fluency; admired Mexican cathedrals; actually came out of his shell to attend balls with señoritas; spent several days in a monastery and interviewed the archbishop of Mexico City as part of an earnest consideration of the Catholic Church, before deciding that he sought a simpler Christianity; and developed a passion for fruit. As part of the victorious army now occupying Mexico, Jackson actually enjoyed himself. For him Spanish always remained the language of romance.

"Tom Fool" Jackson

Returning home on leave, Jackson was prescient: "If there is another war, I will soon be a general. If peace follows, I will never be anything but Tom Jackson."[10] Tom Jackson, however, was an interesting customer in his own right. Jackson's eccentricities—he was a food faddist, devoted to water cures, stale bread (he timed its aging with a watch), and an idiosyncratic exercise program, among other things—became legend among his compatriots, but there was still something winsome about his sincerity. He continued his studies in religion, was baptized (in the Episcopal Church, but only after negotiating with the priest to ensure that he was still free to pitch his Christian tent in whatever denomination he eventually settled on), and continued to enjoy an active social life in the peacetime army. He also continued his self-education by becoming a patron of New York City bookstores, focusing mainly on volumes of history. His actual military duties were slight, and after a tedious and unhappy time posted to Florida, he won an appointment as an instructor at the Virginia Military Institute in Lexington, Virginia.

When a friend asked how he would manage to teach college-level courses to the cadets, given his own academic struggles, Jackson replied:

Thomas Jonathan "Stonewall" Jackson (1824–1863)

"I can always keep a day or two ahead of the class. I can do whatever I will to do."[11] That will required painstakingly memorizing his lectures, spending his evenings, when his eyes were too tired to read, staring at a wall, reciting the lectures in his head. In the classroom, he was unable to deviate from their literal recitation. An unexpected question could set him repeating his lecture from the beginning. The cadets nicknamed him "Tom Fool" Jackson, regarding him as a continual odd duck and an occasional martinet (though they took advantage of his poor hearing—the price of his being a former artillery officer). But they also knew of his reputation, of how in Mexico he had been among the bravest of the brave, and they caught glimpses of it when he was outside the classroom, acting as an instructor of artillery. He was not meant to be a teacher; he was meant to be a soldier.

It was in Lexington that Jackson finally settled on the Presbyterian Church as his spiritual home. It was, naturally, not chosen on a whim but only after continual study of religious doctrine and probing sessions with the local Presbyterian minister, Dr. William Spottswood White. But once in, he was a fiercely committed adherent, albeit one who, with typical eccentricity, more often than not fell asleep in church. Asleep or awake, he lived his life in a state of silent prayer.

Jackson prayed for his cadets before every lecture at VMI. His piety expressed itself, too, in his acting as devoted co-founder, sponsor, and teacher of a black Sunday school that not only taught religion but skirted the law by teaching slaves and their children to read and write. If Jackson bored the cadets, he found a more receptive audience here. His classroom discipline was strict, but he was regarded, in the words of the Reverend White, as "emphatically the black man's friend."[12] He was so much the black man's friend that two of his slave-students asked him to buy them. So Jackson became the slaveholder of Albert, a handyman who eventually earned enough money to buy his freedom, and Amy, a housekeeper. Through marriage he gained another slave, Hetty and her two sons (whom Jackson taught to read). He also took in a slave who had been orphaned, a girl named Emma.

Jackson's religion brought him romance as well. In 1853 he married Elinor Junkin, daughter of the Reverend Dr. George Junkin, a Presbyterian divine who was president of Washington College, adjacent to VMI. Elinor Jackson died only fifteen months later, shortly after giving birth to a stillborn son. In 1857, Jackson married again, this time to Mary Anna Morrison (she went by Anna), another Presbyterian minister's daughter. Her father was Dr. Robert Hall Morrison, the first president of Davidson College, and she was a sister-in-law to his old Mexican War colleague, fellow postwar professor, and friend D. H. Hill. Their first child died, but Anna lived, and Jackson was utterly devoted to her. She bore him another child, a daughter, in 1862, who survived. Jackson always loved children. With them his awkwardness and reserve dropped away and he happily joined in their games and adventures. But he knew his own daughter for less than a year before his own tragic death.

The reluctant secessionist

Jackson was a Democrat and a states' rights man, but like most northwestern Virginians, many of his neighbors in the Shenandoah Valley, and Dr. Junkin (a native Pennsylvanian who declared "I would not dissolve this union if the people should make the devil President"[13]), he was also a Unionist. As for slavery, his wife Anna said, after the War, that he would have preferred "to see the negroes free, but he believed that the Bible taught that slavery was sanctioned by the Creator himself, who maketh men to differ, and instituted laws for the bond and the free. He therefore accepted slavery, as it existed in the Southern States not as a thing desirable in itself, but as allowed by Providence for ends it was not his business to determine."[14]

Jackson believed masters had a Christian duty to their slaves. His slaves were part of the family's own daily religious life of Bible readings, prayer, church, and Sunday school. He disliked abolitionists, as agitators attempting to drive the nation into division and war.

He was present, with a detachment of VMI cadets, when one of the most dangerous—indeed, mad—abolitionists, John Brown, was hanged at Charles Town, Virginia. Jackson and the cadets were there to keep the peace. For Virginians like Jackson, all the South wanted was a peaceful

Stonewall Jackson . . . for the Union?

Jackson was a Unionist. So was Robert E. Lee. So was Virginia's governor John Letcher. They all wanted a continuance of the republic in its current form.

Even in late January 1861, after the election of Abraham Lincoln, Jackson remained a Unionist, though he warned that if the North denied Virginia "the rights guaranteed to us by the Constitution of our country," if the North "should endeavor to subjugate us, and thus excite our slaves to servile insurrection in which our families will be murdered without quarter or mercy, it becomes us to wage such a war as will bring hostilities to a speedy close. People who are anxious to bring on war don't know what they are bargaining for; they don't see all the horrors that must accompany such an event. For myself I have never yet been induced to believe that Virginia will even have to leave the Union."* Jackson felt that once Virginia made it clear that she would, indeed, leave the Union if Southern rights were threatened, good sense would prevail in the North.

This was precisely the sort of check that states' rights were supposed to exert on Federal power. Jackson trusted to this check. He was soon to change his mind. Jackson's sister, Laura, remained a Unionist. When battle lines were drawn, the two, formerly devoted correspondents, never wrote one another again. His sister became a nurse and reportedly said that she could mend Union wounded as fast as Stonewall could shoot them.

* Quoted in Byron Farwell, *Stonewall: A Biography of General Thomas J. Jackson* (W. W. Norton & Company, 1992), 144.

abidance by the Constitution. If the North, through men like John Brown or Abraham Lincoln tried to violate Southern rights, to impose their doctrines by armed force, only then would secession be justifiable.

Until then, Jackson's position was to support the Union and "to see every honorable means used for peace, and I believe that Providence will bless us with the fruits of peace. . . . But if after we have done all that we can do for an honorable preservation of the Union, there shall be a determination on the part of the Free States to deprive us of our right which is the fair interpretation of the Constitution, as already decided by the Supreme Court, guarantees to us, I am in favor of secession."[15] But it was more than the defense of slavery that Jackson saw as Southern rights; it was a constitutional system that granted the states extensive sovereign powers that the Federal government was not to trifle with.

The Sword Is Mightier Than the Scabbard

Before Virginia's governor John Letcher had given up hope of reaching a compromise with the Federal government, Jackson told a group of VMI cadets, champing at the bit to put their bayonets into some Yankees, "The time for war has not yet come, but it will come and soon, and when it does come, my advice is to draw the sword and throw away the scabbard."*

* Quoted in James I. Robertson, Jr., *Stonewall Jackson: The Man, the Soldier, the Legend* (Macmillan, 1997), 210.

As Jackson's widow remembered, he "would never have fought for the sole object of perpetuating slavery. It was for her *constitutional* rights that the South resisted the North, and slavery was only comprehended among those rights."[16] What was not comprehended among the rights of the Federal government was the right to invade sovereign states that had joined the Union and now had decided to leave it of their own free will, as decided by their state legislatures. Virginia was, initially, not among the seceding states. But when Lincoln called upon Virginia to raise troops to subjugate its fellow Southern states, the die was cast. Virginia would do no such thing. To do so would be to support Northern tyranny against the South.

Jackson took the long view. He had supported the Union when in good conscience he could. But the Federal government was not God. "Why should Christians be disturbed about the dissolution of the Union? It can only come with God's permission."[17] The Federal government was an institution created by the people of the sovereign states. The people of the sovereign states could change their mind, and the Federal government had no divine mandate forcibly to tell them otherwise.

Jackson's battles

As trained soldiers, Jackson and his cadets were valuable men to the new Confederacy; their task: train Virginia's volunteers into a semblance of an army. Jackson's duties first brought him to Richmond, and then to Harpers Ferry as a Colonel of Virginia volunteers. The Jackson legend began almost immediately. He was taciturn, disciplined, mysterious, devoted to duty, eccentric, and oblivious of appearances. He wore a cadet cap down close over his brow. His horse, "Little Sorrell," originally bought for his wife, looked almost like a pony beneath the six-foot tall Jackson. Among the units trained by Jackson was the First Virginia Brigade, drawn from the Valley, which became known as "the Stonewall Brigade."

From the start Jackson had a strategic and tactical rapport with Jefferson Davis's top military adviser, Robert E. Lee. Jackson believed that "we must give them [the enemy] no time to think. We must bewilder them and keep them bewildered. Our fighting must be sharp, impetuous, continuous. We cannot stand a long war."[18] Lee agreed, and he shared Jackson's desire to take the war to the enemy. But the gentlemanly Episcopalian Lee drew a firmer line on waging war exclusively against the Union army than the stern Presbyterian Jackson did, at least in Jackson's strategic vision for the war. Jackson saw the greatest mercy—and the greatest opportunity for Southern victory—in swift, crushing counterstrokes that would shock the North into letting the South go free.

Jackson told General G. W. Smith that "We ought to invade their country now [the fall of 1861], and not wait for them to make the necessary preparations to invade ours." Jackson's plan was to concentrate Confed-

Seminarians for the South

Within the Stonewall Brigade were the Liberty Hall volunteers from Washington College. Their initial drill master was William Nelson Pendleton, future commander of the famous Rockbridge Artillery, and a West Point graduate, but at the time, rector of Grace Episcopal Church. One quarter of the Liberty Hall volunteers were Presbyterian seminarians. Their commander was a professor of Greek, James J. White, son of Stonewall Jackson's pastor. Pendleton's Rockbridge Artillery was similarly holy. Among its batteries were the cannons "Matthew, Mark, Luke, and John" and among his cannoneers were no less than twenty-five seminarians. And, for a while, Jackson's chief of staff was Robert Lewis Dabney, a man less noted for his martial abilities and experience and more noted as a professor of theology and Presbyterian pastor. If Jackson believed God was on the side of the South, he had plenty of clergymen and seminarians available to confirm his opinion.

One of the Confederate seminarians, Hugh White (another son of the Reverend William S. White), put the matter thus: "We of Virginia are between two fires. If we join the one party, we join friends and allies; if we join the other, we join enemies and become vassals. Our decision then is formed, and we will seek to break the oppressor's yoke. Our only hope, under God, is in a united resistance even unto death."*

---

* Quoted in Robert G. Williams Jr, "Scholar Warriors Volunteer for the South: College Unit Follows Steps of Revolutionary Forebears," *Washington Times*, March 1, 2008, page D3 (the Civil War page).

erate forces to cross the Potomac, seize Baltimore, bring Maryland to the side of the South, force the Federal government from Washington, attack McClellan's army "if it came out against us in open country, destroy industrial establishments wherever we found them, break up the lines of interior commercial intercourse, close the coal mines, seize, and if necessary destroy the manufactories and commerce of Philadelphia, and of other large cities within our reach." The Confederate army would "subsist mainly on the country we traverse" and make "unrelenting war" amidst Northern homes, forcing "the people of the North to understand what it will cost them to hold the South in the Union at bayonet's point."[19]

There is no doubt that to some degree Jackson was right. In this strategy lay the Confederacy's greatest chance for victory, but it was utterly opposed to the vision of Jefferson Davis, which was defensive. Davis certainly understood the military merits of concentration of force but believed he needed to defend the borders of the Confederacy. Even more important, Davis believed he must maintain the South on the moral high ground. The North was the aggressor and he did not want to muddy appearances in the fall of 1861. Whether Jackson's offensive could have been conducted in a way that would have fallen within the parameters of just war, as Lee and Davis thought of it, is debatable. But given Jackson's unbending devotion to orders, chances are that some such compromise could have been made: an invasion made in defense of the South and in a war that hit military targets (railroads, munitions, telegraph wires) while sparing civilians.

In the event, Lee and Jackson's first point of agreement was that Harpers Ferry should be held. The commander on the scene, however, was that brilliant artist of the tactical retreat, General Joseph E. Johnston, who never met a position from which it was not advantageous to fall back. Still Jackson's men, in a defensive sally, did get their first taste of battle, and Jackson was promoted to brigadier general in the Confederate army.

"Tom Fool" Jackson becomes "Stonewall" Jackson

Jackson who was a hypochondriac in peace (driven by intestinal trouble that once caused him to remark that "if a man could be driven to suicide by any cause, it might be from dyspepsia") was a veritable titan in war.

The Secret of Stonewall's Courage

After the Battle of First Manassas, Jackson was asked by Captain John Imboden, "General, how is it that you can keep so cool, and appear so utterly insensible to danger in such a storm of shells and bullets as rained about your head when your hand was hit?"

Jackson replied, "Captain, my religious belief teaches me to feel as safe in battle as in bed. God fixed a time for my death. I do not concern myself about that, but to be always ready, no matter when it may overtake me. Captain, that is the way all men should live, and then all would be equally brave."*

---

* Quoted in Allen Tate, *Stonewall Jackson: The Good Soldier* (J. S. Sanders & Company, 1991), 94-5.

At First Manassas, when General Bernard Bee rode by exclaiming, "They are beating us back! They are beating us back!" Jackson calmly replied, "Then, sir, we will give them the bayonet." He was similarly unruffled when a bullet struck a finger on his left hand. Bee used Jackson's example to reform his men: "Look, men, there stands Jackson like a stone wall! Rally 'round the Virginians."

At the battle's height, as Stonewall's men braced for a Union charge, a Confederate officer rode up to Jackson and said: "General the day is going against us."

"If you think so, sir, you had better not say anything about it."

He counseled his own men: "Reserve your fire till they come within fifty yards, then fire and give them the bayonet. When you charge, yell like furies." Jackson's men helped turn the tide. As the Federals broke and ran, Jackson said: "Give me ten thousand men and I will be in Washington tomorrow morning."[20] Had they been, Stonewall Jackson might now be remembered as the founder of his country.

As it was, he deepened his men's confidence that he was a cool-headed general who knew how to smite the enemy. With victory won, Jackson turned to another important matter that had been preying on his conscience. He sat down and wrote a letter to the Reverend William S. White: "In my tent last night, after a fatiguing day's service, I remembered that I had failed to send you my contribution to our colored Sunday School. Enclosed you will find my check for that object, which please acknowledge at your earliest convenience, and oblige, Yours faithfully, T. J. Jackson."[21]

The hero of the valley

In October 1861, Jackson was promoted to major general and given command of Confederate forces in the Shenandoah Valley. Jackson astonished his own troops, and the Federals, by insisting on a winter campaign. On 1 January 1862, Jackson drove his men on a forty-mile forced march through snow and ice to fight the Yankees at the town of Bath. But the Federals withdrew. Jackson pressed on, despite the frigid weather, pushing his men on to the town of Romney. Jackson's cavalry, under the command of the dashing Ashby Turner, discovered the Federals had abandoned Romney, fearful that Jackson's command of perhaps 6,000 frozen, sick, and hungry men, might be too much for the 18,000 Union troops.

Jackson's victory at Romney, however, was not a happy one. Officers complained to Richmond that they were holding a frozen, strategically unimportant waste, at the orders of a madman. Their lobbying Richmond—even President Davis—led to orders being handed Jackson to withdraw the men. Jackson threatened to resign over this interference with his command. Jackson's protest had the desired effect—the general who had opposed was transferred. But the Federals returned to Romney and once more threatened the Valley.

To the East, the Confederacy braced for McClellan's massive march on Richmond. In the Valley, Jackson saw his task as bedeviling a Union foe much superior to his own in numbers. Jackson had no more than 4,000 men. Union General Nathaniel Banks, who was advancing on Winchester, had nearly 40,000. Naturally, Jackson decided to attack. But his carefully laid plans were foiled by junior officers who made mistakes and took the counsel of their fears (something that Jackson famously said one should never do).

Jackson vowed never to risk such errors again by never again having a council of war. Jackson's plans were now to be known only to Jackson, and to his superior officers, like Lee, from whom he received orders. To the others, his marches and countermarches could seem madness. Confederate General Richard "Dick" Ewell said of Jackson, "I never saw one of Jackson's couriers approach without expecting an order to assault the North Pole!"[22]

Jackson's orders were to keep the Federals occupied in the Valley, in particular to prevent General Banks from crossing the Blue Ridge Moun-

Stonewall Jackson's Way of War

"Always mystify, mislead, and surprise the enemy, if possible; and when you strike and overcome him, never let up in the pursuit so long as your men have strength to follow; for an army routed, if hotly pursued, becomes panic-stricken, and can then be destroyed by half their number. The other rule is, never fight against heavy odds, if by any possible maneuvering you can hurl your own force on only a part, and that the weakest part, of your enemy and crush it. Such tactics will win every time, and a small army may thus destroy a large one in detail, and repeated victory will make it invincible."[*]

* Quoted in G. F. R. Henderson, *Stonewall Jackson and the American Civil War* (Da Capo, 1988), 318–9.

tains and threaten Joseph E. Johnston, who had troubles enough preparing the defense of Richmond against the combined forces of generals McClellan and McDowell. When Ashby Turner brought Jackson word that Banks was moving out of the Valley to support a giant Federal campaign against Richmond, Jackson marched his men more than forty miles in two days to try to cut him off. He met a portion of Banks' army at Kernstown. That portion turned out to be bigger than Jackson expected—three times bigger—and the fighting was ferocious. Trusting to Providence, Jackson refused to admit defeat until his men finally admitted it for him. They could not advance; they could, at best, hold their line against the overwhelming Yankee numbers.

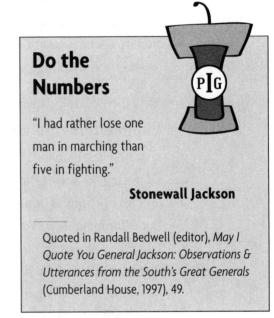

Do the Numbers

"I had rather lose one man in marching than five in fighting."

Stonewall Jackson

Quoted in Randall Bedwell (editor), *May I Quote You General Jackson: Observations & Utterances from the South's Great Generals* (Cumberland House, 1997), 49.

It was a tactical defeat, but it proved a strategic victory. The Federal commander believed that Jackson had actually outnumbered *him* by two to one. That was enough to put the wind up Lincoln, who feared that while McClellan drilled his men for the great march on Richmond, Jackson might slip through the Valley and attack Washington. Lincoln demanded that Banks be retained as a stopper in the Valley. General Frémont was ordered to the Valley as well, and General McDowell was told to stay put at Manassas, in case Jackson crossed the Blue Ridge himself for a northern thrust.

Jackson led the Federals on a merry chase, dodging them (sometimes three separate Union armies) and stinging them at will thanks to the astonishing marches of Jackson's "foot cavalry," which seemed to be one place, then another—and never where one expected (and had reliable reports) that they were. Jackson's Valley Campaign is a standard military study of tactical genius, and much of Jackson's reputation rightly rests upon it. General Richard Taylor, who served with Jackson, said that among the hard-marched troopers, "Every man seemed to think he was on a chessboard and Jackson played us to suit his purpose."[23] So he did, and the short, sharp, shocks that Jackson gave the enemy in the Valley in the spring and early summer of 1862 made him a Confederate a hero. In the scale of Civil War battles, the engagements of the Valley campaign were small-scale affairs. Jackson never had more than 16,000 men but he tied up about 64,000 Union troops. The legend that was begun at Manassas became writ large in the Valley.

Chancellorsville and death

If he was the hero of the Valley, he also participated in the big battles as well: The Seven Days Campaign, Fredericksburg, Second Manassas, and Sharpsburg. But his apotheosis was at Chancellorsville, the most brilliant Confederate victory of the war, its battle plan drawn up by Lee and Jackson over a campfire. Lee was holding back the jaws of a pincer movement. At one end, he had a holding force at Fredericksburg, keeping back a Union host more than twice its size. At the other end, Chancellorsville, Jackson had surprised the Federals, attacked, and driven them to entrench their position. There were about 73,000 of them. Lee and Jackson had about 43,000 men. That night, Lee, in conference with Stonewall Jackson, mused, "How can we get at those people?" The answer was a bold flanking movement across the front of the Federal line, shielded by forest, to strike at the Federal right.

The conversation has been recorded as going something like this:

"General Jackson, what do you propose to do?"

"Go around here."

"What do you propose to make this movement with?"

"With my whole corps."

"What will you leave me?"

"The divisions of Anderson and McLaws."

"Well, go on."

That was it. The plan was agreed, and near dusk the next day, Jackson's troops were ready to spring. At 5:15 p.m., General Jackson gave the order.

"Are you ready, General Rodes?" Jackson asked.

"Yes, sir."

"You can move forward then."

With a terrifying rebel yell, the Confederates ripped into the Union line and sent the bluecoats fleeing.

"They are running too fast for us," one Confederate officer remarked to Jackson. "We can't keep up with them."

"They never run too fast for me, sir. Press them, press them!"[24]

Press them they did to the point of creating a Federal rout. Jackson intended to press the attack through the night, but scouting ahead of his own lines to see how he could capitalize on his smashing success, Jackson was shot by Confederate soldiers who mistook him and his staff officers for a Federal patrol. Jackson was badly wounded, but no one knew yet that it was mortal.

When Lee was informed of Jackson's wound, he replied, "Ah, Captain, any victory is dearly bought which deprives us of the services of General Jackson, even for a short time."[25] Lee wrote to his wounded general, "Could I have directed events, I would have chosen for the good of the country to be disabled in your stead."[26] To one of the army chaplains, Lee noted that Jackson's arm had been amputated. "He has lost his left arm, but I have lost my right."[27] Pneumonia claimed Jackson's last breath; his last words were: "Let us cross over the river and rest under the shade of the trees."

The "great and good" Jackson was gone, and with him, perhaps, went the cause of the Confederacy. Lee certainly thought so. He was said to have remarked after the war, "If I had had Jackson at Gettysburg, I should have won that battle, and a complete victory there would have resulted in the establishment of the independence of the South."[28] If there is one reason why the enigmatic, eccentric Jackson—the "Tom Fool" turned audacious and brilliant Cromwellian warrior—became an icon of the South, a symbol of the Lost Cause second only to Lee, this is why.

Jackson's piety was admired by most and suspected by a few. But few could doubt that that large, shambling, dusty man with his cadet cap pulled low over his mystic grey-blue eyes, his terse, ever-controlled speech, delivered victories, that he had a measure of strategy and tactics that put him among the greats. Field Marshal Lord Frederick Roberts ("Bobs"), the commander in chief of the British Army at the turn of the century, said of Jackson: "In my opinion Stonewall Jackson was one of the finest natural geniuses the world ever saw. I will go even further than that—as a campaigner in the field he never had a superior. In some respects I doubt whether he had an equal."[29] In his devotion to duty, Jackson lived his axiom: "You can be whatever you resolve to be." "Old Jack" set his sights high, and Southerners have looked up to him ever since.

Chapter Twelve

A. P. HILL
(1825-1865)

"We will whip the damned hounds yet."[1]

I f George Thomas was the best Union general you've probably never heard of, A. P. Hill was the best Confederate general you've probably never heard of. Gallant "Little Powell" was very different from his fellow Virginian in build, temperament, and politics. Though they both opposed slavery (Hill never owned any slaves), Hill always knew that his first loyalty was to his native state, and was contemptuous of any bullying Yankees who thought they could justify killing Southerners to enforce Northern views.

Ambrose Powell Hill was born a son of the Virginia gentry, whose lineage in Virginia dated back to the seventeenth century, and as befit those roots his father raised him on horseback, a junior cavalier. He was quick and strong intellectually, well-schooled, though with an adolescent (and

Guess What?

- Hill opposed slavery, owned no slaves, condemned lynching, and, *mirabile dictu*, was an ardent Southern patriot, resigning his commission even before his state left the Union

- Hill was a groomsman at Union general George B. McClellan's wedding

- Hill wanted to lead the attack on the third day of Gettysburg—and if he had done so, with his full corps, the Confederates might have won

243

lasting) skepticism about religion (he nevertheless, as a matter of course, attended Episcopal services while in the Confederate army). That skepticism came not from his native Anglicanism but from a Baptist preacher who converted Hill's mother to a piety of worldly renunciation, prohibiting virtually all forms of jollity such as a young man might enjoy. Hill loved his mother, but he didn't love Calvinism. Hill would be one of those who didn't think much of Stonewall Jackson.

A Southerner Opposed to Lynching—Whoever Heard of Such a Thing?

While it might surprise subscribers to the politically correct reductionism that the Civil War was all about slave-liberating Northerners legitimately knocking the stuffing out of racist Southerners, lynching was not a common antebellum Southern recreation. In fact, it was a crime. Murder was murder, whether committed by an individual or a mob. When, in 1850, future Confederate General A. P. Hill heard that a black man—suspected of murdering a white man—had been hanged without trial, he erupted in a letter home:

> "Shame, shame upon you all, good citizens. Virginia must crawl unless you vindicate good order or discipline and hang every son of a bitch connected with this outrage."[*]

Such "outrages" were an affront to the Southern honor of men like Hill. On the other hand, it speaks to the dishonor of the abolitionists that they did not repudiate the murderer and insurrectionist John Brown but made a martyr of him.

---

*Quoted in James I. Robertson, Jr., *General A. P. Hill: The Story of a Confederate Warrior* (Vintage Books, 1992), 22.

But he did, as a young man, think a lot of heroism and battles. Early on in his life he had adopted the Latin tag *"Dulce et decorum est pro patria mori"* as his own (and his *patria* was always unmistakably the land in which he had been born and raised, Virginia). He wanted a career of military glory, and won an appointment to the U. S. Military Academy. His studies at West Point caused him no difficulties, and though a sociable cadet, with a few serious demerits early on, he was dutiful enough to recover his class standing.

In the summer before his third year at the Academy, however, he made a mistake that would plague him all his life. While on leave in New York City the sociable young cadet apparently contracted a social disease. Not only was the disease debilitating—and humiliating—at the time (he had to be sent home to recover), it later led to the ending of one serious courtship, and undermined his health for the rest of his life. Under the stresses of constant campaigning during the War Between the States, the erosion of his constitution, thanks to this disease, made him a man physically used up by 1865. The more immediate consequence of his indiscretion was that Hill graduated a year behind his entering class, which had rushed off to fight in Mexico. Hill was sent to Mexico too—the only man of the class of 1847 to be sent south of the border (perhaps the military authorities felt sorry for him)—but it was in relief of his 1846 classmate Thomas J. Jackson, who had already scooped up the battlefield honors Hill craved.

The young second lieutenant of artillery embarked in flamboyant style. He wore a fire red shirt (his red calico battle shirts would become a signature during the War), blue pants with a holstered sidearm on each hip, and another pair of handguns (and a knife) tucked into his belt. As a signature of rank, he had a saber clanking at his side. His pants were tucked into spurred boots, and on his head: a sombrero. Despite this get up, there is no record of any American sentry mistaking him for the enemy.

Hill did, however, get a small taste of combat in the mopping up operations, more than a small taste of typhoid fever (which nearly killed him), and a gentleman's taste for the señoritas of Mexico, whom he ranked highly. He remained a sociable fellow.

The following year he was stationed at Fort Henry, in Maryland; then he was transferred to Florida, where he spent nearly six years (as well as a year off patrolling the Texas border) absorbing whatever diseases the humid, swampy Seminole country could throw at him. In 1855, he was sent home to Virginia to recuperate, and when his strength returned he found more amenable employment just across the Potomac. He was assigned to the office of the United States Coast Survey (run by the U.S. Navy) in Washington, D.C. His experience on engineering projects in the Florida swamplands made him a suitable candidate, and though Hill's dreams were of martial glory, not desk-bound competence, he proved an expeditious administrator.

A. P. Hill's Ethnic Studies

"'Tis a fact that the ladies of Mexico are beautiful—and oh how beautiful—but very few of them have ever read Wayland's *Moral Science* . . ."

Quoted in William Woods Hassler, *A. P. Hill, Lee's Forgotten General* (University of North Carolina Press, 1957), 35-6.

Not surprisingly, he also proved a social success in Washington with his easy and refined manners. In 1859, they were enough to win him the hand of a striking young widow nine years his junior, Kitty Morgan McClung (Hill always called her Dolly, a name her mammy had given her), a belle of the Kentucky blue grass. Dolly's brother, future Confederate cavalry officer, John Hunt Morgan, was Hill's best man, and his new bride brought Hill back, at least physically, to the Episcopal Church. They made a splendid couple, and did indeed (as far as the marriage went) live happily ever after—ever after, in this case, ending with Hill's premature death. Dolly bore Hill four daughters, one of whom died during the war.

A. P. Hill (1825–1865)

A not-so-reluctant secessionist

At the end of March 1861, a little more than two weeks before Virginia seceded, Hill resigned from the army. For Hill it was a matter of facing facts: Virginia would not abandon her fellow Southern states—and Hill's paramount loyalty was to his family and his native soil.

Hill's ambition was to be a general in Virginia's armed forces, but the Old Dominion was full of officers with West Point educations. Instead, in May, he was commissioned a colonel in the Confederate army, given command of a regiment of infantry, and issued orders to whip them into shape at Harpers Ferry. He did so wearing swashbuckling boots, his red battle shirts (hand-sewn by his wife), buckskin gauntlets, and a black felt hat. He would be distinguished in battle, at least sartorially.

He trained his men hard, but won them over by his easy manner and his sincere concern for their welfare (once even rounding up cattle on his own after the commissary officer told him there was no beef to be had). He proved capable from the start, a colonel who executed his orders with efficiency (no small accomplishment with newly raised troops).

In February 1862, Hill's skill, if not yet his combat leadership (he had been on the field at Manassas but his troops were not engaged), won him promotion to brigadier general. His new assignment was to block the advance of George B. McClellan's massive Union host up the Virginia Peninsula. He saw his first real action of the war at Williamsburg on 5 May 1862, in a fierce collision of blue and grey. Hill

Southern Groomsman for a Northern General

A. P. Hill was a long-standing, close friend of George McClellan, dating back to their days at West Point. In May 1860, Hill was a groomsman when McClellan married Ellen Marcy, a girl who, at one point, Hill had hoped to marry himself. A year later, McClellan would be drilling troops for a massive invasion of Virginia, and Hill would be drilling troops to defend his old home state.

led his men from the front, charging into battle with pistol raised, and, rather confusingly, wearing a blue shirt rather than a red one.

The field was a mess of mud and rain, but the Confederates drove the Federals back to a line of felled timber. With ammunition running low, Hill ordered a bayonet charge that scattered the Federals. The young brigadier earned the plaudits of those who saw him directing troops through the storm of lead, "erect, magnificent, the god of war himself, amid the smoke and the thunder."[2]

His performance won him promotion again. Before the month was out, he was a major general, the youngest in the Confederate army, and was given command of its largest division, which Hill dubbed "the Light Division," no doubt thinking it gave the unit a certain panache. Its brigadier generals certainly did, including men like Maxcy Gregg, commander of the 1st South Carolina. A lawyer in civilian life, Gregg was also one of those Southern renaissance men who was by turns, and among other things, a classicist, an ornithologist, and an astronomer with his own private observatory. The first brigade was full of professional men—doctors, lawyers, prominent businessmen—who had gallantly reassured the ladies of Richmond that "We go cheerfully to meet the foe; rest assured our vile enemy shall never desecrate your homes until they have first trodden over the bodies of our regiment."[3]

McClellan on A. P. Hill's Loyalty to the South

"Hill I am truly sorry you are going to leave us; but to be frank I cannot blame you. If I were in your place, I would do as you are about to do; but I am an Ohioan and will stand by my state, too."

Quoted in William Woods Hassler, *A. P. Hill, Lee's Forgotten General*, 27-8.

"Always ready for a fight"[4]

After Robert E. Lee took command of the army defending Richmond, he called a conference among generals James Longstreet, A. P. Hill, D. H.

Hill, and Stonewall Jackson, who stunned the others by his arrival (everyone believed he was still in the Valley). Lee outlined his daring plan to attack McClellan's right flank; the lead element would be Stonewall Jackson's. Jackson said he could withdraw his men from the Valley and have them ready to attack on 25 June, only two days away. Longstreet and Lee demurred that surely Jackson needed more time. Jackson agreed to the morning of 26 June. As it happened, Jackson would be very, uncharacteristically, late.

By 3:00 p.m. on 26 June, Hill decided he had waited long enough. He ordered his men forward, inaugurating the Battle of Mechanicsville. Hill's impetuosity meant his men had to cross open ground under deadly fire. Artillery captain "Willie" Pegram rushed up support, but Pegram was so badly outnumbered—by about thirty batteries (which quickly pinpointed his position) to six—that he lost more than half his artillerists and four of his six cannons in a matter of minutes.

Hill's action was a mistake, but the Confederates were inspired by the line of bluecoats retreating before them. The Federals reformed at heavily fortified Beaver Dam Creek: 30,000 men in a virtually impregnable position. Hill was not impressed. He ordered his men to attack. With Lee and Jefferson Davis looking on, and dusk falling on the field, Hill threw his forces at the Yankee right flank. His men "made the hills and valleys and woods ring with their Confederate yells as they eagerly pressed forward with anticipation of coming victory."[5] But victory eluded them under the withering fire and the entangling brambles that kept them from reaching the Union line.

Hill, however, refused to give up. Failing on the right and center of the Union line, he tried the left—and the results were worse: Union fire ripped through the charging Confederates. Hill had shown more ardor and personal courage than tactical brilliance at Mechanicsville, but Lee did not criticize him. He valued Hill's spirit. If there was any blame to be laid it was with Jackson who had not only not arrived, not only badly underestimated how long it would take him to reach the field, but had failed to get a messenger to Lee to tell him where he was. Jackson and his men were simply worn out mentally and physically; they had asked too much of themselves.

What to do next? The answer, it turned out, was to walk in and seize the Federal position at Beaver Dam Creek. The Union General FitzJohn Porter had left only a token holding force and withdrawn his men in the night. So it was victory after all—at least on this field.

Porter had withdrawn behind Powhite Creek at Gaines's Mill. The Confederates pursued him and gave him battle once again. Maxcy Gregg's brigade had charged, pushing the Federal skirmish line back, but only to get his own men pinned down by Federals in positions on the high ground. What neither Hill nor Gregg knew was that the Federal line was three lines deep, entrenched or fortified at each line, a total of about 35,000 men, approachable only across a field of fire that was a muddy, swampy mess.

Hill drew up his entire force to come to Gregg's rescue. Longstreet would be in support on his right, and Jackson, reportedly soon to arrive, would be on his left. Longstreet had the lead but his troops got bogged down by the terrain, and were further impeded by Union artillery fire. Hill, champing at the bit again, decided he could not wait. His own artillery opened fire and his men went charging in—unsupported by either Longstreet or Jackson.

Gregg's men got into the first Union entrenchments, but were pushed out in fierce hand-to-hand fighting. All along the line, the Confederates surged forward only to melt back under Union fire—and then surged forward again. The Light Division was becoming considerably lighter. Hill did not recall his troops, but sent orders for them to cease the offensive and hold their bloody ground. Jackson at last arrived, still apparently dazed from exhaustion, and at 7:00 p.m. Lee sent his combined forces against the Union position. The Federals were driven back until darkness became their shield. But the position at Gaines's Mill now belonged to the Confederates.

Hill and his Light Division had distinguished themselves in these, the opening of the Seven Days' Battles, and they would continue to do so. It was a handsome compliment to the young major general that his was the hardest fought regiment in the army; his men were the best in pursuit of the Federals and the most reliable at taking positions.

Another compliment to his leadership was when he rode up to Lee and Jefferson Davis who were surveying the battlefield under enemy fire. Hill said with less than his usual charm, "This is no place for either of you, and as commander of this part of the field I order you both to the rear!" "We will obey your orders," said Jefferson Davis, with a slight smirk. Artillery fire burst closer, but Davis's horse and Lee's trotted only a short distance away. Hill charged back, "Did I not tell you to go away from here, and did you not promise to obey my orders? Why, one shot from that battery over yonder may presently deprive the Confederacy of its President and the Army of Northern Virginia of its commander!"[6] "Little Powell" was more than big enough to stand up for good sense.

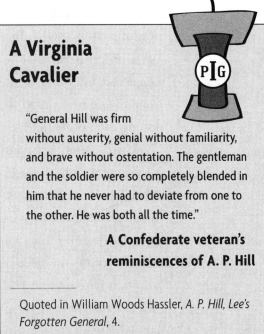

A Virginia Cavalier

"General Hill was firm without austerity, genial without familiarity, and brave without ostentation. The gentleman and the soldier were so completely blended in him that he never had to deviate from one to the other. He was both all the time."

A Confederate veteran's reminiscences of A. P. Hill

Quoted in William Woods Hassler, *A. P. Hill, Lee's Forgotten General*, 4.

At the Battle of Frayser's Farm, Hill's (and Longstreet's) troops again bore the brunt of the fighting, with Hill storming about the battlefield on his horse Prince, encouraging, leading, and even grabbing the standard of the 7th North Carolina and telling them to charge with him or he would die alone. His leadership was inspirational, but at Frayser's Farm he also showed the tactical skill that Lee hoped to see in him. Hill was proving he deserved his stars.

Battles front and rear

Unfortunately, Hill's next enemy was James Longstreet. After a Richmond journalist wrote up Hill's praises to the exclusion of Longstreet, Longstreet had his aide Moxley Sorrel write an indignant reply. Hill was now affronted at what he thought was Longstreet's slighting of the Light Division. Hill refused to communicate with Longstreet's command. Longstreet put him under arrest and Hill challenged Longstreet to a duel. General Lee reconciled the two commanders, at least to the point of tolerating each other, and then sent Hill to join Stonewall Jackson.

Jackson's men were moving north to defend Virginia from the blustering Union general John Pope. Despite orders from Lee to keep Hill well apprised of his plans, Jackson pursued his council of one, with comically disastrous results. Because some generals were informed of changes in movements and others were not, their marching orders became a hashwork of confusion. Jackson was definitely not on his best form. It didn't help that Jackson and Hill didn't like each other. Hill had not forgotten Jackson's failures to support the Light Division during the Seven Days campaign; and the Cromwellian Jackson found it hard to appreciate the Cavalier Hill.

But at the Battle of Cedar Mountain, six miles south of Culpepper, it was Hill and his troops who again carried the day. Jackson's men had engaged the enemy first; when Hill arrived, it was with a perfectly timed and placed assault; the Light Division smashed the Federals and led the pursuit. The battlefield brought Hill a new charger, a grey stallion named Champ. It did not, however, bring him an improved relationship with Jackson.

Nevertheless, Jackson was dependent on Hill's stalwart leadership at the Battle of Second Manassas, which followed on 29 August 1862. Hill's performance was not perfect—in arranging his troops he had left a dangerous 175 yard gap within his front line—but it was bravely led, hard fought, and, against heavy odds, successful. Jackson had perhaps 18,000 effectives on the field. Marching towards him were 63,000 men under the command of Union General John Pope. Hill's men withstood the first Union assault and then gallantly counterattacked, scattering the bluecoats. But this was only the opening round. The Federals came back in force, and the violent collision of armies became one of hand-to-hand combat, among bursting artillery shells, crackling muskets, and smoky fires ignited in the woods and grass. Though some of the Confederates were reduced to fighting with rocks, bayonets, and muskets used as clubs (in the absence of ammunition) they refused to buckle.

In the bloody ebb and flow of battle, the Confederates repelled Federal attacks all day long. Hill, however, had to confess to Jackson, via a messenger, that if the Federals mounted another attack, he would do the best he could, but with no ammunition, his men would be hard-pressed.

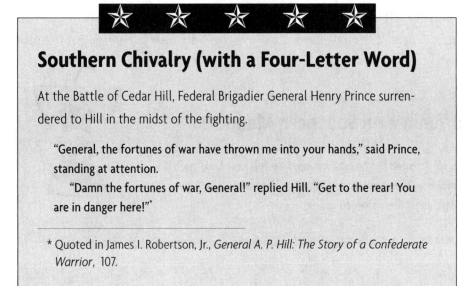

Southern Chivalry (with a Four-Letter Word)

At the Battle of Cedar Hill, Federal Brigadier General Henry Prince surrendered to Hill in the midst of the fighting.

"General, the fortunes of war have thrown me into your hands," said Prince, standing at attention.

"Damn the fortunes of war, General!" replied Hill. "Get to the rear! You are in danger here!"[*]

* Quoted in James I. Robertson, Jr., *General A. P. Hill: The Story of a Confederate Warrior*, 107.

Henry Kyd Douglas, an aide to General Jackson, remembered that "Such a message from a fighter like Hill was weighty with apprehension." Jackson replied, "Tell him if they attack him again he must beat them." Douglas and Jackson rode to meet Hill and listened to his concerns, to which Jackson said: "General, your men have done nobly; if you are attacked again you will beat the enemy back."

Suddenly musket fire erupted along Hill's position. "Here it comes," Hill announced, and immediately rode off to join his men. Jackson called after him: "I'll expect you to beat them."

Beat them he did, and when Hill sent a message to Jackson confirming his success, a grim smile creased Jackson's face. "Tell him I knew he could do it."[7]

The next day the Federals came again, but this time, forming up along-side Jackson were James Longstreet's men, and when Longstreet turned them loose, the grey tide swept the bluecoats away, with Hill's men jumping into the counterattack. And Hill fought well again—and again with a shortage of ammunition—at Ox Hill on 1 September 1862.

Despite such victories, the mountain-bred Calvinist and the Piedmont cavalier fell into another dispute over marching orders. Jackson put Hill under arrest, though he did have the good sense to release him before

A Captured Yankee on Southern Manners

"We were most civilly treated by the rebels, whom we found to be ... men like ourselves; only the rebels were not nearly as profane as our men—in fact, they used no profane language at all. They shamed us."

Quoted in James I. Robertson, Jr., General *A. P. Hill: The Story of a Confederate Warrior* (Vintage Books, 1992), 139.

action at Harpers Ferry and allowed Hill to resume his command until the end of the Maryland campaign.

Bloody roads

Hill seized Harpers Ferry and was given the task of arranging and executing the terms of the Yankee surrender (which under the chivalrous Hill were very liberal) while Jackson moved north into the bloodiest day's fighting of the war, at Sharpsburg. But it was Hill who once more turned the tide. Moving to the sound of the guns, he force-marched his men to the rescue of Lee's army, making a dramatic arrival at the battle field, sweeping away Ambrose Burnside's bluecoats who might otherwise have broken the Confederates, and convincing General McClellan not

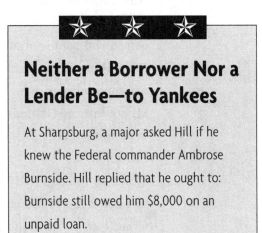

Neither a Borrower Nor a Lender Be—to Yankees

At Sharpsburg, a major asked Hill if he knew the Federal commander Ambrose Burnside. Hill replied that he ought to: Burnside still owed him $8,000 on an unpaid loan.

to press his luck against the valiant Army of Northern Virginia. When the Confederates withdrew, it was Hill's men who slapped the pursuing Federals a bloody repulse.

The campaign concluded, Hill demanded a hearing on his arrest by Jackson. Lee replied that no trial was necessary, because surely an officer of Hill's caliber would never disappoint General Jackson again. Hill was not mollified and reiterated his demand for a hearing. But even the stubborn Jackson, at this point, wanted to let the matter drop. Lee met with his generals, and though he could not reconcile them, he at least restored them to a status of receiving each other with cold and reluctant civility. Lee, in the meantime, named Longstreet and Jackson as the commanders of the First and Second Corps of the army. "Next to these two officers," Lee wrote to Jefferson Davis, "I consider A. P. Hill the best commander with me. He fights his troops well, and takes good care of them."[8]

At Fredericksburg, Hill was charged with anchoring the right side of the Confederate line, but he was apparently distracted with grief. His eldest daughter had died of diphtheria, and the normally ardent commander was noticeably absent from the action. In arranging his line, he had allowed it to be separated by a wide patch of swampy woods, leaving a gap in the center of about 600 yards. When the Federals crashed into Hill's line, they inevitably found the gap, pouring into Maxcy Gregg's unprepared men who were arrayed behind it as a reserve. Gregg was killed, but the Confederates bravely closed ranks and plugged the gap, driving the Federals back and ending the major action on Hill's side of the field.

Before the Light Division left Fredericksburg, Hill had recovered his composure, and his men donated $10,000 to help the poor in the battered, old, picturesque town. It was a typical, chivalrous gesture from Hill's command.

At Chancellorsville, despite their personal animosities, Hill and Jackson cooperated as well as they ever did, with the Light Division joining Jackson's audacious sweep across the Federal front, and filing in as the reserve to pursue the Federals that Jackson drove from the field.

But just as Jackson was shot down at dusk scouting ahead of Confederate lines, so too Hill and his staff were shot at by Confederate troops only fifty yards away. Hill had been riding ahead calling out for the Confederates to cease fire. But in the darkness, the grey-clad infantry thought it was a Yankee trick. Hill plunged from his horse at the crackle of close-range musketry and was miraculously unscathed. When he heard that Jackson was hit, he went immediately to help his commander. It was Hill who cradled Jackson's head and bandaged his arm to stanch the bleeding. Hill called for a surgeon, before moving out to secure the position around Jackson.

Unfortunately, Hill himself was then wounded by Federal shell fire. He nevertheless regained his horse and directed troops into position until he could be relieved by J. E. B. Stuart as temporary commander of the Second Corps. Hill returned to command four days later, but Jackson would not return at all. In his final feverish hours he was heard to call out: "Order A. P. Hill to prepare for action!"

After Jackson's death, Lee appointed General Richard Ewell, a Jackson favorite, commander of the Second Corps. It was a popular choice among Jackson's men. But Lee had a promotion for A. P. Hill as well. In a letter to President Jefferson Davis, Lee had said that Hill was "upon the whole . . . the best soldier of his grade with me,"[9] recommended him for promotion to lieutenant general, and proposed that the Army of Northern Virginia should now be divided into three corps, rather than two. Jefferson Davis approved, and the Third Corps went to A. P. Hill.

Corps commander

The Third Corps' first action was Gettysburg, but their corps commander was terribly sick, ashen-faced, tired, and perhaps distracted by pain. Nevertheless, it was his men who stumbled into the Yankees first and precipitated the greatest battle of the war. As dusk crept up on the first day of battle, Lee asked Hill whether his men could press the attack. The normally belligerent cavalier said no, his men had marched and fought themselves out. It was then that Lee turned to the usually equally belligerent Richard Ewell who came to the same conclusion about the Second Corps. It was not an auspicious beginning for the newly configured Army of Northern Virginia, and these were not the answers that Stonewall Jackson would have given.

On the second day, Hill's men were to act in support of Longstreet. The troops of the Third Corps most deeply involved, those under General Richard Anderson, were badly managed—in part because Hill assumed that Longstreet would coordinate their attack and Longstreet assumed that they would remain under Hill's direction. Hill again seemed insufficiently aggressive, dispirited in the wake of Longstreet's sluggishness, and disengaged from his responsibilities.

On the third day, Hill, unlike Longstreet, was an enthusiast for the planned assault on the Union center. He asked permission to lead the attack and Lee should have given it to him and allowed Hill to commit the entire Third Corps to the charge (instead of holding most of it in reserve—a role that would have been better served by Longstreet, who was always better at counterpunching). Had "Little Powell" led the charge at the Union line, with the entirety of the Third Corps, with all the celerity of a commander convinced of the plan's worth, the Confederates might have won the battle of Gettysburg.

Instead, a surly, insubordinate Longstreet was charged with making an attack he was convinced would fail, and which he did everything possible to delay and cancel. Longstreet was the wrong man for the job; Hill would have been the right one. Moreover, Hill's relationship with Longstreet was very nearly as cold as his relationship had been with Jackson; and as on the second day, neither commander took responsibility for directing Hill's men in the attack; each general assuming it was the other's prerogative or responsibility. The result, of course, was a disaster.

On 14 October 1863, Hill thought he had found his redemption, when he caught a large body of Federals napping at Bristoe Station, Virginia, not far from Manassas. But in his haste to attack the Federals before they could escape, he neglected to reconnoiter the ground. His precipitate assault did, indeed, catch the Federals by surprise, but as General Henry Heth's division was hurried to pursue the fleeing Yankees, it ran into a flank attack by blue-coated troops concealed behind a railroad cutting. Hill had seen the risk—though he had only a vague idea of enemy numbers behind the railroad tracks—but assumed that his artillery could keep the Federals at bay, and was simply eager to fight. He didn't realize that concealed behind those tracks were three Union divisions that had a clear killing ground to enfilade the attacking Confederates.

When the entrenched Federals opened fire, cutting a swathe through the grey-clad ranks, the Confederates reformed and redirected their attack at the Yankees behind the railroad tracks. It was a brave but dangerous choice. They managed to break through the first Union line, but were trapped by the second and driven back with heavy losses. James I. Robertson, one of Hill's best biographers, estimates that Hill lost a man—killed, wounded, or captured—every two seconds of the battle. Hill's impetuosity had its place, but not here, and probably never as a corps commander, a role that actually never suited Hill. He needed to be in among the fighting men, not directing the movements of a corps.

Hill knew he had blundered and confessed as much in his official report. The next day, after the Yankees had continued their retreat, Hill rode over the ground with Lee and repeatedly apologized for his costly error. Lee offered Hill no excuses. But as was often the case, he issued no sharp rebuke either, knowing it was beside the point. Hill knew he had erred, and knew he had disappointed Lee. Finally Lee said, "Well, well, General, bury these poor men and let us say no more about it."[10] Hill, however, could never let the dead bury their dead at Bristoe Station. For the rest of the war, his failure there, and his increasingly faltering health, depressed his spirits—and his effectiveness.

On the first day of the Battle of the Wilderness (5 May 1864), Hill fought his corps like his old self (even if physically he was ailing), directing his troops with remarkable skill in a very hot fight. But his physical disabilities began to tell that night, and not enough was done to prepare the next day. Hill had expected (and so did Lee) that Longstreet would be up with reinforcements. Longstreet, however, was late, and when the Federals hit Hill's battered lines on the morning of 6 May, the Southerners were unprepared for the ferocious attack. Though in tremendous pain, Hill gallantly rode up and down the lines encouraging the troops, organizing the defense, even directing batteries of enfilading artillery fire at the front. When Longstreet's men finally rolled onto the field, Hill led his men in a counterattack against the Federals (so far in advance was Hill that he was nearly captured by lead units of the Union army).

Two days later, an enfeebled Hill asked Lee to give command of the Third Corps to another general, at least temporarily. Lee reluctantly granted his request, giving the Third Corps to Jubal Early, while Hill remained with the troops aboard an ambulance. He eventually returned to command, and battered as he was, he and Lee endured together, the great slogging match between the counterpunching Army of Northern Virginia and the relentless, hard-pounding Ulysses S. Grant, all the way through most of the siege of Petersburg.

On 19 June 1864, a woman saw Lee and Hill during Sunday services at an Episcopal church. The woman described Hill as "a small man, but [one who] has a very military bearing, and a countenance pleasing but inexpressibly sad."[11] Hill's physical state was an apt reflection of the state of the Confederacy, battling on, with a remembrance of past happiness and nobility, now turned inexpressibly sad and worn down. But as Lee proved himself a master of defensive tactics in these final months, so did Hill, whose leadership rebounded even if his health did not.

By the winter of 1864, his strength, vitality, and even his ability to concentrate were visibly failing. The swashbuckling Hill now found it difficult and painful to mount a horse. But he remained intent on his duties, and rode his lines. He was returning from an early morning conference with Lee on 2 April 1865 when he met his fate. The Confederate line had been broken and Hill was determined to rally his men. Lee admonished him to be careful. Careful was not a word easily applied to Hill.

In his search for the front, the desperately sick Hill rode along a no-man's land. Along the way, he captured and sent to the rear, under escort, two Federal infantrymen. With his remaining companion, courier George Tucker, he rode on, until he found two more Yankees leveling muskets at him. Hill drew a revolver and called on them to surrender. Instead, the blast of a .58 caliber bullet smashed through Hill's heart, killing him.

When Lee heard the news, he replied sadly, "He is now at rest, and we who are left are the ones to suffer."[12] Like Jackson in his delirium, Lee in his final moments also called for "Little Powell": "Tell A. P. Hill he must come up." Perhaps no other general, besides Lee, was so much a part of the Army of Northern Virginia. General James Alexander Walker said of him that "of all the Confederate leaders [Hill] was the most genial and lovable in disposition...the commander the army idolized."[13]

Hill fought virtually the entire war. He represented the Virginia of manners, courtly graces, chivalry, and patriotism. If he is little remembered today, compared with Jackson, Longstreet, and J. E. B. Stuart, he deserves to be recognized for the gallant Southern soldier that he was.

Chapter Thirteen

GEORGE B. MCCLELLAN (1826-1885)

"I am in no way responsible."[1]

George McClellan was in the wrong profession—though it didn't seem like it at the time.[2] He rocketed his way through West Point—in which he enrolled before he was even sixteen years old, having been classically educated already, including two years at the University of Pennsylvania—graduating second in his class (he thought he should have been first, a feeling he often had in life) in 1846 at the age of nineteen. His military career was equally meteoric. He went straight to combat in Mexico. Come the Civil War, he was, at age thirty-four, appointed a major general in the United States Army, second in rank only to Winfield Scott. And between these wars, he had been a highly paid railroad executive. Successful in academic and business pursuits, recognized as a gifted administrator, born leader, and supremely well-qualified young military

Guess What?

✦ Lincoln's top commander, McClellan, was a Democrat who loathed abolitionists and disparaged the idea of racial equality

✦ When McClellan led his troops into western Virginia, he threatened to "crush any attempt at insurrection" by the Southern slaves

✦ A failure as commander of the Army of the Potomac, he made quite a decent governor of New Jersey

officer, "chock full," as one colleague noted, "of big war science,"[3] McClellan seemed bound to succeed. He was the "Young Napoleon."

McClellan himself noted, "I find myself in a new & strange position here—Presdt, Cabinet, Genl Scott & all deferring to me—by some strange operation of magic I seem to have become *the* power in the land. I almost think that were I to win some small success now I could become Dictator or anything else that might please me—but nothing of that kind would please me—*therefore* I *won't* be Dictator. Admirable self denial!"[4] Admirable, indeed, because he seemed well suited to the role. He was a resentful subordinate, a man convinced that, in his words, "I can do it all,"[5] but also one never to take blame for a failure, which was always someone else's fault. Deference he accepted as his due. He had an ill-disguised contempt for his commander in chief, for General Scott (whom he forced into retirement), and for anyone else who might second-guess, interfere, offer contrary ideas, or provide anything less than blind and complaisant support of his every demand—and his every excuse.

When he married, it was to a Presbyterian who converted him to a Calvinism rather different in kind from Stonewall Jackson's. Jackson took comfort from the doctrine of predestination that he had nothing to fear on the battlefield—God would collect him in His own good time. McClellan took predestination to affirm that he was God's elected military savior of the Union. This messianic impulse—common amongst Northern abolitionists—perhaps should have steered Little Mac to a career in politics, a calling he did eventually heed; though, ironically, he was a political enemy of the abolitionists.

From his days at the academy, McClellan disdained Yankees and gravitated to Southerners, at least those of a gentlemanly sort. McClellan was very much an adherent to the cult of the gentleman, which is no bad thing in itself, but with McClellan, it was more the snobbery of a Philadelphia doctor's son than it was the aristocratic poise and *noblesse oblige* of the Southern planter class.

Though a conservative Democrat who loathed abolitionists (on occasion accusing them of "rank & open treason"[6]), a moderate on the issue of slavery (he took a slave-servant named Songo with him to Mexico), and a man who preferred Southern gentlemen for company, McClellan was nevertheless a firm Unionist. He once told Navy Secretary Gideon Wells that he detested "both South Carolina and Massachusetts, and should rejoice to see both States extinguished." These two states, he argued, had always been seats of extremism, driving otherwise reasonable Americans to quarrel.

The great moral crusade for McClellan was the preservation of the Union—not the abolition of slavery. Slavery was a constitutional right, as affirmed by the Supreme Court, and so therefore deserving of every legal protection. The idea of racial equality was repugnant to him, if not just flat-out ridiculous: "I confess to a prejudice in favor of my own race, & can't learn to like the odor of either Billy goats or niggers"[7] (a sentiment he confessed to, incidentally, *after* the war). He did, however, also volunteer that he would have found—had it been in his power and been his responsibility—an equitable way to abolish slavery that both adequately compensated and protected the slave-owner while liberating and assisting the slave. But then again, McClellan always believed that he had the right plan for everything.

Apprenticeship in Mexico

Though doctors benefited much more in prestige than in pay in mid-nineteenth century America, things came easily to young McClellan growing up in Philadelphia. He had a strong family and parents who emphasized education. McClellan's mind was quick, and he never had to study much to excel. Such precocious acuity had the downside of making him dogmatically certain of his opinions.

Originally it was assumed he would be a lawyer. But the prospect was so dull, and, to his parents, the attractions of a free education seemed so inviting, that West Point became his alma mater—and once in, he considered himself a professional soldier. One of his earliest professional prejudices, honed in Mexico watching the rabble of rowdy volunteers and citizen-soldier officers (appointed through political connections), was that war was a job for those trained to the task: civilians should butt out—or take their orders and their training from those qualified to give them. Later, Abraham Lincoln would not be among those deemed so qualified.

He had, as the British say, a "good war," seeing action, performing admirably, learning from Winfield Scott's masterful campaigning, and leading the life of a gay young blade (he embarked for war even more fully and colorfully armed than A. P. Hill, with saber, bowie knife, pistols stuffed in his belt and a double-barreled shotgun in his hand). He scoffed at danger, ate and drank the best Mexico could provide (when not in the field), and romanced a señorita named Nachita, who, a friend reported, "cried uninterruptedly for the space of a week" after he left Mexico City, "but as she has done the same thing several times before for others, don't cut your throat."[8] He also continued his military education—something he would do throughout his life, even while a railroad executive—picking through the volumes in the library of a Catholic seminary, looking "for something readable among their shelves of bad theology"[9] (a very McClellan comment), and latching onto Bernal Diaz's riveting first-person account of Cortez's conquest of Mexico, reading it in the original Spanish.

McClellan found peacetime service dull, though he was given far more special assignments than most young officers, in no small part because one of his patrons was the Secretary of War, Jefferson Davis, who, like most people, thought highly of this young lieutenant who radiated professionalism. Even when he botched an assignment, as he did while investing a northern route for the transcontinental railroad, he did so in a way that stood on his dignity, or rather on his assumption that whatever he believed to be true was true. In this case, without adequate scouting, he believed there were obstacles in his path—only there weren't—a failing that would repeat itself during the War.

More to his taste, perhaps, was an assignment that took him to Europe with two officers much his senior (he dismissed them as old fuddy-duddies). The party had hoped to inspect the armies of both sides in the Crimean War, but had to make do with the Allied forces, and with some other travels. It was from this jaunt that McClellan came back with a design for "the McClellan saddle" (based on a Hungarian model as adapted by the Prussians) that became standard issue to the U.S. Cavalry for the rest of its existence. He also taught himself Russian well enough to translate Russian books. McClellan, indeed, was something of a linguist. He could read books in German, Spanish, or French, and translated a book on French bayonet tactics.

When he left the service to become a railroad executive, he was more than once tempted to resign (if he had been allowed to) in order to rejoin the colors to fight Mormons (in the bloodless "Mormon War") or to join a mercenary unit that might independently extend America's manifest destiny farther south, as filibusters like William Walker attempted to do. But the circumstances were never right—not until the war to restore the Union.

Before that occurred, however, he made one last peacetime conquest. After nearly six years of diligent wooing, he married Miss Ellen Marcy in May 1860. She had rejected his proposal of marriage in 1854, been compelled by her parents to break her engagement to A.P. Hill in 1856, and had enjoyed many suitors in between, most of them military swains, as her father was himself an officer. The marriage was an extremely happy one; whatever his other failings, McClellan was an admiringly loyal husband. They had two children, a girl, Mary ("May"), and a boy named after his father, but as there could only be one "Little Mac," the other became little Max.

The price of generalship

Men often become more cautious in their forties, as life experience, family responsibilities, and physical decline set in. War, too, is a sobering experience, and McClellan had seen war, though he gave every appearance of not being in the least traumatized by it. McClellan was still only in his thirties when he reached high command. He believed he was predestined by Providence to save the Union. He was certain that only he knew what to do in the crisis. But it was what he knew that perhaps was the problem. "There is only one safe rule in war," he said: "to decide what is the very worst thing that can happen to you, & prepare to meet it."[10] Compare this principle to Robert E. Lee's contrary one that Richmond was never so safe as when it was *undefended* (that is, rather than wait and prepare for the worst to happen, seize opportunities to upset the balance of your opponent). Lee, like McClellan, believed in defensive entrenchments. He was not imprudent, but his goal was ever and always to drive the enemy back and threaten him where he felt he was vulnerable, and to use fortifications as pivots for offensives.

McClellan had various grand offensive strategies as well, of course, though Scott thought them impractical, and Lincoln, though generally supportive of McClellan, doubted them too. More important than this, however, was McClellan's consistent magnification of the enemy, often to three times its actual size. His evidence for these miscalculations seemed based less on actual intelligence than either on his own fears or his own grandiose imagination: if he was to save the Union, surely it would have to be against nearly insurmountable odds. The battles of the Young Napoleon would be among the greatest in history.

They were anyway—certainly in American history. But there is no excuse for not seeing things as they are (at which Lee excelled) and for taking the counsel of one's fears (an apothegm of Stonewall Jackson's). McClellan consistently saw things as he imagined them to be and, as he himself said, thought the only safe rule was to prepare oneself to meet the very worst that could happen.

The first campaigns

McClellan started his Civil War service, it is sometimes forgotten, in the West. In April 1861, he became a major general of Ohio volunteers (he was at the time a resident of Ohio, as an executive with the Ohio and Mississippi railroad). By May he was commanding the Department of the Ohio, which included Ohio, Illinois, and Indiana for starters, but soon began annexing other neighboring areas into its responsibilities, which is what brought McClellan to western Virginia, and his first shift from raising, supplying, and training troops to fighting them.

Western Virginia was sympathetic to the Union. It was also crucial to Federal transportation and communications, because the Baltimore and Ohio railroad passed through it. When reports reached McClellan's desk of Confederate activity in the area, with Johnny Rebs threatening to burn the railroad bridges, he was authorized to act. Entering slave-holding Virginia, he issued a proclamation stating that he would not only not interfere with slavery, which was no more illegal now than it had ever been, but pledged that "with an iron hand," he would "crush any attempt at insurrection" by the slaves.[11] The burnt bridges were rebuilt and a small detachment of Confederates at Philippi was scattered (and six were killed) by Federal artillery, prompting Northern newspaper headlines about "the Philippi Races." To cap it all, pro-Union politicians in western Virginia organized to have their counties secede from the state—one act of secession of which Lincoln approved.

As commander of an army of occupation, McClellan reaffirmed his commitment to defending the property rights of all, whether secessionist or Unionist, and he maintained a strict discipline. There was no winking at depredations against slaveholders. He also sounded a note that seemed right and proper, but would prove frustrating to his commander in chief: he promised "not to move" into action "until everything is ready" and he would not "depart from my intention of gaining success by manoeuvring rather than by fighting; I will not throw these men of mine into the teeth of artillery & intrenchments, if it is possible to avoid it."[12] To be fair, he also pledged to "move with the utmost rapidity & energy" when "everything is ready."

McClellan was very popular with his troops. He turned them into fine model soldiers, and he was immensely careful with their lives. He was not, however, careful in his judgments of others. McClellan, of all people, severely rebuked one of his brigadier generals in the Rich Mountain campaign in western Virginia for accurately reporting that the enemy force he was assigned to divert outnumbered him. He added, "I confess I feel apprehensive unless our force could equal theirs." McClellan responded with abuse, threatening to replace Brigadier General Thomas A. Morris—who had already proven his worth in the successful surprise attack at Philippi—telling him, in another McClellan turn of phrase, "I propose taking the really difficult & dangerous part of this work on my own hands." McClellan's column would "decide the face of the campaign. . . . I have spoken plainly—I speak officially—the crisis is a grave one, & I must have Generals under me who are willing to risk as much as I am."[13]

As McClellan's authoritative biographer Stephen Sears acknowledges, McClellan's "risk was in fact slight." But the self-dramatization and the rush to blame others—even before anything has gone wrong—these are very much the McClellan touch that President Lincoln later came to know so well. In fact, a reinforced Morris (McClellan gave in with an extra regiment) faced an equal number of Confederates, about 4,000 troops on either side. McClellan and his column of 7,000 men, meanwhile, met 1,300 Confederates (less than half the number McClellan expected) at Rich Mountain.

He confessed his nervousness to his wife: "I realize the dreadful responsibility on me—the lives of my men, the reputation of the country, and the success of the cause. . . . I shall feel my way and be very cautious, for I recognize the fact that everything requires success in my first operations. You need not be alarmed as to the result; God is on our side."[14]

Needless to say, the Battle of Rich Mountain (11 July 1861) was not the epochal event McClellan thought it was, though it was a Union victory, affirming, for the newspapers anyway, McClellan as the Young Napoleon. To Brigadier General William Rosecrans, McClellan was a good deal less than that. Rosecrans had led the assault on Rich Mountain and thought McClellan had abandoned him by not committing the rest of the column to the attack. In a subsequent Federal pursuit of the enemy, McClellan himself was free in assigning blame to every officer not named McClellan: "Unless I command every picket & lead every column I cannot be sure of success."[15] Were he alive today, McClellan would no doubt be in favor of cloning.

To this point, McClellan's war had been one of distant musketry, heard, not seen or felt; of plans achieved or miscarried, not executed on a hot battlefield. He had done every task of preparation and planning skillfully and well. But for one so liberal with criticism, he had not yet himself been in the firing line against the Confederates. This was unusual for Civil War generals, who actually had a 50 percent higher chance of being killed or wounded than enlisted men. He might have been wise to keep himself back from the action, but it was certainly unusual.

More important than the Battle of Rich Mountain and its aftermath, however, was the Federal defeat at First Manassas. The government in Washington was in panic. Who else could they turn to but the Young Napoleon? He accepted their summons and became the commander of the Army of the Potomac, a name that he gave the army.

McClellan told his wife, "Who would have thought, when we were married, that I should so soon be called upon to save the country?"[16] The key words being, of course, "so soon"; in the long run, it was inevitable that McClellan should save his country. He rode on cap-waving excursions (or inspections) among the men, eliciting huzzahs and raising morale (both theirs and no doubt his), but he was also a diligent administrator, orderly in his methods, and decisive in enforcing discipline. When it came to organization and preparation, he was everything he thought himself to be.

His signal failing was his system of intelligence. Allan Pinkerton, the famous detective, was the man charged by McClellan to gather and report news of the enemy. Pinkerton and his men proved better at passing on wild rumors and the ingratiating exaggerations of deserters than anything else. But Pinkerton's consistent inflation of enemy numbers was exactly what McClellan wanted to hear, because it fit his own vision of the challenge before him. Winfield Scott was entirely more skeptical, and accurate, in assessing the size of the Confederate army, and confident that it posed no risk to Washington.

McClellan, typically, regarded him as either "a *dotard* or a *traitor . . .* he is a perfect imbecile. He understands nothing, appreciates nothing & is ever in my way." Lincoln was no better. McClellan dismissed him as an "idiot" and took up calling him "the Gorilla." Both men were condemned for not recognizing that "the enemy have from 3 to 4 times my force" (in fact, McClellan outnumbered the enemy, and would always do so, usually by odds of at least two to one) and for not seeing "the true state of affairs," which was actually a false state of affairs.[17]

McClellan threatened that "if he [Winfield Scott] *cannot* be taken out of my path, I will resign and let the admin[istration] take care of itself. . . . The people call upon me to save the country—I *must* save it and cannot respect anything that is in the way."[18] McClellan won the dispute, Scott was retired, and in November 1861, the commander of the Army of the Potomac became also general in chief of the army. When the president asked him if he felt capable of performing two such weighty jobs at once, McClellan reassured him, "I can do it all."[19]

McClellan could do it all, but believed that Lincoln and his cabinet could do next to nothing, and needed to be kept far away from his areas of responsibility. He repeatedly snubbed the president, refusing to meet with him whenever the great general thought it inconvenient or tiresome. He was surly to congressmen and cabinet members (and anyone else) who pressed him for his plans . . . unless of course he was himself leaking these plans to the *New York Herald*. He was, as ever, quick to assign blame to others, whether for military defeats (such as the ill-attempted Federal attack at Ball's Bluff on 21 October 1861) or even for the fact that the Army was becoming extremely adept at parading, but of little proven use at fighting. "If it is so the fault will not be mine,"[20] might well serve as the emblematic McClellan quote, a motto for his personal coat of arms.

Vive le Général McClellan!

McClellan, "the Young Napoleon," was flattered to have on his staff three French royals from the House of Orange: the Prince de Joinville, the Duc de Chartres, and the Comte de Paris. They helped bring France's famed success in arms to the Army of the Potomac.

McClellan as commander

Of McClellan's great on to Richmond drive, advancing up the Peninsula, one might wish to say as little as possible—for McClellan's sake. But of course, the great commander wouldn't quite see it that way. For him, it was a tremendous struggle against politicians in Washington who continually connived against him because he was a Democrat and not an abolitionist radical, against overwhelming Confederate numbers (which were, in fact, much smaller than his own), and pulled off one of the greatest tactical withdrawals of all time from the gates of Richmond (in other words, was handily defeated by Robert E. Lee's smaller army).

McClellan had his supporters in the press (chiefly among Democrat-leaning papers) and certainly in the ranks. But Lincoln and his cabinet and many of the Republican-leaning newspapers and even some of McClellan's officers and men were beginning to have their doubts about a commander who was so cautious, so full of contempt for his civilian masters (though he stopped well short of countenancing a military coup, which was sometimes—perhaps merely to blow off steam—discussed by others), and who, while dutiful in the hours he spent in preparing his army, was rarely on the field of battle.

Whether humbugged by "Prince John" Magruder, whose humble Confederate outpost convinced McClellan that he faced the bulk of the Confederate army (inspecting Magruder's positions, Joe Johnston quipped, "No one but McClellan could have hesitated to attack"[21]) or making ludicrous assessments of his enemy whose audacity and daring with inferior numbers would drive him to abandon his march on Richmond ("I prefer Lee to [Joseph E.] Johnston—the former is too cautious & weak under grave responsibility—personally brave and energetic to a fault, he yet is wanting in moral firmness when pressed by heavy responsibility & is likely to be timid & irresolute in action"[22]), McClellan's record is frankly embarrassing to consider.

It is one thing to have arranged a battle as best one can and fail. It is quite another, however, to bleat, as McClellan did before the Battle of Mechanicsville (26 June 1862), "I am in no way responsible...as I have not failed to represent repeatedly the necessity for reinforcements.... If the result...is a disaster, the responsibility cannot be thrown on my shoulders."[23] Or take this dispatch, written in the early morning hours of 28 June, after the Confederates had driven his men back in a desperate frontal assault of the sort the McClellan would never have dared contemplate, "I have lost this battle because my force was too small. I again repeat that I am not responsible for the result.... [T]he government has not sustained this army. If you do not do so now the game is lost. If I save this army now, I tell you plainly that I owe no thanks to you or any other persons in Washington. You have done your best to sacrifice this army."[24]

One cannot imagine Grant or Lee writing such words. They had neither the ego, nor the self-deception, nor the weakness of character, nor the submission to panic that lies behind them. And it is surely, at a minimum, a lack of gratitude, if not an unbalanced sense of conspiracy, to assert that the Secretary of War for the Union wanted the army to be sacrificed, either out of bullheaded civilian stupidity or in order to discredit McClellan politically. Despite McClellan's complaints—driven in part by Lincoln's withholding of troops to protect Washington—the Army of the Potomac lacked for nothing, thanks to the generosity and resources of the Federal government. Though he hardly gave him credit for it, Lincoln was McClellan's great defender, even if an exasperated one. It was he who returned McClellan to command the Army of the Potomac after General Pope's defeat at Second Manassas, and it was he who recognized that even if McClellan could not lead men into battle, he was a genius at organizing them and preparing them for it. But McClellan did not raise his own units the way a Bedford Forrest did, equipping the men with supplies paid for out of his own pocket. It was the Confederate army that was always strapped for resources, yet Confederate generals didn't bemoan their fate, the way McClellan did, as a spoiled, egocentric child.

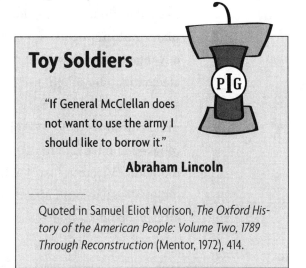

Toy Soldiers

"If General McClellan does not want to use the army I should like to borrow it."

Abraham Lincoln

Quoted in Samuel Eliot Morison, *The Oxford History of the American People: Volume Two, 1789 Through Reconstruction* (Mentor, 1972), 414.

Where some saw failure—for which he blamed others—he saw himself as a grand strategist and masterful tactician extracting chestnut victories from the fire of war: "the officers & men feel that I saved the day," he said at Williamsburg, as his army slogged its way up the Peninsula. Whether they did or not, McClellan always knew that this was true: he *had* saved the day from the "utter stupidity & worthlessness" [25] of his corps commanders and the treacherous, two-faced, conspiring, interfering politicians in Washington. In McClellan's mind there was no man so indispensable as himself: "I feel too that I must not unnecessarily risk my life—for the fate of my army depends upon me & they all know it."[26] One wonders if he ever needed to remind them. It is certain that Lincoln had to remind McClellan that his constant appeals for more troops would leave the Federal government with no more than 25,000 troops to cover every other theatre of the war.

The fate of the Army of the Potomac under McClellan's command was to skedaddle from Richmond. Even when McClellan was privy to Lee's plans, outnumbered him more than two to one, and had every possible advantage over him, as at the Battle of Sharpsburg, the daring Confederate commander fought McClellan to a draw, or perhaps a tactical Confederate victory. When Lee withdrew from the field, McClellan declined to pursue him save for a half-hearted, *pro forma* attempt. He was too relieved to have had his army survive the battle. He reported that "at that moment—Virginia lost, Washington menaced, Maryland invaded—the national cause could afford no risks of defeat."[27] To his wife he was more effusive, content that "God has in his mercy a second time made me the

McClellan on Why Lee Defeated Him in the Battle for Richmond

"I think I begin to see his [God's] wise purpose in this.... If I had succeeded in taking Richmond now the fanatics [abolitionists] of the North might have been too powerful & reunion impossible."

George McClellan

Quoted in Stephen W. Sears, *George B. McClellan: The Young Napoleon* (Ticknor & Fields, 1988), 235.

instrument of saving the nation."[28] McClellan's record is thus one of bluster and recrimination, failure and refusal to confront failure, leavened only by his capacity for organization and training, at which he was indeed expert. It was fighting at which he lacked. Rather than a general, he should have been a bureaucrat . . .

. . . or perhaps a politician. In the political arena, his enormous ego put him at one with many another seeker of public office. And as a politician, his ideas were not ones easily dismissed. As a general he had been appalled by the way General John Pope had waged war on Southern civilians as well as on Southern troops. He thought that to restore the Union meant to fight the war in such a way that respected Christian values and that presented the Union as something the people in the South would *want* to rejoin. That meant treating civilians with every proper consideration. It meant fighting solely to preserve the Union, not to wage a radical, ideological war to extinguish an institution recognized as legal by the Constitution and the Supreme Court and that was, however unfortunate, a cornerstone of Southern life.

Early in their relationship, McClellan had said of the "well-meaning baboon," the president of the United States: "The Presdt is perfectly honest & is really sound on the nigger question."[29] In fact, of course, the president proved far less "sound" than McClellan hoped, which was one reason why he ran against him for president in 1864 as the nominee of the Democratic Party. But there were other more admirable reasons. He was shocked when, two days after the Battle of Sharpsburg, Lincoln suspended the writ of habeas corpus and imposed military courts on civilians accused of hindering the war effort or assisting the enemy. McClellan believed that the Emancipation Proclamation violated the Constitution as did Lincoln's suspension of traditional American civil rights. Such overthrowing of the Constitution made a mockery of McClellan's cause of restoring and preserving the Constitutional Union (as he saw it). He was committed to fighting secession, not to forcing through the wants and desires of an abolitionist cabal. McClellan believed that the "infamous" Emancipation Proclamation and the suspension of habeas corpus had "at one stroke of the pen" changed America's "free institutions into a despotism."[30] Nevertheless, he allowed himself to be persuaded that, as a serving soldier, the course of duty required him to keep his opinions private, and to address the army on the need of submitting to civil authority.

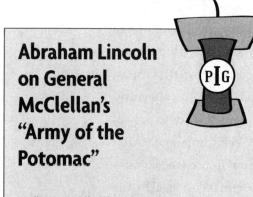

Abraham Lincoln on General McClellan's "Army of the Potomac"

"So it is called, but that is a mistake; it is only McClellan's bodyguard."

Quoted in Stephen W. Sears, *George B. McClellan: The Young Napoleon* (Ticknor & Fields, 1988), 331.

The president, however, had lost patience with McClellan, as well as the political will to defend the Democrat general from his Republican enemies. On 5 November 1862, just after the midterm elections, Lincoln ordered him relieved from duty. McClellan was now free of military constraints. If he wished, he could oppose Lincoln as a rival politician—and that is exactly what happened.

Citizen McClellan

Lincoln resisted all efforts—after the humiliation of Ambrose Burnside at Fredericksburg and Joseph Hooker at Chancellorsville—to restore McClellan to command, though he recognized that among many in the army there was a strong sympathy for Little Mac. Such "McClellanism" was regarded as a threat, but not so great a one as to risk restoring a commander in whom the president had utterly lost confidence.

In the summer of 1864, the Democratic Party elected General McClellan as its candidate for president. McClellan was a pro-war Democrat— that is, one who believed that the Union must be restored before there could be peace. But the party's platform and its chosen vice presidential candidate were in favor of an immediate armistice, to be followed by negotiations to restore the Union. McClellan refused to budge from his principles, while simultaneously trying to fudge the differences between the wings of the Democratic Party.

The Democrats had expected that by nominating McClellan, they would win the soldier vote. But the peace plank of the Democratic platform made that impossible. In the event, Lincoln defeated McClellan handily, with the general capturing only three states: New Jersey, Delaware, and Kentucky. The margin in the electoral college was 212 votes for Lincoln to 21 for Little Mac. It was a trouncing defeat, though to the general's credit he had taken the high road in the campaign, doing as little electioneering as possible, behaved as a gentleman, and accepted the electoral voice of the people as the voice of God's will. He was indeed a better politician than he was a soldier.

He finally resigned his commission only to find that his political notoriety made it impossible for him to resume his role as a railroad executive. He considered becoming a mercenary, including putting himself at the service of the French Emperor Maximilian of Mexico, which would have been an outcome devoutly to be wished—had he been more successful in French uniform than Federal blue.

But instead of returning to arms, he relied on his investment income to live the life of a European exile, a role that suited him better still. He delighted in interviews with Helmuth von Moltke, chief of the Prussian general staff, and the famed Swiss military strategist Antoine-Henri, Baron de Jomini, marveled at Rome, and enjoyed the high reputation he had in the cities of Europe. He did not return home until 1868, in time to see Ulysses Grant elected president. He also found that he was now again employable, and so pursued engineering and railroad work. He did not return to politics until 1876, when he enthusiastically endorsed and campaigned for the Democratic Party candidate for president, Samuel J. Tilden, against the Republican (and eventual winner) Rutherford B. Hayes. That, in turn, led to New Jersey's Democratic Party electing

McClellan as its gubernatorial candidate in 1877—and this was an election he won.

Moreover, he governed well, trimming spending, abolishing direct state taxes on individuals, and bringing to bear all the skills of organization and management that he had developed as a general and businessman. This was his métier. He served but a single term, and then returned to private life. His last political hurrah was campaigning for Grover Cleveland, though political rivals denied him his hope of being appointed Cleveland's secretary of war. McClellan died at age fifty-eight in 1887. His son, George B. McClellan Jr. ("Max"), took up the profession that should have been his father's, becoming a congressman from New York and then mayor of the Big Apple (1904-09). That bloodless field of conflict was McClellan's true home.

Part IV

★ ★ ★ ★ ★ ★ ★ ★

CALL IN THE CAVALRY

A CAVALRY QUARTET: WADE HAMPTON, PHIL SHERIDAN, J. E. B. STUART, AND GEORGE ARMSTRONG CUSTER

Wade Hampton (1818-1902)
"Charge them, my brave boys, charge them!"[1]

Guess What?

- ❧ Confederate cavalryman—and former slave owner—Wade Hampton fought segregation on Philadelphia railroad cars

- ❧ Phil Sheridan loathed Texans, Southerners in general, and the idea that enemy civilians (or at least their property) weren't a legitimate military target

- ❧ The war caused Jeb Stuart to change his son's name

- ❧ During the war, Custer, a Union officer, stood as best man for a Southern officer getting married on a Virginia plantation

Wade Hampton was to the manor born. One of the largest landholders in the South, educated in the Southern gentlemanly tradition, skilled with guns and horses, courtly with women, experienced in politics, one would expect that he was cut from the same scarlet cloak as the dashing cavalryman he served under, J. E. B. (Jeb) Stuart. But that would be wrong.

Part of it was simply age. Stuart was still in his twenties when the war began; Hampton was a twice married, once widowed, forty-three-year-old man, with six children, one of whom he had had to bury eighteen months after his first wife died. (Two more children would be born to him in the course of the war.) He was neither a West Pointer nor a professional cavalry officer, but Hampton seemed more the mature, sober statesman—and even soldier—than the cavalier Stuart.

And there was another difference: Stuart and his favorites were Virginians—and this, in the mind of Stuart and many other Southerners (especially Virginians) meant a great deal. A Virginia cavalier was several cuts above anyone else, no matter how aristocratic his origins, no matter how wealthy or distinguished he might be. If one wanted proof that states' rights was more than a political slogan—that it was a lived reality—one need look no further than the fierce attachment, loyalty, and pride of Virginians to their native soil, and to the culture that they associated with it.

South Carolina, of course, felt the same way, and Wade Hampton (actually Wade Hampton III) was a member of its ruling class. He was not only a planter, he was the inheritor of a military and political tradition. His grandfather Wade Hampton had fought Cherokees (who had murdered his family), been an officer of dragoons in the American War of Independence, a brigadier general in the War of 1812, and an enormously successful planter, in addition to serving in the state legislature and the U.S. House of Representatives. His father, Colonel Wade Hampton, had been a cavalryman, a military aide to Andrew Jackson, and a man of expansive generosity (and, as it turned out, an expansive capacity for debt, which his son would have to straighten out). He married well, to Ann Fitzsimmons, whose brother served as governor and U.S. senator from South Carolina.

Wade Hampton III was a worthy scion of this dynasty. He was big, strong, tall, and active, and keen on hunting, fishing, and riding. Quiet, good-tempered, well-mannered (he was opposed to dueling, though proficient with guns), upright, schooled as a lawyer but working always on his estates, he was a reluctant (yet *noblesse oblige*) politician, serving in the state assembly and senate before the war, where he was a voice of moderation, counseling against secession (as had his father and grandfather) and opposed to reopening the slave trade. He was, at the same time, an owner of several thousand slaves.

Hampton on John Brown, Murderer of the Union

"I have not, sir, heretofore apprehended a dissolution of the Union—I have always desired its preservation.... But—I say this with deep conviction of its truth, though with profound regret—unless an entire revolution of public sentiment takes place at the North—unless that spirit of hostility towards us, that seems to have spread like some dread pestilence through-out their land, is rebuked, and speedily and effectually by the good and true men of the North...unless that religion which preaches rapine and murder is superseded...I do not see how the Union *can be* or *should be* preserved."

Wade Hampton, speaking in the South Carolina Senate after the Northern abolitionists championed John Brown as a martyr

Quoted in Walter Brian Cisco, *Wade Hampton: Confederate Warrior, Conservative Statesman* (Brassey's Inc, 2004), 49.

Hampton was one of that tribe of Southern planters who, though uneasy about slavery, saw no way round it save an obligation to be a good master, which meant treating his slaves with all Christian charity, not separating their families, caring for them when they were sick (with the same doctors that treated his own family), and showing them that he valued their work. He was, however, certainly no abolitionist. Abolitionists, in his mind (and in the minds of many others, not just in the South), were dangerous and ignorant extremists who knew nothing of the reality of Southern slavery and threatened the Union with their agitation. They were "trampling the Constitution and the Bible alike under their feet," while they "impiously appeal to a *higher law* than is found in either, to sanction their enormities."[2]

All in all, Hampton was a high-minded, middle-aged man of position and responsibility, a conservative who believed in temperance, prudence, caution, and duty. When war came, he saw his duty clearly enough. His properties spread over South Carolina and Mississippi. He was a Southerner, and he would stand by his people. He knew that men of his estate raised regiments of their own and offered them to the governor. He did the same, though in his case he modeled his military muster upon that of the ancient Romans, creating Hampton's Legion, which he recruited and fitted out with a gubernatorial agreement that he and the state would share some of the expenses. He imported artillery pieces and Enfield rifles from England, and planned to distribute them among one company of artillery, six companies of infantry, and four of cavalry. With Southern gallantry, he told the governor that he was willing himself to enlist, if he was unworthy of a commission. The governor dismissed that with a stuff and poppycock and commissioned him a colonel. Now the colonel was the commander of a legion of a thousand men. Riding at the head of his legion, leaving behind his estates and their several thousand slaves, his was a thoroughly classical beginning.

Hampton's Legion saw action at First Manassas, where the Legion stood, like Jackson's men, as a stone wall repelling the fierce Union assault that nearly surrounded it. Hampton had one horse killed beneath him by an artillery shell, but kept his men in good order, maintaining a steady stream of well-directed fire. Leading by example, he picked up a rifle and fired his own volleys at the Yankees. Hit by shrapnel in the face, temporarily blinded by blood, he continued to issue orders until he was convinced to turn over command. His performance on the field won the praise not only of General P. G. T. Beauregard but of Jefferson Davis, who visited the wounded warrior to offer his personal thanks and congratulations for a battle well fought.

Hampton was made a brigadier general in May 1862, and his legion served everywhere from Dumfries, were it was to harass Yankee movements, commercial and military, on the Potomac and Occoquan Rivers; to the Peninsula, where it covered Joseph E. Johnston's retreat and smacked the pursuing Federals at Eltham's Landing along the York River; to the defense of Richmond, where, at the Battle of Fair Oaks/Seven Pines, Hampton gave the memorable order to his men, not to fire "until you can feel the enemy on your bayonets."[3] What Hampton soon felt was a Minié ball in his boot, which regimental doctors operated on while he remained in the saddle directing his men in the fight. The wound left Hampton with a permanent limp and brought him new orders.

He returned from his convalescing to find the army reorganized, his legion broken up, and he assigned first as a brigadier under Stonewall Jackson's command and then as a brigade commander of cavalry under the newly elevated Major General Jeb Stuart.

Riding with Stuart

In some ways, Stuart and Hampton complimented each other. Hampton admired the keen, tactical soldier and inspirational leader that Stuart could be, while privately deprecating Stuart's fondness for conducting the Confederate equivalent of a medieval court full of gaiety, pomp, display, and flirtation.

Most of all, he detested what he saw as blatant favoritism of the Virginian Stuart for his fellow Virginians. Stuart's cavalry was divided into two brigades, the other commanded by Brigadier General Fitzhugh Lee, Robert E. Lee's nephew. This, the Second Brigade—Stuart had originally designated it the First Brigade until Robert E. Lee reminded him that Hampton was the senior brigadier—was composed entirely of Virginia cavalry. Hampton's brigade was made up almost entirely of units from the lower South. William Henry "Rooney" Lee (Robert E. Lee's son) would eventually get a brigade as well, and Hampton certainly liked him better than Fitzhugh Lee whom he regarded as an arrogant git, and just the sort of man Stuart would favor because he was a Virginian.

Hampton never shook the conviction that as long as Stuart held command, his non-Virginian troopers would be given the hardest assignments and the least consideration. Not only were his men the dray horses of the cavalry, but Hampton felt that he needed to be the responsible counterpoint to his cavalier commander. Typical of their relationship was an incident during the Confederate advance into Maryland in early September 1862. It was Hampton who stood by with his men at the pickets and skirmished with the Federals, while Stuart danced with the cream of Confederate society in Urbana, Maryland, at an impromptu ball (music furnished by the regimental band). Though, to his credit, the Virginia cavalier was quick into action once aware of the Yankee intrusion.

John Esten Cooke, who wrote a book about serving with Jeb Stuart, penned an encomium to the South Carolinian general who never uttered an oath, he said, could never be flustered, and was always a paragon of courage, composure, leadership, and paternalism to his men. "It was plain," he wrote of Hampton, "that he thought nothing of personal decorations or military show, and never dreamed of 'producing an impression' upon any one.... After being in his presence for ten minutes, you saw that he was a man for hard work, and not for display."[4]

Dances aside, Hampton's men saw plenty of action in the Maryland campaign. They fought in cavalry charges and stand up fights, and in Stuart's Chambersburg raid that resulted in another merry—and to the Federals, embarrassing—circumnavigation of McClellan's army, which helped convince President Lincoln that McClellan was not only hapless but dispensable.

Stuart celebrated his success with more dances and romantic rendezvous. Hampton went back to watch with the pickets, and launched his own cavalry raids, proving that Stuart was not the only Confederate commander who could bedevil the Yankees.

But while the Confederate cavalry were getting worn down from hard service, the Yankees were getting stronger, with fresh mounts, more experience, and more men. At the battle of Brandy Station, 9 June 1863, the biggest cavalry battle of the war, Federal cavalry under the command of John Buford caught Stuart's men napping. The Confederates quickly regained their balance, and counterattacked effectively enough to hold their ground. Hampton, fighting with saber and pistol, killed his share of the enemy. But falling, too, was his brother Frank, who, like Horatius at the bridge, had tried to block the advance of an entire Union division with no more than three dozen men.

Frank Hampton had been gut shot, and his handsome head split by saber blows. That was the reality of close-quarters cavalry combat, which could be very personal. During the Gettysburg campaign, on 2 July 1863, Wade Hampton fought the battlefield equivalent of a duel: riding out to trade shots—officer's pistol versus private's carbine—with a Union soldier. They fought by the Marquis of Queensberry's Rules, with Hampton pausing when the bluecoat's gun misfired and needed ramming out. Hampton won the duel, wounding the Yankee through the wrist, but a Union cavalry officer then burst out of the woods and brought a saber crashing down on Hampton's head. The South Carolinian kept his wits and chased his attacker off, but now bore a four inch head wound—and it would get worse.

After getting his head patched, he confronted the Sixth Michigan of twenty-three-year-old brigadier general (just promoted from lieutenant) George Armstrong Custer in a sharp skirmish. They met again the next day, in a larger engagement, a thundering blue versus thundering grey collision of cavalry, a giant melee of men and horses, clashing sabers and avenging pistols. Blasting and bashing his way forward, Hampton was blindsided by Union reinforcements, one of whom charged behind him and struck two more cleaving blows to his skull (one merely reopened the existing wound). As the Confederates turned about, they had to charge through a field of Yankee artillery and rifle fire. Taking his horse leaping over a fence, Hampton's hip was smashed by searing shrapnel. But he kept his head—and his saddled leg, at least for now—and survived.

"General Hampton Cannot Be Spared"

Meanwhile, the cavalry of the Army of Northern Virginia was expanded from a division into a corps. Jeb Stuart remained a major general, but joining him at that rank were Wade Hampton and Fitzhugh Lee, with Hampton retaining his seniority over the latter, so that when Stuart was killed at Yellow Tavern (11 May 1864), command fell to Hampton—or it did eventually. At first Lee, who had mixed feelings about Hampton, gave the South Carolinian not command over the entire corps but only seniority over the cavalry divisions when they operated together. Lee had no doubts about Hampton's gallantry. He had praised him highly and repeatedly denied efforts to have him transferred out of the Army of Northern Virginia ("General Hampton cannot be spared"[5]). But for all his youth and rashness, Lee had liked and trusted Stuart. He was not yet sure if Hampton had the capacity and *élan* for corps command of the cavalry of the Army of Northern Virginia. It took three months, and a few battles, to convince Lee that Hampton was the man.

Hampton on Leadership

"You must not believe a word about my being 'reckless.' I am the personification of discretion. But to make men fight well the officers must *lead*."

Quoted in Walter Brian Cisco, *Wade Hampton: Confederate Warrior, Conservative Statesman*, (Brassey's Inc., 2004), 72.

The first was the Battle of Haw's Shop, fought 28 May 1864, where Hampton's men fought an old man's way, dismounted and relying on marksmanship rather than on an impetuous charge; and it seemed to work. Hampton discharged his mission (which was finding the dispositions of the Union infantry) and fought his men well before withdrawing them safely from a Union line that was being reinforced by General Custer.

At Trevilian Station, on 11 June 1864, he pursued and caught Phil Sheridan (and Custer). Asked what he proposed to do now that he had the Yankees in sight, he replied: "I propose to fight!"[6] And his proposal was to fight in his style—what he came to call "riding infantry": dismounted troopers, scattered through the woods and other cover, though the battle turned on a charge of the Sixth Carolina Cavalry (which included cadets from what is now the Citadel) led by Hampton. Hampton could not prevent Sheridan, the next day, from ripping up Southern railroad tracks, but he had, in the second biggest cavalry battle of the war, held the field against the Yankees and proven his mettle, yet again, as a combat commander.

It also highlighted something else about Hampton—he was adept at raiding raiders. He had done this before, on 1 March 1864, ambushing a column of Federal cavalry, under Colonel Judson Kilpatrick (a frequent Hampton nemesis), who had orders to raid Richmond. Instead, the raiders became the raided. He did it again at the end of June 1864, when he captured one hundred Yankee raiders who were fleeing—across Hampton's headquarters as it turned out—from charging Confederate cavalry. (Hampton rode down with his orderlies, pistols drawn, to order and accept the Federals' surrender.) Such performances won him his official promotion to corps commander. And he kept himself in Lee's good graces with raids of his own, including his famous "Beefsteak Raid" in September 1864 that relieved the Federals of nearly 2,500 head of cattle.

Hampton's men participated in the defense of Petersburg, where on 27 October 1864, Hampton's second son, Thomas Preston, a young but already twice-wounded staff officer, impulsively joined a cavalry charge. Hampton sent his eldest son, Wade IV, charging after him to bring him back. Hampton and his staff followed. They arrived just as Preston fell from his horse, mortally wounded. As they gathered around him, Wade IV was hit. Hampton cradled Preston while he died. Wade IV, hit in the back, would pull through. Hampton mourned only a moment and then returned to directing the battle. But there would be a new grit in his opposition to the Yankees—a grit made only more unappeasable by the destruction of his homes in South Carolina and what he saw as the barbarous Yankee way of war.

In January 1865, Lee endorsed Hampton's transfer to South Carolina to defend his native state from the depredations of William Tecumseh Sherman. Jefferson Davis approved and promoted Hampton to lieutenant general. That made him the highest ranking Confederate cavalry officer in the war. The other cavalry officer to reach lieutenant general was Bedford Forrest, but Hampton held pride of place through seniority.

Hampton refused to give in to counsels of despair. He continually insisted, argued, and acted on the conviction that Sherman could be stopped and that the Confederate States of America could still preserve their independence from the United States. He was, of course, wrong. But he was so committed to the cause that not only did he refuse to believe the first reports of Lee's surrender, but he resolved that even if that were the case, and even if his new commander in North Carolina, Joseph E. Johnston, surrendered, he would ride west and continue the struggle from Texas. He would even, failing that, go to Mexico and fight for the Emperor Maximilian, or so a group of Union officers heard him say during Johnston's surrender.

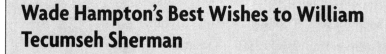

Wade Hampton's Best Wishes to William Tecumseh Sherman

"From my heart I wish that every old man and boy in my country who can fire a gun would shoot down, as he would a wild beast, the men who are desolating their land, burning their homes, and insulting their women."

Quoted in Edward G. Longacre, *Gentleman and Soldier: The Extraordinary Life of Wade Hampton* (Rutledge Hill Press, 2003), 230.

In the end, Hampton did no such thing, but reconciled himself to trying to restoring his family's fortunes in South Carolina and Mississippi. He had land, but it was burnt out. His possessions had been robbed from him. The slaves were gone, save for a few who remained to work for Hampton. He had money, but only in Confederate script, now worthless. His homes were cinders. But he bent his back to the task, building a house and plowing the fields, planting them not with cotton or tobacco, but with crops that would feed his family and the former slaves. When creditors called in his debts in 1868, the only way he could begin meet his obligations was to auction his properties.

Hampton the Politician

One aspect of his life that he did not have to restore was his status as a political leader in South Carolina, even though as a Confederate general, he was barred from political life: "Disenfranchised, an unpardonable and unrepentant rebel, I live solely to try to help my State, and failing that, to suffer with her."[7]

> ### Wade Hampton—Die Hard
>
> "My own mind is made up. As to my course I shall fight as long as my government remains in existence, for I shall never take the 'oath of allegiance.' I am sorry that we paused to negotiate, for to my apprehension, no evil can equal that of a return to the Union."
>
> Quoted in Edward G. Longacre, *Gentleman and Soldier: The Extraordinary Life of Wade Hampton*, 243.

When South Carolinians debated the adoption of a new state constitution that would be acceptable to the Reconstruction authorities, Hampton roared against the very thought: "Are the people of the State, willing, by the adoption of a new and totally different constitution, to ignore all the teachings of the past, to subvert the whole order of society, to change, in a moment, its whole organization, and, in a word, to commit political suicide?" Or, in other words, to create a "constitution representing not the views and interests of the people of South Carolina, but of Mass[achusetts]."[8]

The population of South Carolina—like the population of Alabama, Florida, Louisiana, and Mississippi—was predominantly black. One man, one vote in South Carolina—especially minus the votes of former senior Confederate officers, politicians, and prominent landowners—meant a revolution in the politics of the state, if the black vote was led (as Hampton came to fear it would be) by white carpetbaggers and scalawags rather than by the planter class (his original hope). Nevertheless, Hampton sought a moderate course: he accepted emancipation and the awarding of civil rights to blacks, but argued that such civil rights be restored to former Confederates, that the Southern states not be treated as conquered vassal states of the North, and that all voters meet education and property qualifications.

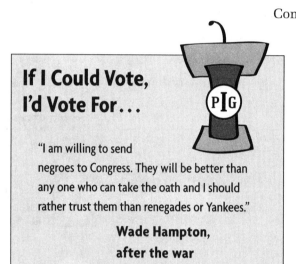

If I Could Vote, I'd Vote For...

"I am willing to send negroes to Congress. They will be better than any one who can take the oath and I should rather trust them than renegades or Yankees."

Wade Hampton, after the war

Quoted in Walter Brian Cisco, *Wade Hampton: Confederate Warrior, Conservative Statesman*, 188.

In 1868, in a Republican landslide (even with voting rights returned to former Confederates), South Carolina became the first state to elect a black majority legislature. Led by white carpetbagging politicians, it also became notorious for graft and corruption. Hampton could bemoan his state's fate, but his personal situation preoccupied him just as much. He tried various business ventures, which failed, considered but eventually declined the idea of serving as a mercenary officer in the Egyptian cavalry, and finally subsisted by renting land to black farmers on the part of his former Mississippi estate that his creditors had allowed him to keep. He had buried another child and his second wife. Hampton's fortunes really did seem to have gone with the wind.

But in 1876, in a heated, occasionally violent, and contested election (contested, indeed, for five months after the fact, with two sitting legislatures, each proclaiming itself authentic) Hampton became governor, though his opponent vacated the governor's office only after the contested *presidential* election was resolved in favor of Republican Rutherford B. Hayes, who agreed to end the military occupation of the Southern states. Hampton's platform was, typically, one of moderation and racial reconciliation, but his most strident supporters where the "red shirts" whose clothing proclaimed their loyalty and whose violence confirmed it. They were led by a former Confederate officer named Martin Gary, whom Hampton always regarded with distaste.

Gary quickly became a political enemy, but he could not match Hampton's popularity. Hampton was elected almost unanimously to a second term, which he didn't serve because the state legislature immediately elected him to the United States Senate (the very day he had a leg amputated because of a hunting accident). Hampton's cautious, responsible, paternalistic conservatism represented that of his class. But by the end of

Black and White in Philadelphia

When a Philadelphia ticket master told Wade Hampton that his two black servants could not ride in his car with him, because Pennsylvanians "did not like to ride with negroes," Hampton erupted that "one of them is the nurse of my children" and that "I thought them good enough to ride with me, and therefore quite good enough to ride with his fellow-citizens, and that they should get into my car. So I brought them there and kept them there."*

* Quoted in Edward G. Longacre, *Gentleman and Soldier: The Extraordinary Life of Wade Hampton*, 186.

Hampton's second Senate term, a new political revolution had roiled South Carolina. The "Bourbons," the old political aristocracy, had been annihilated by Martin Gary's successor "Pitchfork Ben" Tillman. Proclaiming an openly racist, anti-aristocratic, populist platform, he worked to undo all the good work Hampton had done, and successfully denied Hampton a third term. The former cavalryman was stunned—"I never expected to see my friends bolt for Tillman"[9]—but he had continued to suffer many personal losses over the years: the death of friends and family and, at the end of his days, even the loss of his humble home and all his possessions in a fire.

He finished his working life in Democrat Grover Cleveland's administration as commissioner of railroads. When the Republican William McKinley was elected president, the job went to former Confederate and current Republican James Longstreet. Hampton then retired to South Carolina. He had served his state all his life and he had lost almost everything he ever possessed, save honor. His last words were a fitting epitaph for a man who gave all he could for the Palmetto State: "God bless all my people, black and white."[10]

Wade Hampton: Patriot

"If we were wrong in our contest [for Southern Independence], then the Declaration of Independence was a grave mistake, and the revolution to which it led was a crime....If Washington was a patriot, Lee cannot have been a rebel; if the enunciation of the grand truths in the Declaration of Independence made Jefferson immortal, the observance of them could not have made Davis a traitor."

Quoted in Walter Brian Cisco, *Wade Hampton: Confederate Warrior, Conservative Statesman*, 319.

Philip Sheridan (1831-1888)
"The only good Indians I ever saw were dead."[11]

In physique Sheridan was shaped like the Fighting Irish leprechaun of Notre Dame. He was only five feet five inches tall, mostly body with scant legs, long arms attached to ready fists, and slit eyes that burned defiance. Abraham Lincoln described Sheridan as "a brown, chunky little chap, with a long body, short legs, not enough neck to hang him, and such long arms that if his ankles itch he can scratch them without stooping."[12]

Sheridan was never put off by the size of an opponent. During the war, he once took a dislike to the "saucy and impertinent manner" of a brawny, six-foot-tall train conductor. He handled things the Sheridan way. He thrashed him with his fists, threw him off the train, and then returned to his conversation with General George Thomas.

Sheridan was the son of an Irish immigrant, a road laborer, and he never harkened after anything softer than a soldier's life. It was soldiering that determined nearly everything about him: his loyalties and prejudices, his sense of duty and honor, his ideas of justice and order. He was a soldier's soldier of a certain type: demanding, hard-swearing, but also one who burned the midnight oil to make sure his troops were adequately provisioned (he had been trained as a quartermaster) and with battle plans adequately laid. No officer was more diligent in gathering intelligence about topography and troop movements. And he was tough. Grant liked him for the same reason Lincoln liked Grant: because he was willing to fight. Like Bedford Forrest, he knew that war means fighting and fighting means killing; he once told a Federal officer, "Go in, sir, and get some of your men killed."[13] It wouldn't do to hang about when it was battles and fighting that won wars.

He grew up in the small town of Somerset, Ohio, took the usual smattering of small town education enlivened by small town boyish truancies and became a store clerk and bookkeeper—but one with ambitions to win a congressional appointment to the United States Military Academy. He succeeded when Congressman Thomas Ritchey's previous candidate flunked out. It was a pretty turn of events for a store clerk who had only happened to make the acquaintance of the congressman as a customer. As Lana Turner was discovered at Schwab's Drug Store, so Phil Sheridan was discovered behind the counter of Finck & Dittoes. It can be argued who had the finer career.

He crammed for the entrance exam, and kept cramming to keep up his grades, and found it impossible to refrain from fighting with his fellow cadets, (which resulted in a year-long expulsion). Nevertheless he graduated, albeit a year behind, and with a nice record in demerits, and was posted where such young men were sent—as an infantry officer on the

★ ★ ★ ★ ★

Disrespect for a Senior Officer?

When Sheridan graduated from West Point, the superintendent of the Academy was Robert E. Lee, whose army Sheridan would hound at the end of the war. Sheridan never had any time for Southern gentlemen; he was untroubled by such manners himself.

Texas frontier, where he hunted, socialized with Mexican families (developing sympathies that would be important later), and had occasional scrapes with Indians. He followed up this useful experience with similar scrapes with Indians in the Pacific Northwest, one of whom sent a bullet brushing across his nose, exploding into the neck of the orderly beside him. But he also acted as a sort of colonial administrator to the tribes that fell in his purview—not only punishing them when they applied war paint, but attempting to rid them of superstitions and to enforce the white man's law (against murder, among other things). The justice might have been of a frontier variety, but though short and Irish, Sheridan had most assuredly taken up the white man's burden, as well as an Indian mistress.

Sheridan, the Quartermaster and Fighting General

When the Union divided, Sheridan won swift promotion. His first major task took him not to blood-drenched battlefields, but to the disorderly red-ink accounts of General John C. Frémont's quartermaster. Frémont's chaotic administration of Missouri—full of pomp and abolitionist circumstance, but rather lacking in practical aptitude, except for the graft of his quartermaster—led to the quartermaster's court-martial. Sheridan was drafted by General Henry Halleck to help make sense of the financial misdeeds and audit the accounts. Using the keen eye of a professional clerk and bookkeeper, he executed his duties with dispatch.

It's likely that few people who think of Sheridan think of him wearing green eye-shades, but it was a fitting way for him to enter the war. For him, there were no great political issues involved. He cared neither for abolitionism or states' rights or any of the other arguments roiling the political waters of the Republic. He was an Irish immigrant's son. America had been good to him, the army had been good to him, he followed his orders, and just as books had to balanced, rebels had to be punished, and there was no need for any gasconading—or sentimentality—about it. He did say to a group of friends, family, and well-wishers, "This country is too great and good to be destroyed."[14] But that was about the extent of his politics.

Henry Halleck was enamored of Sheridan's wizardry with accounts, and soon posted him a commissary officer. Sheridan, however, convinced Halleck that he should also be chief quartermaster for the Army of Southwest Missouri, and so it was done. Sheridan took the same practicality that he had employed analyzing accounts to the more vigorous task of expropriating the property of Southern-sympathizing civilians for the use of the army. He would not, however, unlike Frémont's quartermaster, condone thievery that cost the U.S. Treasury. Sheridan condemned soldiers who stole farmer's horses, then sold them to the army, as simple thieves who would not be tolerated, even as he was pressured to tolerate them by a superior officer.

Sheridan was an excellent quartermaster, but as an experienced Indian-fighter he was itching to get his licks in against the Johnny Rebs. He got his chance. In May 1862, he was commissioned a colonel of the Michigan cavalry, and only days later was involved in the first major raid by Union cavalry, ripping up railroad ties in Mississippi and bending them into the sort of bowties that Sherman and Sheridan considered their contribution to dressing up the Southern countryside. As Sheridan had impressed Halleck in accounting, so did Sheridan impress the likes of General William Rosecrans who saw in Sheridan an aggressive officer who was an excellent scout, with a sound analysis of topography and intelligence, and most of all a desire and a talent for fighting.

One of Sheridan's tutors in command was General Gordon Granger. Confronted by Confederate guerillas, Granger once expostulated: "We must push every man, woman, and child before us or put every man to death found in our lines. We have in fact soon to come to a war of subjugation, and the sooner the better."[15] Sheridan had no qualms fighting such a war. By September 1862, he was promoted brigadier general.

A month later, Sheridan fought in the biggest and bloodiest battle ever fought on Kentuckian soil, the Battle of Perryville. The Confederates under the ever-lamentable leadership of Braxton Bragg, suffered more than 3,000 casualties, the Federals more than 4,000. The stakes were high. In Lincoln's famous words: "I hope to have God on my side, but I must have Kentucky. I think to lose Kentucky is nearly the same as losing the whole game."[16] Luckily for the Union, Braxton Bragg was master at losing entire games. In this case, he won a tactical victory on the battlefield, which he turned into a strategic defeat by vacating Kentucky to the Union. Sheridan acquitted himself well, though he was not involved in the major part of the action. Blessed with the high ground and a manpower advantage of four to one, he thrashed the grey coats before him. But at the end of the battle both armies felt they had lost, because neither pursued their gains.

Sheridan closed 1862, with another battlefield triumph at Murfrees-boro, Tennessee, where his troops thwarted the initial Confederate

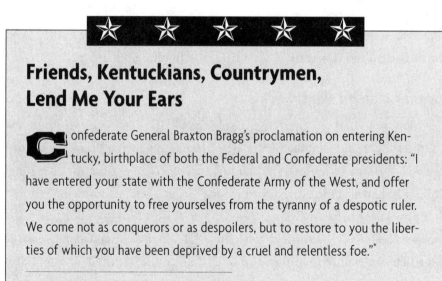

Friends, Kentuckians, Countrymen, Lend Me Your Ears

Confederate General Braxton Bragg's proclamation on entering Kentucky, birthplace of both the Federal and Confederate presidents: "I have entered your state with the Confederate Army of the West, and offer you the opportunity to free yourselves from the tyranny of a despotic ruler. We come not as conquerors or as despoilers, but to restore to you the liberties of which you have been deprived by a cruel and relentless foe."*

* Quoted in Roy Morris, Jr., *Sheridan: The Life & Wars of Phil Sheridan* (Vintage Civil War Library, 1993), 83.

advance, and then under extreme pressure (his men ran out of ammunition and suffered 40 percent casualties) performed a gritty fighting withdrawal. A brigadier general said of Sheridan's conduct that "I knew it was hell when I saw Phil Sheridan, with hat in one hand and sword in the other, fighting as if he were the devil incarnate." A devil, perhaps, but a calm one too, as he lit and puffed on a cheroot during the fight. When he emerged from the battle, he told General Rosecrans, "Here we are, all that are left of us."[17] General Grant credited Sheridan's tenacity with saving Rosecrans's army and making possible the Union victory. Sheridan's service was recognized the following spring, when he was elevated to major general at the age of thirty-two.

He fought at Chickamauga and Chattanooga: in the former, having to extricate his men in another fighting withdrawal (but unlike Rosecrans he didn't flee from the field) and in the latter he was one of the leaders of the massive blue surge up Missionary Ridge. Resting under the sight of the enemy, he lifted a flask to the Confederates above, saying "Here's to you!" The response was an explosion that splashed his face with dirt. "That is ungenerous," he shouted "I shall take those guns for that!"[18] And he did—and led the Yankee pursuit of the fleeing Southerners.

Grant's Man on Horseback

Grant, who had watched Sheridan's charge up Missionary Ridge, knew "Little Phil" to be another fighter who wanted always to press the enemy. He was the sort of man Grant wanted as he took over operations against Robert E. Lee and the Army of Northern Virginia. When someone pointed out how short he was, Grant replied, "You'll find him big enough for the purpose before we get through with him."[19] Likewise, when General George Meade told Grant of Sheridan's boast that he could "thrash hell out of Stuart any day," Grant responded, "Did Sheridan say that? Well, he generally knows what he's talking about. Let him start right out and do it."[20]

Sheridan performed poorly for the irascible General George Meade. Scouting and screening for the Army of the Potomac were not duties fit for Sheridan's talents, or so he thought. What he wanted to do was raid the enemy, and Grant supported him, giving him an independent command that allowed him to chase down Jeb Stuart, bring him to battle, and kill him—which gave Sheridan an ungallant pleasure. There was much about Sheridan's way of war—the Union way of war—that was ungallant. Most famous, in this category, was Sheridan's destruction of the farms of the Shenandoah Valley, an act of rapine that Virginians knew as "the burning."

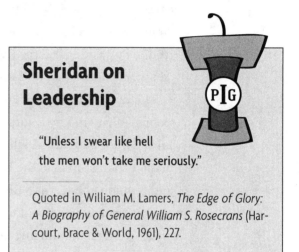

Sheridan on Leadership

"Unless I swear like hell the men won't take me seriously."

Quoted in William M. Lamers, *The Edge of Glory: A Biography of General William S. Rosecrans* (Harcourt, Brace & World, 1961), 227.

Sheridan took the view that the prospect of Southern independence was so outrageous that not only must the South be subjugated by war, but Southern civilians must be punished for desiring a country of their own and for defending their homes from invading armies. This attitude would, incidentally, make him a top notch enforcer of martial law during Reconstruction, during which time he sided with the Radical Republicans.

Grant's famous order that he wanted the Shenandoah Valley made a "desert," that all its livestock and food should be confiscated or destroyed, that all its people should be displaced, "so that crows flying over it for the balance of the season will have to carry their provender with them"[21] was in perfect accord with Sheridan's own views; and it fell to him to expand the Union program of devastation of the Valley that had already begun. Grant told him, "If the war is to last another year, we want the Shenandoah Valley to remain a barren waste."[22]

There were real battles along the way (like the battle for Winchester on 18 September 1864, which claimed the life of Confederate Colonel George S. Patton, grandfather of the World War II general), but the campaign quickly took on an ugly patina. Not content with waging war on civilians, Sheridan's men treated, as a matter of policy, endorsed by General Grant, Confederate cavalryman John S. Mosby's rangers not as soldiers but as "ruffians" and "murderers" who could be executed without trial—even as Sheridan organized his own ranger force (which sometimes operated under the guise of captured Confederate uniforms, and was notorious for its thievery).

The one bit of legitimate glory for Sheridan was when he rallied his troops—shattered by a surprise attack launched by the Valley's defender, Jubal Early—and turned what would have been a deeply embarrassing rout of the Federal forces at the Battle of Cedar Creek (19 October 1864) into an annihilation of Early as a threat to the Federal army. At one point a fleeing Yankee colonel yelled out to Sheridan, "The army is whipped," only to be put down with the stinging reply, "You are, but the army isn't,"[23] as the general stormed past on his mount Rienzi. Sheridan also showed courage and dash—though Lee's army was broken at this point—when he led the Union charge that won the battle of Five Forks (1 April 1865), where he led Rienzi

Phil Sheridan, Humanitarian

"I do not believe war to be simply that lines should engage each other in battle, and therefore do not regret the system of living on the enemy's country. These men or women [or children] did not care how many were killed, or maimed, so long as war did not come to their doors, but as soon as it did come in the shape of loss of property, they earnestly prayed for its termination. As war is a punishment, if we can, by reducing it advocates to poverty, end it quicker, we are on the side of humanity."

Quoted in Roy Morris, Jr., *Sheridan: The Life & Wars of Phil Sheridan*, 179.

leaping over the Confederate defenses and in amongst the battered men in butternut and grey, who surrendered to the sharp little general.

But for a man who allegedly wanted to bring the war to an early conclusion—in the interests of "humanity"—Sheridan's reaction to news that Lee was surrendering was distinctly odd, though distinctly in character: "Damn them, I wish they had held out an hour longer and I would have whipped hell out of them."[24] If denied that pleasure, he did join in with other Federal officers in ripping up the belongings of Wilmer McLean, in whose Appomattox home the surrender took place, to make off with souvenirs. Sheridan bought the table where the surrender had been signed and then, as a *beau geste*, gave it to the boy general, and Sheridan favorite, George Armstrong Custer as a present for Custer's wife.

Phil Sheridan's Maxim of War: The Only Good Confederate Is an Impoverished Confederate

"Death is popularly considered to be the maximum of punishment in war, but it is not; reduction to poverty brings prayers for peace more surely and more quickly than does the destruction of human life."

Quoted in Richard O'Connor, *Sheridan the Inevitable* (Bobbs-Merrill Company, 1953), 197.

Post-War Pugilist

Sheridan ended the war as one of three burly musketeers—Sheridan, Sherman, and Grant—who had done more than any other generals to win the war for the Union, and had done so by waging war with a brutality that would make them notorious in the South for generations. To Sherman, Sheridan was "a persevering terrier dog." To Grant, Sheridan had "no superior as a general, either living or dead, and perhaps not an equal."[25] They succeeded each other as the top general of the postwar United States Army—Grant, Sherman, and Sheridan—and to Sheridan (under Sherman's watch) goes the credit for creating a postgraduate college for officers (at Fort Leavenworth).

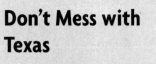

Don't Mess with Texas

"If I owned hell and Texas, I would rent out Texas and live in hell."

General Philip Sheridan.

Quoted in Roy Morris, Jr., *Sheridan: The Life & Wars of Phil Sheridan*, 280.

Sheridan did not mellow after the war. Fully backed by Grant, he governed Texas and Louisiana as a martinet. He deposed governors and mayors and others as he saw fit, openly despised Southerners, Texans in particular, and sided with Republicans, freed blacks, and carpetbaggers in every dispute. Despite his later reputation as an Indian exterminator, Sheridan also showed a marked preference for putting the political screws to Texans rather than protecting them from Indian raids, which he dismissed as a distraction.

His real distraction, however, was Mexico where he and General Grant (the general who thought our Mexican war was immoral) were ready and eager to intervene on the side of the Juaristas in their war against the French-supported government of the Austrian Archduke Maximilian. While American military adventurers plied both sides of the war, it is generally true that Southerners supported the Archduke (as cavaliers should) while Unionists supported the Mexican rabble. The Unionists won this war too, and Maximilian was eventually executed by a firing squad of ungrateful Mexicans.

Sheridan ended his career as he began it, as an Indian fighter, though now he was a lieutenant general rather than a shavetail. His strategy was that of the Shenandoah: he reduced the Indians less by fighting them in open battle (such battles were fought, but the Indians' hit and run tactics made them inconclusive) than by attacking the Indians in winter, when they did not expect paleface campaigns and were bedded down with their families and were vulnerable. In addition, he endorsed the free slaughter of the buffalo as a way to drive the Indians from the plains. A hunter himself, he was not entirely opposed to animals—he was instrumental, in fact, in creating Yellowstone National Park and ensuring that its wildlife was preserved—he just wanted to starve the Indians. Sheridan, who became rotund with age, well appreciated hunger as a military tool in driving one's enemy to submit.

The Indians, of course, were not entirely innocent or undeserving of Sheridan's wrath. There were Indian outrages aplenty—scalpings and mutilations and murders and rapes and raids (sometimes committed with rifles given to them by the government as peace offerings), that sickened Sheridan and fully justified in his own mind the harshest retribution, though that retribution was not always directed at the proper tribes or groups of savages. And Sheridan had lost friends to the Indians—most spectacularly, in the disaster at Little Big Horn in 1876, where his "brave boy" George Armstrong Custer met his fate.

Sheridan's ultimate fate was more pleasant. A bachelor for his first forty-four years, he broke his fast from the opposite sex by marrying a woman half his age, Irene Rucker, whose military family (her father was a colonel and assistant quartermaster of the army), had trained her well for life with Sheridan. This last great conquest brought him four children, three girls and a son who became a military aide to Theodore Roosevelt

Sheridan's "Forerunners of Civilization": Buffalo Hunters and Cowboys

"Those men [buffalo hunters] have done more in the last two years and will do more in the next year to settle the Indian question than the entire regular army has done in the last thirty years. They are destroying the Indians' commissary; and it is a well known fact that an army losing its base of supplies is placed at a great disadvantage. Send them powder and lead if you will, and for the sake of peace let them kill, skin, and sell until they have exterminated the buffalo. Then your prairies will be covered with speckled cattle and the festive cowboy, who follows the hunter as a second forerunner of civilization."

General Philip Sheridan

Quoted in Richard O'Connor, *Sheridan the Inevitable*, 326.

but died, only thirty-seven years old, of a heart attack—the same malady that claimed his father at the age of fifty-seven.

J. E. B. Stuart (1833-1864)
"If you want to have a good time, jine the cavalry!"[26]

There's a special place in the Confederate pantheon for Jeb Stuart because he personified one of the archetypes of the South—the gay cavalier, who mocked danger, flirted with women, kept prayer book in hand, knew horseflesh, loved racing, and responded to the plink of a banjo. Stuart not only kept a banjo player with him throughout his campaigns, he actually stole the best banjo player in the Confederate army from another unit and claimed him as his own.[27]

Stuart was born James Ewell Brown Stuart in southwestern Virginia, the son of a lawyer and politician (and veteran of the War of 1812), whose father before him had commanded Virginians in the Battle of Guildford Court House during the American War for Independence. The Stuarts were Scotch-Irish Presbyterians who had achieved prominence in Virginia. His mother's family was equally distinguished, well-to-do, and noted for its political connections. His mother was as known for her piety as his father was noted for his charm. Stuart inherited both.

Educated in the usual Virginia fashion—with a smattering of the classics—he won an appointment to West Point, where he earned the mocking nickname "beauty." But the existing portraits we have of him—before his face was covered in a luxuriant cinnamon-colored beard—show a man of perfectly respectable looks. He had arresting blue eyes, a captivating voice, an easy manner, and a strong, athletic physique. Free spirit that he was, he enjoyed his time at West Point, earned the demerits to prove it, but did well enough to graduate thirteenth in his class academically (allegedly, he intentionally tried to lower his academic scores so that he would be assigned to the cavalry rather than the engineers, for he was already a horseman).

He served in Texas, with a unit of mounted riflemen, and was then one of the officers handpicked by Secretary of War Jefferson Davis for his elite 1st and 2nd Cavalry being organized in St. Louis. From there he was assigned to Fort Leavenworth, in the Kansas Territory, and met the daughter of another cavalry officer and Virginian, Colonel Philip St. George Cooke. Colonel Cooke's daughter Flora, a rather homely lass but a pious Episcopalian like Stuart's mother, was swept off her feet by the gallant cavalier. A bit bewildered by the suddenness of the thing, Colonel Cooke nevertheless assented to the couple's marriage in November 1855. Two years later Stuart became a father, and a little over a year later, he set his little daughter a good example by being confirmed in the Episcopal Church.

In Kansas, then torn by sectional rivalry, Stuart's cavalry was charged to keep the peace, and the young 1st Lieutenant got his first glimpse of John Brown, the abolitionist terrorist who thought of himself as leading a holy war against slavery. Stuart got his second glimpse three years later, through a crack in the door of the firehouse at Harpers Ferry where John Brown had barricaded himself, his band of would-be insurgents, and his captives. At Harpers Ferry, Stuart acted as an aide to Robert E. Lee, commander of the Marines dispatched to arrest Brown, (Lee had also been Stuart's superintendent at West Point).

Jeb Stuart: Southern Patriot

"I had rather be a private in Va.'s army than a general in any army to coerce her."

Quoted in Burke Davis, *Jeb Stuart: The Last Cavalier* (Burford Books, 1957), 47.

It wasn't only abolitionist rowdies who occupied Stuart in Kansas. He charged into action against the Cheyenne, one of whom shot Stuart in the chest at near point-blank range. It was a credit to Stuart's sturdy constitution that he was able to treat the wound as a mere bagatelle.

After the election of Abraham Lincoln, but before South Carolina's secession, Jeb Stuart wrote to Jefferson Davis (then serving as United States Senator from Mississippi) offering his services to any Southern army that might soon be formed. Stuart's loyalty was to Virginia above all else, but he could not imagine Virginia abandoning her fellow Southern states if secession led to war. Secession was inevitable, and war, he thought, was likely to follow. If it didn't, and if Virginia had no need for him in her officer corps, well then, he might just have to become a lawyer, a dread prospect.

The Happy Warrior

Lincoln's decision to wage war on the South spared Stuart the humiliation of having to trade his cavalry saber for a lawyer's shingle. He resigned a captain and was commissioned a lieutenant colonel of Virginia infantry, assigned to the command of Stonewall Jackson. Jackson transferred him to the cavalry, where Joseph E. Johnston promoted him to colonel. Stuart's dash—and efficiency—were apparent from the start. In one early engagement (Stuart was wearing a blue coat and his old U.S. Army cavalry pants), he found himself amidst dozens of Federals, began giving them imperious orders, and then told them to surrender. They did, assuming they were surrounded by unseen Confederates, and he led them away as prisoners of war.

To train his green cavalry, he would keep them in the saddle all hours, ride them into trouble (under fire, surrounded by the enemy), and then laugh and get them out again, always coolly, always daring danger. He looked for men who relished hard-riding, who thought cavalry work was "fun" ("You don't want to go back to camp, I know; it's stupid there, and all the fun is out here. I never go to camp if I can help it"[28]), and who shared his disdain for shell-fire (he even organized a special company, Company Q, eventually abolished, to drain off from his other units the lazy, malingering, cowardly, and dull—and anyone who didn't enjoy racing past whizzing bullets was certainly dull). As he instructed his troopers: "You are brave fellows, and patriotic ones too, but you are ignorant of this kind of work, and I am teaching you. I want you to observe that a good man on a good horse can never be caught. Another thing: cavalry can *trot* away from anything, and a gallop is unbecoming a soldier, unless he is going toward the enemy. Remember that. We gallop toward the enemy, and trot away, always."[29]

Stuart had a habit of finding himself amidst the enemy—and not always by intent. At First Manassas, when his men were ordered onto the field, he called out to the unit of Zouaves before him, "Don't run, boys. We're here!" only to realize that the troops bore the stars and stripes of the Union, and what started as a greeting became a cavalry charge. But

Stuart's Strategy

"If we oppose force to force we cannot win, for their resources are greater than ours. We must substitute *esprit* for numbers. Therefore I strive to inculcate in my men the spirit of the chase."

Quoted in Burke Davis, *Jeb Stuart: The Last Cavalier* (Burford Books, 1957), 51.

such was life in the cavalry—though life with Stuart's cavalry was far different from life with, say, Sheridan's.

With his plumed hat, scarlet cloak, thigh-high riding boots, courtly manners with women, love of fun, and affection for flowers (both giving them and receiving them as a conqueror's garlands), he was the Middle Ages come to life, which was no coincidence, as the South was enraptured by the books of Sir Walter Scott. The knightly ideal was not remote from Virginia cavaliers, but few took it as far as Stuart did. He gave his camps names like *Qui Vive* and *Quien Sabe*, and surrounded himself with the Southern equivalent of a medieval court that included a minstrel (or in this case a banjo plucker), a "fighting bishop" (the Reverend Major Dabney Ball), relations of the "King" (Robert E. Lee's son Rooney and nephew Fitzhugh), a foreign mercenary come to join the Round Table (the Prussian Giant, Heros

---

★ ★ ★ ★ ★

A Wartime Re-Christening

Jeb Stuart's young son, born in 1860, had been named after his maternal grandfather, Philip St. George Cooke. But Cooke, though a Virginian, had cast his lot with the Union. Stuart said of Cooke's decision, "He will regret it but once, and that will be continuously." But it also meant that Jeb's son needed a new name, for the name of a traitor to his native state would certainly not do. He wrote his wife offering several suggestions. Among them: "How would you like the name of *Stuart* Stuart? It would be novel and I think pretty, but J. E. B. would be most suitable." In fact, he judged it so suitable that the young lad became James Ewell Brown Stuart Jr., and, Jeb assured his wife, "You will find that very few will ever know that his name was ever other than *Jimmie*."[*]

* Quoted in Burke Davis, *Jeb Stuart: The Last Cavalier*, 77.

von Borcke, who after the war flew the Confederate battle flag from the ramparts of his ancestral castle), a golden knight errant (John Pelham, an Alabama-born West Pointer,[30] of romantic blond good looks, a bang up reputation as an athlete, and a fearlessness that petrified those it didn't inspire, earning him the nickname "the Gallant Pelham"), and a fierce pet raccoon for a watchdog.

But all of this should not blind us to how skilled an officer he was. Joseph E. Johnston wrote of him that "He is a rare man, wonderfully endowed by nature with the qualities necessary for an officer of light cavalry. Calm, firm, acute, active, enterprising, I know of no one more competent than he to estimate the occurrences before him at their true value. If you add a real brigade of cavalry to this army, you can find no better brigadier general to command it."[31] In September 1861, he was duly promoted. In seven years in the regular army he had been promoted from second lieutenant to captain (which was accounted rapid promotion). But from March to September 1861, he had been promoted from first lieutenant in the United States Army to a brigadier general in the forces of the Confederate States of America. No one doubted that his swift elevation was merited. He was twenty-eight years old.

Stuart's men were with General Joseph E. Johnston on the retreat from the Peninsula and with Lee during the defense of Richmond. It was during this latter service that his men leapt to prominence with their celebrated raid that had them riding round McClellan's entire army, humiliating the Federal commander and having a daredevil's good time

A Soldier's Wish

"I think it's a foregone conclusion that we shall ultimately whip the Yankees. We are bound to believe that, anyhow; but the war is going to be a long and terrible one, first. We've only just begun it, and very few of us will see the end. All I ask of fate is that I may be killed leading a cavalry charge."

Jeb Stuart

Quoted in George Cary Eggleston, *A Rebel's Recollections* (Louisiana State University Press, 1996), 117.

doing it. (One of the Federal cavalry officers pursuing Stuart was his father-in-law; and there were some who thought General Cooke was more hesitant in the field than usual.)

Stuart for his part, relished the danger (though he was perturbed once when a bullet sliced off half his prized moustache), and it was part of his character that he could perform his duties with the utmost skill, with the soberest estimate of the military realities of his situation, while indulging a rambunctious, fun-loving, cavalier spirit. His personality was such that if he could not entirely win over Wade Hampton (who chafed under the supremacy of the Virginians), he could warm the odd heart of Stonewall Jackson and even wheedle jokes out of him (and present him with a fine new uniform as a gift that left the western Virginian touched, and his staff delighted with amusement as they chided him to try it on). Lee regarded Stuart almost as a son. And Stuart delighted Southern-sympathizing women wherever they could be found.

Nevertheless, he spoke often of the possibility of death—though in no morbid way. When he was chided for exposing himself too often to the enemy, he remarked that he was easily replaceable. He once explained his troop movements to one of his officers so that in case he was killed on the campaign, the officer could explain why Stuart had acted as he did. He was utterly committed to the cause and told his wife Flora that it was his wish that his son should "never do anything his father would be ashamed of" and should "never forget the principles for which his father struggled."[32]

Those principles were, of course, the defense of his native Southland and of the sovereign rights of the state of Virginia. Slavery he accepted as part and parcel of the South's way of life, but like most men of his class, station, and background he was sympathetic, in a paternal way, towards blacks, as were many of his men. On one occasion they discovered that Yankees had stopped at a Virginia plantation and made off with a black carriage driver's watch. The Confederates rode down the blue-bellies, and Confederate Captain William Blackford told them: "Do you see those pine saplings? Well, those ladies back there [at the plantation] tell me you treated them with respect; if you hadn't, I would be hanging every one of you by your halter straps. Now, one of you took a watch from an old Negro back there. Hand it up to me."[33] The watch was surrendered and returned to its rightful owner.

Stuart took pride in such knight errantry among his men. Blackford noted that "next to having a staff composed of handsome men about him, he liked to see them mounted on fine horses." And lest you, as a decadent modern reader, suspect something awry from the mention of "handsome men" I can assure that you're wrong. For him it was simply a matter of having knights worthy of their calling—handsome, daring, well-bred, on fine horses, laughing at hazards, and dancing and singing the night away. And lest Stuart's fondness for balls, flirtations, and girls bearing flowers lead your thoughts down another immoral alley, we have it on the good authority of his staff officers that Stuart was utterly innocent in these matters.

Stuart was a man who stood by his vows. He told his mother, at the age of twelve, that he would never drink alcohol—and he never did. He even left orders that if he were wounded he was not to be given medicinal whiskey. He was also a keen supporter of religious revivals among the men, and told one scoffer that he regarded no calling higher than that of a clergyman. It might be hard today to find hearts so pure, but surely it is harder when Virginians, and others, no longer aspire to the spirit of the Virginia cavalier, no longer think of chivalry as an ideal to be pursued, or of knighthood as a practice for the current age. Such ambitions are gone with the wind, ground out, as Stuart eventually was, by the ruthless determination of the likes of Phil Sheridan.

Fighting to the End

But before Sheridan caught up with him, Stuart had his fun, including his celebrated raid on the headquarters of General John Pope. For Stuart it was a matter of settling a score. Pope's cavalry had ambushed him, and while Stuart had made his escape, he had lost some of his *accoutrements*, including his famous plumed hat. Stuart's revenge came in typical Stuart fashion. Riding in search of the enemy, Stuart found a black man on horseback singing "Carry Me Back to Old Virginny." The black Virginian told Stuart he knew exactly where Pope was, and led him there.

The Union troops were bedding down. One Federal officer said to another, "I hope Jeb Stuart won't disturb us tonight." Then, as if on cue, gunfire, chaos, and the Rebel Yell burst into his ears, "There he is, by God!"[34]

Pope, as it turned out, was not in his camp, but Stuart obtained the general's coat nevertheless (he offered a prisoner exchange of the coat for his hat), and the Union foe was thrown into confusion. During the raid a buffalo robe remained in Federal hands only because it was guarded by a Newfoundland, and Stuart's animal-loving cavaliers would never shoot a dog—no matter how prized the booty.

Stuart's men fought in all of Lee's campaigns—Second Manassas, Sharpsburg (followed by Stuart's rollicking Chambersburg raid, his second circumnavigation of McClellan's army), Fredericksburg, Chancellorsville (where Lee put Stuart in command of the Second Corps after Jackson's fatal wound), and Gettysburg.

Stuart styled himself "The Knight of the Golden Spurs," after a female admirer in Baltimore sent him such a pair following his Chambersburg raid. But for some, the sheen wore off those spurs after his performance at Gettysburg, where his men circled round the enemy army, and raided their way through Pennsylvania, but lost track of the Federal Army and lost contact with Lee. Lee, as was his custom, had left Stuart with a great deal of discretion regarding his orders—but he did not expect Stuart to leave him blind to the movements of the Federals.

In fact, the Battle of Brandy Station in June 1863 and the Gettysburg campaign that followed shortly thereafter revealed a problem that would only grow worse. The Confederate cavalry that had benefited greatly by the superiority of Southern horsemanship was getting worn out by casualties, hard campaigning, and a shortage of good replacements in both men and horses. Stuart's audacity and joyful spirit (even as he endured the loss of his daughter to illness, the gallant Pelham to shrapnel, and other losses that brought him to tears) were beginning to elicit more criticism than kudos. As the tide of war grew grimmer, the gay cavalier seemed out of place. He was accused of being shallow, vain, immature, and self-centered; he was no longer dashing, he was reckless. War had lost its glamour, and too many had died for his critics to accept Stuart as an inspiring or admirable *beau ideal*.

Nevertheless, he could still cut a dash, he still had the confidence of General Lee, (who always knew when to forgive and forget the inevitable shortcomings of a subordinate), and he still had the confidence of his men. And he remained spirited enough that when he saw Phil Sheridan and a substantial body of cavalry, more than 10,000 troopers, advancing towards Fredericksburg, he pursued to cut them off from what he assumed was to be a raid on Richmond. It was really a baited trap to lure Stuart to his death. Stuart had no more than 4,500 men. Six miles from Richmond, he moved to block Sheridan at Yellow Tavern, where blue and grey met in battle on 11 May 1864. Stuart took his place at the van of his army—where he promised he would always be.

"General, I believe you love bullets," said his bugler.

"No, Fred, I don't love 'em any more than you do. I go where they are because it's my duty. I don't expect to survive this war."

Colonel Charles Venable admonished Stuart: "Men behind stumps and fences are being killed, and here you are out in the open."

His response was to laugh. "I don't reckon there is any danger."[35]

When the Federals charged, Stuart was behind a thin grey line of men from Company K. Stuart fired at the bluecoats with his pistol as they galloped past him, and he fired again, when the Federals retreated, repelled by a Confederate countercharge. Amidst this flowing and ebbing tide of blue, a fleeing Federal private suddenly turned and fired a .44 caliber bullet into Stuart. Stuart knew it was a mortal wound. He rallied his men and turned command over to Fitzhugh Lee: "Go ahead Fitz, old fellow. I know you will do what is right." As he was taken from the field, he urged retreating Confederates to "Go back! Go back! and do your duty as I have done mine, and our country will be safe. Go back! Go back! I had rather die than be whipped!"[36] He died the following night, assuring everyone, for as long as his strength lasted, that he was resigned to death if it was God's will.

Stuart's wife grieved forever. She outlived her husband by fifty years, never remarried, and every day wore black as a sign of her mourning. Lee confessed, after Stuart's death, that he could "scarcely think of him without weeping." As perhaps we should all weep when we ask if it was really necessary, if it was really just, to kill men such as Stuart for their devotion to their native state and the cause of Southern independence.

George Armstrong Custer (1839-1876)
"Come on, you Wolverines!"

Custer, always known as Armstrong or Autie to his friends (or Fanny to his West Point classmates, in honor of his girlish golden curls), was the North's equivalent of Stuart. At West Point, he wasn't much for studying but he loved to ride and was popular with his fellows for his love of fun and pranks (and racking up of demerits). His friends were mostly Southerners. He liked to read Southern chivalric romances. His family was ardently Democratic, loathing abolitionists, Whigs, and Republicans.

When Custer opted to fight for the Union (he had been born in and sent to West Point from Ohio and spent half his boyhood in Michigan), it was not to eradicate the Southern way of life. He admired it. Early in the war, he even attended, as best man, the wedding of a paroled Southern officer at a Virginia plantation. Then he hung around for nearly a fortnight courting one of the belles, until he realized that McClellan was evacuating from the Peninsula.

Custer did not fight for the Union because he disagreed with states' rights. Nor did he fight because he wanted to abolish slavery (during the war he adopted one runaway slave as a servant). He fought for the Union because of the oath of allegiance to the United States he had taken at West Point. Throughout his life, Custer showed unstinting loyalty to his friends, devotion to his family, and gratitude to his benefactors. For all his carefree optimism, he never wanted to let any of them down. When he had earned some minor distinction at First Manassas, Custer rode into Washington, D.C., to introduce himself to Congressman John A. Bingham (a Republican) who had sponsored his nomination to the United States Military Academy. He thought it the right thing to do. The Congressman remembered the encounter:

> Beautiful as Absalom with his yellow curls, he was out of breath, or had lost it in embarrassment. And he spoke with hesitation: "Mr. Bingham, I've been in my first battle. I tried hard to do my best. I felt I ought to report to you, for it's through you I got to West Point. I'm...."
>
> I took his hand. "I know, you're my boy Custer!"[37]

The Boy General

Born a blacksmith's son, he was without social distinction, but also without worries and with the luck of the Irish (though his heritage was German) for most of his life. He grew up in a large boisterous family where politics was meat and drink. But for Custer fun was ever the lure.

Like Stuart, he was a flirt, but unlike the Virginian, it is often supposed that he did not keep his affairs strictly within the confines of Christian propriety. He also liked a drink, though he later took the pledge—and, like Stuart, once on the wagon he never fell off. He was the most popular cadet at West Point because he was the most irrepressible, the king of demerits, and the sort who would ask the Spanish professor how to say, "Class dismissed," *en español*, and when the poor sap said it, lead his fellow cadets out of the room. Unlike other cadets who found West Point a place of drudgery, Custer loved it, even as he violated its rules and absorbed all its punishments: "Everything is fine. It's just the way I like it."[38] After his first year at the Point, he wrote: "I would not leave this place for any amount of money because I would rather have a good education and no money, than to have a fortune and be ignorant."[39]

The impish blacksmith's son could resist no chance for a jape, avoided studying (he smuggled novels into class instead), but was nevertheless a bright lad, however sorry his grades. He graduated last in his class. Worse, or perhaps even better, he ended his West Point career court-martialed for failing to break up—indeed, for refereeing—a fight between two cadets. (Custer was not a brawler himself. His wit, which got him into so much trouble, also kept him out of fights, which he saved for the battlefield).

He graduated—or was court-martialed—straight from West Point to the front, serving at First Manassas and then on the Peninsula. Custer was fearlessly brave, a good scout (and considered a dispensable one, as he was sent up in balloons for aerial reconnaissance), leapt to the initiative in action, and took pride in never confessing to fatigue or hunger—all of which endeared him to his superior officers. It was after a successful reconnaissance that General McClellan, whom Custer greatly admired, turned to the young lieutenant and said, "Do you know, you're just the young man I've been looking for, Mr. Custer. How would you like to come on my staff?"[40] He did, and was given a brevet rank of captain.

Their regard for each other was mutual. McClellan said of Custer, "in these days Custer was simply a reckless, gallant boy, undeterred by fatigue, unconscious of fear; but his head always clear in danger and he always brought me clear and intelligible reports of what he saw when under the heaviest fire. I became much attached to him."[41]

After Lincoln dismissed McClellan, Custer joined the staff of General Alfred Pleasanton, and it was Pleasanton who really sent Custer's star soaring by recommending the brevet captain for promotion to brigadier general—which promotion was endorsed by Washington, becoming official 29 June 1863—jumping him over captains, majors, and colonels. Custer was twenty-three, the youngest general in the Union army, and with characteristic flair he not only had stars sewn on his collar, but fancied himself up with a crimson tie, a broad-brimmed black hat, and a black velvet jacket that radiated gold braid. No matter that it made him a mark for enemy sharpshooters, Custer thought the men should be able to spot their general in the field. That, with his uniform and his distinctive goldilocks curls and blond moustache, they certainly could.

Custer in Command

Custer's command was the second brigade of the third division of the Cavalry Corps of the Army of the Potomac, consisting of the First, Fifth, Sixth, and Seventh regiments of Michigan cavalry and a battery of artillery. These were the men he led into battle at Gettysburg with the cry: "Come on, you Wolverines!"

His first charge at Gettysburg, on 2 July 1863, was repulsed by Wade Hampton's men. But Custer, whose horse was shot from beneath him, was cited for gallantry by his commander, Brigadier General Judson "Kill-Cavalry" Kilpatrick. On the next day, the day of Pickett's charge, Kilpatrick's men were ordered to shield the flank at Little Round Top. Custer, however, was detached to the command of General David McMurtrie Gregg whose men were in place to protect Meade's rear from Jeb Stuart's cavalry, the "Invincibles," who had the same undefeated aura about them as did the infantry of Robert E. Lee's Army of Northern Virginia.

The fighting had already grown hot when Custer was given the orders he wanted, to lead a charge into the enemy. The honor fell to the 7th Michigan, Custer's most inexperienced troops. The blue-coated cavalry charged into Confederate shot and shell and crashed into an intervening fence, which didn't inhibit hand-to-hand fighting with sabers, pistols, and carbines between Virginians and Michiganders. The Federals were driven back but reformed themselves to meet a Confederate counter-charge. Now at the head of the First Michigan, his best regiment, Custer thrust his sword in the air and shouted, "Come on, you Wolverines!" The clashing opponents collided with such fury that horses tumbled over each other—and this time, though the gun smoke, the point-blank discharges, and the clanging, bloodied sabers, it was the Confederates who pulled back. The invincible Virginians had been stopped. "I challenge the annals of warfare to produce a more brilliant or successful charge of cavalry,"[42] wrote Custer in his official report. This wasn't bragging—though Custer was often, wrongly, accused of that—it was boyish enthusiasm.

Indeed, the key to understanding Custer is that he pursued all his endeavors with boyish ardor, spirit, and pluck. He was tough, of course. He was proud of being able to endure any hardship. But he also thrived on action. He rejoiced in the field (and later on the Great Plains) surrounded by fast horses, good dogs (dogs recognized him as one of their natural masters), a variety of other animals (such as a pet field mouse), and an assortment of hangers-on, including, during the war, a runaway slave named Eliza who became his cook (she said she wanted to try "this freedom business"), a ragamuffin boy servant named Johnnie Cisco and another named Joseph Fought, who repeatedly deserted his own unit to be with Custer. Later in the war, Michigan troops petitioned *en masse* to serve under the golden-haired general.

Custer maneuvered friends and family onto his staff or into his units, including his brother Tom. And if it was cronyism it was cronyism that rewarded the brave, for all the Custers were gallant. His brother Tom won the Congressional Medal of Honor for his bravery at Saylor's Creek (he was shot in the face, and survived to fight again).

A lot of people wanted to be with Custer. That included his bride, Elizabeth "Libbie" Bacon, whom Custer married in February 1864 after her father, Judge Daniel Bacon, could no longer keep the Boy General from his daughter. The Custers were the Bacon's social inferiors, and Custer had a reputation as a ladies

> ## Son of the Morning Star
>
> "I left home when but sixteen, and have been surrounded by temptation, but I have always had a purpose in life."
>
> **Custer to his future father-in-law**

man. But, well, at least that ringleted fellow was a general, and not a blacksmith. And if Judge Bacon had strong doubts before the marriage, he should by rights have quickly buried them (though apparently he never did), for few couples in history seem to have been happier than Libbie and Armstrong.[43] Indeed, his charming, well-bred, pious wife followed her vibrant enthusiast of a husband to camp whenever it was considered safe to do so. And on one occasion, after the war, while on the Great Plains, he was court-martialed and suspended from duty for a year, because he decided to swing by and visit his wife while on a campaign.

Jeb Stuart kept his wife away from camp, thinking it no place for a lady. Custer welcomed his wife, and thought Stuart's flirtations with other women along the campaign trail was no behavior for a husband. But then again, Stuart employed his banjo players for evening entertainments of dancing and singing, and it seemed only right and proper to that cavalier that ladies be invited. Custer kept a band too—but he used it to for purely martial purposes: to inspire the men, to prepare a charge. There's something admirable about the Custer way.

Phil Sheridan's Golden Boy

In March 1864, Custer fell under the command of Phil Sheridan. Sheridan learned to like the cut of Custer's jib—a man as eager to fight the enemy as he was. As an aide to General Meade noted, "fighting for fun is rare ... [only] such men as ... Custer and some others, attacked whenever they got a chance, and of their own accord." And it gained him a reputation. When Libbie was introduced to President Lincoln in Washington, old Abe replied, "So this is the young woman whose husband goes into a charge with a whoop and a shout."[44]

Custer whooped and shouted his way through the Battle of the Wilderness, Trevilian Station, Yellow Tavern (where Stuart was struck down), the Shenandoah Valley,[45] and the final campaign at Appomattox. Custer's star rose ever higher, as he closed out the war a major general of volun-

The Custers of Camelot

"There was a bright and joyous chivalry in that man [Custer], and a noble refinement mingled with constant gaiety in the wife [Libbie], such as I fear is passing from the earth."

Journalist Charles Godfrey Leland on the Custers after the war

Quoted in Jay Monaghan, *Custer: The Life of General George Armstrong Custer* (University of Nebraska Press, 1971), 283.

teers and a brevet major general in the regular army. Not bad for a twenty-five-year-old.

Custer was a magnanimous victor. He liked the South and Southerners. Yes he had defeated them, and in his mind they deserved to be defeated, but he did not believe they should be abused and trampled upon simply because the Federal government now had the power to do so. He had his band play Dixie after he captured worn out grey troopers near the end of the war, and he became a political ally of President Andrew Johnson against the Radical Republicans. Already marked down as a McClellan man and a Democrat, Custer was winning himself political enemies.

But Sheridan was able to keep Custer gainfully employed, bringing him to Texas. That assignment, however, proved temporary, despite Sheridan's best efforts. The War Department reduced Custer in rank to captain and assigned him to the 5th Cavalry. Custer wanted to find something better. Grant wrote a letter of recommendation for him to become a mercenary general in the Mexican army, but Custer's application for leave was denied. Still, Custer hoped something would turn up—and it did, a lieutenant colonelcy in the 7th Cavalry, which at least had the promise of adventure, as the 7th was posted on the Great Plains.

Into the 7th Cavalry would come his brothers, Tom and Boston, a nephew, Autie Reed, and a brother-in-law, as well as such men as Captain Myles Keough, who had fought for the pope in Italy, Lieutenant

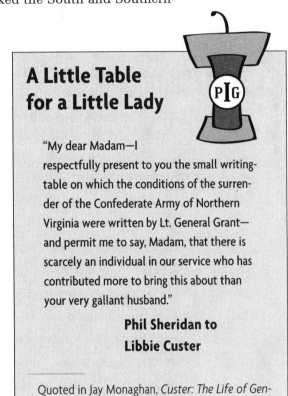

A Little Table for a Little Lady

"My dear Madam—I respectfully present to you the small writing-table on which the conditions of the surrender of the Confederate Army of Northern Virginia were written by Lt. General Grant—and permit me to say, Madam, that there is scarcely an individual in our service who has contributed more to bring this about than your very gallant husband."

Phil Sheridan to Libbie Custer

Quoted in Jay Monaghan, *Custer: The Life of General George Armstrong Custer*, 246.

Reconstruction = Simple Destruction

"I believe that every man who voluntarily engaged in the Rebellion forfeited every right held under our government—to live, hold property. But...for the Government to exact full penalties, simply because it is constitutionally authorized to do so, would, in my opinion, be unnecessary, impolitic, inhuman, and wholly at variance with the principles of a free, civilized and Christian nation, such as we profess to be."

Custer on the policy of Reconstruction

Quoted in Marguerite Merrington, *The Custer Story: The Life and Intimate Letters of General George A. Custer and His Wife Elizabeth* (Devin-Adair, 1950), 187-8.

Charles DeRudio, who had fought against the pope as an Italian nationalist, and Captain Louis Hamilton, the grandson of Alexander Hamilton. He was surrounded by friends, but also by a few enemies like Captain Frederick Benteen and Major Marcus Reno.

Sheridan took no nonsense from Indians, and he set Custer out to destroy any hostiles. Sheridan's Indian policy was harsh, but to his mind, realistic: "The more we can kill this year, the less will have to be killed the next year for the more I see of these Indians the more I am convinced that they will all have to be killed or be maintained as a species of paupers."[46] Custer executed this policy—and he saw the barbarities that justified it: the child rapes and murders of abducted white girls by the Indians, the disemboweling of white boys, the perfidy of Indian promises (not so very different from the cliché of broken government promises to the Indians). And, like Sheridan, he saw the Indian Bureau as corrupt. Unlike Sheridan, he said so in ways that made him an enemy of General Grant, whose Indian policy was more conciliatory than was Sherman's or Sheridan's.

The romantic in Custer—and there was very little of anything else—relished living and fighting amongst the Indians. He was, if anything, sympathetic to their plight. He conceded that they were savage—and the New England pantywaists who called them noble savages had no idea what they were talking about—but he believed they could be civilized, Christianized, and he repudiated any talk of exterminating the Indians. He went further, stating, "If I were an Indian, I often think that I would greatly prefer to cast my lot among those of my people who adhered to the free open plains, rather than to submit to the confined limits of a reservation, there to be the recipient of the blessed benefits of civilization, with its vices thrown in without stint or measure."[47] The modern stereotype of Custer as a crazed Indian-killer is a coarse, blatant slander. The old image, of Custer as a hero, is a simple truth (and one enunciated by former Confederates, like Joseph E. Johnston).

The Battle of the Little Big Horn, Custer's Last Stand, is the crown of thorns of the Custer legend. What actually happened at the battle must also be, in some measure, a matter of mystery and conjecture. But one thing can be said with certainty: the dash and bravery, the willingness to take risks, his belief that disciplined cavalry could defeat Indian numbers greater than their own, all of which had served him so well in the past, deserted him here. It is very likely that the image of Custer being among the last to die, if not the very last to fall on what is now Custer's Hill, is a true one. And with his death, as the journalist foretold, a paragon of a "bright and joyous chivalry" passed from the earth.

Part V

★ ★ ★ ★ ★ ★ ★ ★

BEATING RETREAT

Chapter Fifteen

WHAT IF THE SOUTH HAD WON?

So just suppose that Abraham Lincoln had let the South go. What if he had said:

We part as friends. We hope to reunite as friends. There will be no coercion of the Southern states by the people of the North. No state shall be kept in the Union against its will. Such a turn of events would be contrary to every principle of free government that we cherish. But we ask the Southern states, to which we are bound by mystic chords of memory and affection, that they reconsider their action. If not now, then later, when the heat of anger has subsided, when they have seen the actions of this administration work only for the good of the whole and not for the partisan designs of a few; when this administration shows by word and deed that it is happy to live within the confines of the Constitution, that we will admit of no interference in the established institutions of the several states. I trust that by our demeanor, by our character, by our actions, by our prosperity and our progress we will prove to our separated brethren that we should again be more than neighbors, we should be more than friends, we should in fact be united states, for a house

Guess What?

☞ If there had been no Civil War, the South would have abolished slavery peaceably (as every other country in the Western Hemisphere did in the nineteenth century)

☞ The Confederate States of America might have helped the Allies win World War I sooner

☞ If the South had won the war, Cuba would be a state of the re-United States

united is far stronger, will be far more prosperous, and will be far happier, than a house divided, a house rent asunder by rancor, a house that undermines its very foundations by separation.

To the people of Maryland, Virginia, Delaware, Kentucky, Missouri, Tennessee, and Arkansas, I have a special message. I tell you that this government will raise no arms against the states of the Southern Confederacy. We will wage no war of subjugation against these states. And I confirm, yet again, that I have neither the right, nor the power, nor the desire to abolish slavery within these states or any other where it is lawfully established. What I do desire, as do all the Northern states, is that we be once again a nation united in peace, amity, and common government. Let us through prayer and good graces work to achieve that end. I ask that all good men of the United States, and those now separated from us, work peaceably to achieve the reconciliation that is our destiny and our hope. Four score years ago we created a new nation, united in principle. I pray that sharing the same God, the same continent, and the same destiny, we might unite again in common principle and common government.

Had Lincoln given that speech would "government of the people, by the people, and for the people have perished from the earth"? No, it would have been confirmed, as the Southern states would have enjoyed that very thing and not have been brutalized into accepting a government that they did not want and that did not represent their interests. Would slavery have persisted until this very day? No, it seems certain it would have been abolished peaceably, as it found itself abolished everywhere else in the New World in the nineteenth century. Imagine that there had been no war against the South, and subsequently no Reconstruction putting the South under martial law, disenfranchising white voters with Confederate pasts, and enfranchising newly freed slaves as wards of the Republican Party. Without that past, race relations in the South would have been better, not worse, and the paternalist planters would have arranged, over time, to emancipate their slaves in exchange for financial compensation.

Sorry to break the news to you, but Southern Democrats aren't Nazis

It is sometimes said today—among the politically correct, with their cartoonish views of history—that Lee was the equivalent of Rommel in a Confederacy that was the equivalent of the Third Reich...though the South, of course, waged no aggressive war, committed no Holocaust against the Jews—in fact, included the Jewish Judah P. Benjamin as its, in succession, secretary of state, secretary of war, and attorney general, the first Jewish cabinet officer in North America—and had as its governing ideology states' rights and an even more limited federal government than the United States. Pretty fascist, huh?

The comparison, to anyone with an ounce of sense, or historical imagination, is risible. Far from being sympathetic to National Socialism, the antebellum South was more wedded to economic and governmental libertarianism (no tariffs, no taxpayer-funded "internal improvements," no overweening national government trampling on states' rights) than was the North. The Confederate Constitution limited the president to one six-year term. There was no Holocaust in the South, or anything remotely like it. George Washington and Thomas Jefferson were slave-owners and so was Jefferson Davis, and Davis was no more evil than they were. In fact, he saw himself, in many ways, as their inheritor. Thomas Jefferson's grandson died fighting for the Confederacy. John Marshall's grandson was on Lee's staff. Relatives of Washington, Patrick Henry, and other Virginia patriots, lined up with the Confederacy. So did the grandson of the author of the "Star-Spangled Banner," Francis Scott Key.

Southern ideas were about as far from National Socialist ideas as can be imagined. The South had little truck with nationalism (as opposed to federalism and state loyalties) and "progressive ideas" (like Marxism). Its people insisted on their liberty to a degree that not even the Federal government could tolerate. If they would not take orders from Abraham Lincoln, and often wondered why they should take them from Jefferson Davis, it is hard to imagine they would have had any interest in being harangued by a paper-hanging corporal with a toothbrush moustache.

There would have been—and were—no more ardent anti-Nazis than the people of the South. As the historian Samuel Eliot Morrison noted, writing of the 1940 election between President Franklin Delano Roosevelt and Wendell Wilkie, though Southerners distrusted the New Deal, "the South in general, with its gallant tradition, applauded the President's determination to help the Allies; and ahead of

Books Yankees Don't Want You to Read

If the South Had Won the Civil War, by MacKinlay Kantor (Forge, 2001).

By the author of the novel *Andersonville,* this "counterfactual" was a sensation when in was first published in *Look* magazine in 1960. Cleverly done, with some interesting implications of a Southern victory and Union defeat (for instance, Secretary of State William Seward lacks the political capital to buy Alaska, leaving it a Russian outpost in North America, which later heightens Cold War tensions), Kantor envisions the peaceful end of slavery in the South and the inevitable reunion of the three Republics—Southern, Northern, and Texas. This illustrated edition has rather nifty artist's renditions of doughboys and G.I.s with Texan, Confederate, and Federal insignia, fighting side by side.

any other part of the country, prepared mentally for the war that the nation had to fight."[1] The America First movement—which strove to keep America out of any European war—was most popular in the Midwest and among the descendants of Irish and German immigrants, many of whom had earned their citizenship fighting for Abraham Lincoln.

If the South had won the war, its natural ally would have been Britain, through ties of trade and culture. Sheldon Vanauken, in his imagining of a Confederate victory at the close of his book *The Glittering Illusion: English Sympathy for the Southern Confederacy*, actually saw the Confederacy becoming part of the British Empire, with the result that rather than entering the Great War in the rather dilatory fashion arranged by the schoolmasterish President Woodrow Wilson, Southern regiments charged in from the start, ensuring an Allied victory in 1916 rather than 1918. In MacKinlay Kantor's classic rendering of Confederate victory, *If the South Had Won the War*, North and South eventually reunite, in large part because of common service on the side of Britain in both World Wars.

Confederate Cuba? *Si!*

If the South had won, would the Plains Indians still be running free? Some like to imagine so. Certainly, the South had Indian allies, the most famous being the Cherokee Brigadier General Stand Watie, but so did the North. Still, some folks of a peculiar ideological stripe (paleo-libertarians, they're likely to be called) would have you think that if the South had won the War, Indians and Confederates would have rubbed along amicably ever after: the Indians hunting buffalo on the plains; Confederate statesmen elucidating the finer points of *laissez-faire*.

For folks of this ilk, Lincoln fought to create an American Empire that moved from subjugating the South, to threatening the Emperor Maximilian's Mexico, to exterminating the Indians, to conquering the Philippines. But the idea that the South was not "imperialist," by this definition, is absurd. Thomas Jefferson, one of the idols of the paleo-libertarian school, was the president who called America "an empire of liberty." He believed in "manifest destiny" before the term was invented. (He also believed that the United States should invade and conquer Canada.) It wasn't Northerners who annexed Florida, it was Andrew Jackson who said he'd be happy to take Cuba next (and who was no small shakes as an Indian fighter either). It wasn't Northerners who tore Texas from Mexico; and it was Southern boys who were most ardent for the Mexican War and a Southern president, James K. Polk, who said that thanks to the Treaty of Hidalgo, ending that war, "there will be added to the United States an immense empire, the value of which twenty years hence it would be difficult to calculate."[2]

It was Southerners, too, who had dreams of a cotton kingdom extending into Latin America, and Southern politicians (like Secretary of War Jefferson Davis and Mississippi Governor John A. Quitman) who supported American "filibusters," like the Tennessean William Walker, who looked to carve out little empires in Baja California or Nicaragua. In fact, if one imagines that the South had won the war, it's a near certainty that the South would have annexed Cuba, a long held Southern dream. And think of the implications of that: no Cuban missile crisis, another Southern beach spot for Yankee snow birds, no shortage of Cuban cigars.

In fact, if the South had won—we all would have had it made, to quote a Southern partisan. But while it's fun to imagine, there's not much point in thinking about what didn't happen. Southerners are conservatives, and conservatives are realists. As much as Lee and Longstreet, Davis and Hampton, we need to find our war in post-bellum America.

And if the Old South had its charms and grace and merit, it would be churlish—not to say idiotic—not to count the many blessings we have as citizens of the United States. We should cherish what we have in the Southern tradition. We should enjoy the unity we have as united states, even if we had rather that unity had been reached without the terrors and brutalities and injustices of the War and Reconstruction. And we should remember that men like Lee and Jackson, Stuart and Hill, while Southern heroes, should be American heroes as well. We're all in this together.

Deo Vindice.

AFTERWORD
by Jefferson Davis

y first object in this work [*The Rise and Fall of the Confederate Government*] was to prove, by historical authority, that each of the States, as sovereign parties to the compact of the Union had the reserved power to secede from it whenever it should be found not to answer the ends for which it was established. If this has been done, it follows that the war was, on the part of the United States Government, one of aggression and usurpation, and, on the part of the South, was for the defense of an inherent, unalienable right.

My next purpose was to show, by the gallantry and devotion of the Southern people, in their unequal struggle, how thorough was their conviction of the justice of their cause; that, by their humanity to the wounded and captives, they proved themselves to the worthy descendants of chivalric sires, and fit to be free; and that, in every case, as when our army invaded Pennsylvania, by their respect for private rights, their morality and observance of the laws of civilized war, they showed that they are entitled to the confidence and regard of mankind.

In asserting the right of secession, it has not been my wish to incite to its exercise; I recognize the fact that the war showed it to be impracticable, but this did not prove it to be wrong; and, now that it may not be again attempted, and that the Union may promote the general welfare, it is needful that the truth, the whole truth, should be known, so that crimination and recrimination may for ever cease, and then, on the basis of fraternity and faithful regard for the rights of the States, there may be written on the arch of the Union, *Esto perpetua.*[1]

NOTES

Chapter 1: A Country of Their Own

1. Declaration of the Immediate Causes which Induce and Justify the Secession of South Carolina from Federal Union, 20 December 1860, formally adopted 24 December 1860.

2. Declaration of Independence cited in ibid.

3. Declaration of Independence cited in ibid.

4. Quoted in Shelby Foote, *The Civil War: A Narrative, Fort Sumter to Perryville* (Random House, 1958), 5.

5. Ibid.

6. Jefferson Davis, First Inaugural Address, 18 February 1861.

7. Abraham Lincoln, First Inaugural Address, 4 March 1861.

8. Abraham Lincoln, letter to Horace Greeley, 22 August 1862.

9. Abraham Lincoln, speech in Springfield, Illinois, 16 June 1858.

10. Abraham Lincoln, First Inaugural Address, 4 March 1861.

11. Quoted in Frank E. Vandiver, *Their Tattered Flags: The Epic of the Confederacy* (Texas A&M University Press, 1970), 24-5.

12. Abraham Lincoln, Fourth Lincoln-Douglas Debate, 18 September 1858.

13. Quoted in William C. Davis, *Jefferson Davis: The Man and His Hour* (HarperCollins, 1991), 181-2.

14. Robert E. Lee, letter to Mary Lee, 27 December 1856.

15. Quoted in Eugene Berwanger, *The Frontier Against Slavery* (University of Illinois Press, 1967), 133.

16. Abraham Lincoln, Speech in Peoria, Illinois, 16 October 1854.

17. Alexis de Tocqueville, *Democracy in America* (Anchor Books, 1969), 343.

18. Richard Taylor, *Destruction and Reconstruction: Personal Experiences of the War* (J.S. Sanders & Co., 1998), 245.

19. Jefferson Davis, *The Rise and Fall of the Confederate Government*, Volume One, (Da Capo Press, 1990), 131.

20. Tocqueville, op. cit., 369.

21. Major General J. F. C. Fuller, *Grant & Lee: A Study in Personality and Generalship* (Indiana University Press, 1982), 18.

22. George Cary Eggleston, *A Rebel's Recollections* (Louisiana State University Press, 1996), 27-8.

23. Richard Weaver, *The Southern Tradition at Bay* (Regnery, 1989), 82.

24. Quoted in David McCullough, *John Adams* (Simon and Schuster, 2001), 521.

25. Allen Tate, *Jefferson Davis: His Rise and Fall* (J.S. Sanders & Co., 1998), 287.

26. Quoted in Clifford Dowdey, *The History of the Confederacy* (originally published under the title, *The Land They Fought For*) (Barnes and Noble Books, 1992), 69.

Chapter 2: The Gunpowder Trail

1. Quoted in Richard Brookhiser, *Alexander Hamilton: American* (Free Press, 1999), 202. Aaron Burr, candidate (failed, as it turned out) for governor of New York, was part of the scheme.

2. Thomas Jefferson, letter to John Holmes, 22 April 1820.

3. Lieutenant J. E. B. Stuart was the messenger.

4. Quoted in James M. McPherson, *The Battle Cry of Freedom: The Civil War Era* (Oxford University Press, 1988), 209.

5. Abraham Lincoln, First Inaugural Address, 4 March 1861.

6. Ibid.

7. President Jefferson Davis, First Message to the Confederate Congress, 29 April 1861.

8. Abraham Lincoln, speech to Congress, 12 January 1847.

9. Abraham Lincoln, First Inaugural Address, 4 March 1861.

10. Quoted in Douglas Southall Freeman, *Lee* (an abridgment in one volume, by Richard Harwell, of the four-volume *R. E. Lee*) (Charles Scribner's Son, 1991), 110.

11. Quoted in Clifford Dowdey, *Lee* (Stan Clark Military Books, 1991), 120-21.

12. Ibid.,135.

Chapter 3: Dixie Rising, 1861–1863

1. You can also find it in Thomas DiLorenzo's *The Real Lincoln: A New Look at Abraham Lincoln, His Agenda, and an Unnecessary War* (Three Rivers Press, 2003), 140.

2. Quoted in James I. Robertson, *Stonewall Jackson: The Man, the Soldier, the Legend* (Macmillan, 1997), 264.

3. Quoted in Shelby Foote, *The Civil War: A Narrative, Fort Sumter to Perryville* (Random House, 1958), 351.

4. Quoted in Stephen W. Sears, *George B. McClellan: The Young Napoleon* (Ticknor & Fields, 1988), 168.

5. Quoted in Dabney H. Maury, *Recollections of a Virginian in the Mexican, Indian, and Civil Wars* (Charles Scribners' Sons, 1894), 161.

6. Quoted in Clifford Dowdey, *Lee* (Stan Clark Military Books, 1991), 217.

7. Quoted in Shelby Foote, *The Civil War: A Narrative, from Fort Sumter to Perryville*, (Random House, 1958), 513.

8. For Lee's attitude to Pope see Joseph L. Harsh, *Confederate Tide Rising: Robert E. Lee and the Making of Southern Strategy, 1861-1862* (Kent State University Press, 1998), 113-14 and 196, and Emory M. Thomas, *Robert E. Lee: A Biography*, (W. W. Norton & Company, 1997), 249-50.

9. Quoted in Shelby Foote, *The Civil War: A Narrative, Fort Sumter to Perryville* (Random House, 1958), 642.

10. Douglas Southall Freeman, *R. E. Lee: A Biography,* v. II, (Charles Scribner's Sons, 1934), 343.

11. Among those jailed for secessionist sympathies was the grandson of Francis Scott Key, author of "The Star Spangled Banner."

12. General R. E. Lee's "Proclamation to the People of Maryland," 8 September 1862.

13. Quoted in Foote, op. cit., 703.

14. Quoted in Douglas Southall Freeman, *Lee's Lieutenants: Cedar Mountain to Chancellorsville*, (Charles Scribner's Sons, 1971), 350.

15. Quoted in Jeffrey Wert, *General James Longstreet: The Confederacy's Most Controversial Soldier* (Touchstone, 1994), 221.

16. Quoted in Douglas Southall Freeman, *R. E. Lee: A Biography, Volume II* (Charles Scribner's Sons, 1934), 446.

17. Quoted in Burke Davis, *Gray Fox: Robert E. Lee and the Civil War* (Burford Books, 1956), 168.

18. The Battle of Murfreesboro (31 December 1862 to 2 January 1863) is also known as the Battle of Stones River.

19. Quoted in Frances H. Kennedy (editor), *The Civil War Battlefield Guide,* (Houghton Mifflin, 1990), 107.

20. Quoted in Shelby Foote, *The Civil War: A Narrative, Fredericksburg to Meridian* (Random House, 1963), 233-4.

21. Quoted in John M Taylor, *Duty Faithfully Performed: Robert E. Lee and His Critics* (Brassey's, 1999), 117.

22. Quoted in Shelby Foote, *The Civil War: A Narrative, Fredericksburg to Meridian,* (Random House, 1963), 315-16.

23. Quoted in Carl Sandburg, *Storm Over the Land* (Harcourt Brace, 1942), 181.

24. Quoted in Burke Davis, *Gray Fox: Robert E. Lee and the Civil War* (Burford Books, 1956), 225.

25. Quoted in Douglas Southall Freeman, *R. E. Lee: A Biography, Volume III* (Charles Scribner's Sons, 1934), 79.

26. Quoted in Foote, op. cit., 563.

27. Quoted in Thomas, op. cit., 300.

Chapter 4: The Long Goodbye, 1863–1865

1. Gary Gallagher, *The Confederate War: How Popular Will, Nationalism, and Military Strategy Could Not Stave Off Defeat* (Harvard University Press, 1997), 30.

2. He had performed a similar rock-like task at Murfreesboro.

3. Quoted in Frances H. Kennedy (editor), The Civil War Battlefield Guide (Houghton Mifflin, 1990), 159.

4. Quoted in James M. McPherson, *Battle Cry of Freedom: The Civil War Era* (Oxford University Press, 1988), 680.

5. Quoted in Kennedy, op. cit., 173.

6. Quoted in ibid., 176.

7. Clifford Dowdey, *Lee* (Stan Clark Military Books, 1991), 449.

8. Quoted in Robert Leckie, *The Wars of America* (Castle Books, 1998), 495.

9. Quoted in and Emory M. Thomas, *Robert E. Lee: A Biography*, (W. W. Norton & Company, 1997), 339.

10. Quoted in McPherson, op. cit., 778.

11. Quoted in Dowdey, op. cit., 485.

12. Quoted in Thomas, op. cit., 342.

13. Quoted in Kennedy, op. cit., 253.

14. Quoted in ibid., 349.

15. Quoted in ibid., 362.

Chapter 5: Robert E. Lee

1. Letter from Robert E. Lee to his son G. W. Custis Lee, 5 April 1862.

2. Theodore Roosevelt, *Thomas Hart Benton: The Story of His Life and Work* (Charles Scribner's Sons, 1906), 36.

3. Quoted in Douglas Southall Freeman, *Lee* (Charles Scribner's Son, 1991), 106–7.

4. Quoted in Emory Thomas, *Robert E. Lee: A Biography*, (W. W. Norton & Company, 1997), 173.

5. Quoted in Clifford Dowdey, *Lee* (Stan Clark Military Books, 1991), 83.

6. Quoted in Thomas, op. cit., 123.

7. Quoted in Dowdey, op. cit., 85.

8. Scott and Lee quoted in ibid., 127-8.

9. Quoted in Dowdey, op. cit., 91.

10. Quoted in Thomas, 133.

11. Quoted in Freeman, op. cit., 76.

12. Quoted in Thomas, op. cit., 123.

13. Quoted in ibid., 157.

14. Quoted in Dowdey, op. cit., 103.

15. Quoted in Thomas, op. cit., 167.

16. Field Marshal Viscount Wolseley, *The American Civil War: An English View, The Writings of Field Marshal Viscount Wolseley*, edited by James A. Rawley, (Stackpole Books, 2002), 69.

17. Wolseley, op. cit., 63.

18. Shelby Foote, *The Civil War: A Narrative, Red River to Appomattox* (Random House, 1974), 630.

19. Colonel Charles S. Wainwright, *A Diary of Battle: The Personal Journals of Colonel Charles S. Wainwright, 1861-1865* (Da Capo Press, 1998), 520-21.

20. Ulysses S. Grant, *Personal Memoirs: Ulysses S. Grant* (Modern Library, 1999), 580.

21. Lord Acton to Robert E. Lee, 4 November 1866.

22. R. E. Lee to Lord Acton, 15 December 1866.

23. Edward Porter Alexander, *Fighting for the Confederacy*, edited by Gary W. Gallagher (The University of North Carolina Press, 1999), 530-33.

24. Robert E. Lee to Jefferson Davis, 20 April 1865.

25. Dowdey, op. cit., 611.

Chapter 6: George H. Thomas

1. General Thomas to General Rosecrans at a council of war at the Battle of Murfreesboro, 1 January 1863, see discussion and controversy of this most famous quote of Thomas in Freeman Cleaves, *Rock of Chickamauga: The Life of General George H. Thomas* (Oklahoma University Press, 1948), 131-2 and Peter Cozzens, *No Better Place to Die* (University of Illinois Press, 1990), 172-3.

2. Quoted in Freeman Cleaves, *Rock of Chickamauga: The Life of General George H. Thomas* (Oklahoma University Press, 1948), 4.

3. Quoted in ibid., 41.

4. Quoted in Thomas B. Van Horne, *The Life of Major-General George H. Thomas* (Charles Scribner's Sons, 1882), 6.

5. Quoted in Cleaves, op. cit., 54.

6. Letter from Major George H. Thomas to Governor John Letcher, 12 March 1861.

7. Quoted in W. F. G. Shanks, *Personal Recollections of Distinguished Generals*, (Harper and Brothers, 1866), 71-2.

8. Quoted in ibid., 66.

9. Quoted in Van Horne, op. cit., 75-6.

10. Quoted in Freeman, op. cit., 112-3.

11. Quoted in Donn Piatt and Henry V. Boynton, *General George H. Thomas: A Critical Biography* (Kessinger Publishing, 2006), 205.

12. Quoted in Freeman, op. cit., 131-2.

13. Quoted in ibid., 162.

14. Quoted in Shanks, op. cit., 67.

15. Quoted in ibid., 273.

16. Quoted in James H. Wilson, *The Life of Charles A. Dana* (Harper Brothers, 1907), 265.

17. James H. Wilson, *Under the Old Flag, Volume I* (Appleton, 1912), 272.

18. Quoted in Van Horne, op. cit., 156.

19. Quoted in Frances H. Kennedy (ed.) *The Civil War Battlefield Guide* (Houghton Mifflin, 1990), 157.

20. See Cleaves, op. cit., 28.

21. Quoted in Lloyd Lewis, *Sherman: A Fighting Prophet* (Harcourt, Brace & Company, 1932), 375.

22. Both quoted in Cleaves, op. cit., 225.

23. Rustling and Thomas quoted in ibid., 266.

24. Quoted in Van Horne, op. cit., 213.

25. Quoted in Cleaver, op. cit., 293.

26. Quoted in ibid, 296.

Chapter 7: William Tecumseh Sherman

1. Quoted in Charles Bracelen Flood, *Grant and Sherman: The Friendship that Won the Civil War* (Farrar, Straus and Giroux, 2005), xiii.

2. See Basil Liddell-Hart, *Sherman: Soldier, Realist, American* (Da Capo Press, 1993), 205-6.

3. Quoted in Lee Kennett, *Sherman: A Soldier's Life* (HarperCollins, 2001), 34.

4. Liddell-Hart, op. cit., 205.

5. William T. Sherman, *Memoirs of W. T. Sherman* (Penguin, 2000), 19.

6. Quoted in Liddell-Hart, op. cit., 23-4.

7. Quoted in ibid, 26.

8. Kennett, op. cit., 233.

9. Quoted in Liddell-Hart, op. cit., 44.

10. Quoted in ibid, 73-4.

11. Quoted in ibid., 65.

12. Quoted in Kennett, op. cit., 110.

13. Quoted in Michael Fellman, *Citizen Sherman: A Life of William Tecumseh Sherman* (Random House, 1995), 78.

14. Quoted in ibid., 131.

15. Quoted in Stanley P. Hirshson, *The White Tecumseh: A Biography of William T. Sherman* (John Wiley & Sons, 1997), 93.

16. Quoted in Kennett, op. cit. 125-6.

17. Quoted in Fellman, op. cit., 100.

18. Quoted in Liddell-Hart, op. cit., 53.

19. Quoted in Kennett, op. cit., 173.

20. Quoted in Fellman, op. cit.,139.

21. Quoted in Hirshson, op. cit., 133-4.

22. Quoted in Kennett, op. cit., 192.

23. Quoted in ibid., 196.

24. Quoted in ibid, 228.

25. Quoted in ibid., 234.

26. Quoted in Fellman, op. cit., 197.

27. Quoted in Burke Davis, *Gray Fox: Robert E. Lee and the Civil War* (Burford Books, 1956), 168.

28. Quoted in Kennett, op. cit., 254.

29. Quoted in Hirschson, op. cit., 303 though I've taken the liberty of correcting the spelling.

30. Quoted in Fellman, op. cit., 311.

Chapter 8: James Longstreet

1. William Miller Owen, *In Camp and Battle with the Washington Artillery of New Orleans,* (Louisiana State University Press, 1999), 157.

2. General G. Moxley Sorrel, *At the Right Hand of Longstreet: Recollections of a Confederate Staff Officer,* (Bison Books, 1999), 23-4.

3. H. J. Eckenrode and Bryan Conrad, *James Longstreet: Lee's War Horse* (University of North Carolina Press, 1986), 3.

4. General James Longstreet, *From Manassas to Appomattox* (Da Capo, 1992), 29.

5. Ibid., 30.

6. Sorrel, op. cit., 26.

7. Quoted in Wert, op. cit., 77.

8. Quoted in ibid., 77.

9. Quoted ibid., 152.

10. Sorrel, op. cit., 32.

11. Eckenrode and Conrad, op. cit., 80.

12. Ibid., 131.

13. Sorrel, op. cit., 113.

14. Ibid., 115-16.

15. Wert, op. cit., 196.

16. Ibid., 200.

17. Ibid., 221.

18. Ibid., 93.

19. Arthur J. L. Fremantle, *Three Months in the Southern States, April-June 1863* (Greenhouse Publishing, no date) 254 and 242.

20. Eckenrode and Conrad, op. cit.,m 167.

21. Larry Tagg, *The Generals of Gettysburg,* (Da Capo, 2003), 251.

22. Wert, op. cit., 184.

23. Longstreet, op. cit., 395.

24. Quoted Wert, op. cit., 313-14.

25. Quoted in ibid, 357.

26. Quoted in ibid, 273.

27. Quoted in Jean Edward Smith, *Grant* (Simon & Schuster, 2001), 327.

28. Quoted in Wert, op. cit., 403.

29. Quoted in William Garret Piston, *Lee's Tarnished Lieutenant: James Longstreet and His Place in Southern History* (University of Georgia Press, 1987), 106.

30. Quoted in Wert, op. cit., 410-11.

Chapter 9: Nathan Bedford Forrest

1. Forrest's recipe for success—get their first with the most men—is often rendered in this vernacular version, but the plainer, "Well, I got their first with the most men," is what he actually said.

2. Quoted in Andrew Nelson Lytle, *Bedford Forrest and His Critter Company* (J. S. Sanders & Company, 1992), 357.

3. Quoted in ibid., 304-5.

4. Richard Taylor, *Destruction & Reconstruction: Personal Experiences of the Late War* (J. S. Sanders & Company, 1998), 205

5. John Allan Wyeth, *That Devil Forrest: A Life of General Nathan Bedford Forrest* (Louisiana State University Press, 1989), 132.

6. Ibid., 557.

7. Lytle, op. cit., 22.

8. Quoted in Robert Selph Henry, *"First with the Most" Forrest* (Bobbs-Merrill Company, 1944), 25.

9. Quoted in Brian Steel Wills, *A Battle from the Start* (HarperCollins, 1992), 30.

10. Lytle, op. cit., 28.

11. Quoted in Wills, op. cit., 31.

12. Accounts of this incident vary. This is the version accepted by Andrew Nelson Lytle and by Forrest's earlier authorized biographers. See Lytle, op cit., 24-7. Later biographers are skeptical because of the lack of contemporaneous written evidence to confirm this account.

13. Quoted in Wills, op. cit., 53.

14. Quoted in in ibid., 54.

15. Quoted in Hurst, 80.

16. Quoted in Wills, 64.

17. Quoted in Robert M. Browning Jr., *Forrest: The Confederacy's Relentless Warrior* (Brassey's Inc., 2004), 20.

18. Quoted in Wills, op. cit., 102.

19. Quoted in ibid., op. cit., 119.

20. Quoted in ibid., 122.

21. Quoted in ibid., 124.

22. Quoted in Hurst, op. cit., 130. Hurst and Wills assess the reliability of this account and some of its variations, Hurst on 127-30, Wills on 122-7.

23. Quoted in Wyeth, op. cit., 212-13.

24. All quoted in Wills, op. cit., 141-2.

25. Quoted in Lytle, op. cit., 238.

26. For a detailed discussion of the incident see Wills, op. cit., 179-96, and Shelby Foote, *The Civil War: A Narrative, from Red River to Appomattox,* (Random House, 1974), 108-12.

27. Quoted in Wills, op. cit., 215.

28. Quoted in Lytle, op. cit., 304-5.

29. Quoted in ibid., 336.

30. Quoted in Wyeth, op. cit,, 467.

31. Quoted in Lytle, 351-2.

32. Quoted in Wills, op. cit., 316.

33. Quoted in ibid., op. cit., 320.

34. Quoted in Hurst, op. cit., 267.

35. Quoted in ibid., 286.

36. Quoted in ibid., 313-14.

37. Quoted in ibid., 307.

38. Quoted in ibid., 378.

Chapter 10: Ulysses S. Grant

1. Quoted in Josiah Bunting III, *Ulysses S. Grant* (Times Books, 2004), 58.

2. Ulysses S. Grant, *Personal Memoirs* (The Modern Library, 1999), 3.

3. This famous quotes sets off J. F. C. Fuller's study of *The Generalship of Ulysses S. Grant* (Da Capo Press, 1991).

4. Grant, op. cit., 12.

5. Ibid, 13.

6. Quoted in Bunting, op. cit., 17.

7. Grant, op. cit., 17-18.

8. Ibid., 21.

9. Ibid., 24.

10. Quoted in Bunting, op. cit., 19.

11. Grant, op. cit., 43.

12. Quoted in Brooks Simpson, *Ulysses S. Grant: Triumph over Adversity, 1822-1865* (Houghton Mifflin Company, 2000), 32.

13. Quoted in Geoffrey Perret, *Ulysses S. Grant: Soldier and President* (Random House, 1997), 57.

14. Grant, op. cit., 53.

15. Quoted in Perret, op. cit., 119.

16. Quoted in Simpson, op. cit., 75-76.

17. Quoted in Perret, op. cit., 122.

18. Grant, op. cit., 127.

19. Quoted in John Mosier, *Grant* (Palgrave Macmillan, 2006), 35.

20. Grant, op. cit., 21.

21. See ibid., 142; also quoted in Jean Edward Smith, *Grant* (Simon & Schuster, 2001), 129.

22. Grant, op. cit., 143.

23. Quoted in Simpson, op. cit., 105.

24. Quoted in ibid., 96.

25. Quoted in Fuller, op. cit., 95.

26. Grant, op. cit., 161-2.

27. Quoted in Simpson, op. cit., 134.

28. Quoted in Perret, op. cit., 208.

29. Grant, op. cit., 303.

30. Quoted in Bunting, op. cit., 58-9.

31. Both quoted in Smith, op. cit., 364.

32. Major General J. F. C. Fuller, *Grant and Lee: A Study in Personality and Generalship* (Indiana University Press, 1982), 147.

33. John Russell Young, *Around the World with General Grant* (Johns Hopkins University Press, 2002), 384.

34. Grant, op. cit., 580.

35. Ibid.

36. Ibid., 581.

37. The source is John G. Wilson in his book *General Grant* (Appleton, 1913), p. 367. It is quoted by among others, John Mosier in *Grant* (Palgrave Macmillan, 2006) and J. F. C. Fuller *Grant and Lee: A Study in Personality and Generalship* (Indiana University Press, 1982). Fuller at least prefaces the quote with "he is reported to have said . . . ."

38. Quoted in Bunting, op. cit., 114.

39. Quoted in ibid., 116.

Chapter 11: Thomas Jonathan "Stonewall" Jackson

1. Quoted in Allen Tate, *Stonewall Jackson: The Good Soldier* (J. S. Sanders & Company, 1991), 34. This is one of the maxims Jackson wrote in a notebook at West Point. It now serves as the motto over the arch through which pass the "Keydets" of the Virginia Military Institute, where Jackson taught.

2. Quoted in James I. Robertson, Jr., *Stonewall Jackson: The Man, the Soldier, the Legend* (Macmillan, 1997), 25.

3. Quoted in ibid., 26.

4. Quoted in K. M. Kostyal, *Stonewall Jackson: A Life Portrait* (Taylor Publishing Company, 1999), 22.

5. Quoted in Robertson, *Stonewall Jackson*, 42.

6. Quoted in Tate, op. cit., 34.

7. Quoted in Byran Farwell, *Stonewall: A Biography of General Thomas J. Jackson* (W. W. Norton & Company, 1992), 43-4.

8. Quoted in Kostyal, op. cit., 30.

9. Quoted in Farwell, op. cit., 55 and 57.

10. Quoted in Kostyal, op. cit., 40.

11. Quoted in Tate, op. cit., 49.

12. Quoted in Richard G. Williams, *Stonewall Jackson: The Black Man's Friend* (Cumberland House, 2006), 7.

13. Quoted in Robertson, Stonewall Jackson, 208.

14. Quoted in Farwell, op. cit., 134.

15. Quoted in Robertson, Stonewall Jackson, 207.

16. Quoted in Kostyal, op. cit., 56.

17. Quoted in ibid., 56.

18. Quoted in Robertson, Stonewall Jackson, 269.

19. Quoted in G. F. R. Henderson, *Stonewall Jackson and the American Civil War* (Da Capo, 1988), 132-3.

20. These famous Jackson battlefield quotes are a composite compiled from various accounts.

21. Quoted in Tate, op. cit. 92.

22. Quoted in Henderson, op. cit., 331-2.

23. Quoted in Kostyal, op. cit., 107.

24. Quoted in Shelby Foote, *The Civil War: A Narrative, Fredericksburg to Meridian* (Random House, 1963), 233-4.

25. Quoted in Clifford Dowdey, *Lee* (Stan Clark Military Books, 1991), 353.

26. Quoted in Robertson, *Stonewall Jackson*, op. cit., 739.

27. Quoted in Burke Davis, *Gray Fox: Robert E. Lee and the Civil War* (Burford Books, 1956), 205

28. Quoted in Wilmer L. Jones, *Generals in Blue and Gray, Volume Two,* (Stackpole Books, 2006), 114.

29. Quoted in Mort Künstler and James I. Robertson, *Jackson & Lee: Legends in Gray* (Rutledge Hill Press, 1995), 9.

Chapter 12: A. P. Hill

1. Quoted in William Woods Hassler, *A. P. Hill, Lee's Forgotten General* (University of North Carolina Press, 1957), 35-6. In a letter to a friend early in the war, Hill wrote lamenting, "how many old friends, upon whom we would have staked our last dime, have shown the cloven foot and are now

most bitter in this war of subjugation—yet notheless [*sic*] by the blessing of God, and hearts that never grow faint, we will whip the damned hounds yet and then God grant that a gulf as deep and wide as hell may interpose between us . . . ."

2. Quoted in James I. Robertson, Jr., *General A. P. Hill: The Story of a Confederate Warrior* (Vintage Books, 1992), 22.

3. Quoted in ibid, 60.

4. This was D. H. Hill's characterization of both Robert E. Lee and A. P. Hill. Quoted in Edward Porter Alexander, *Fighting for the Confederacy: The Personal Recollections of Edward Porter Alexander*, edited by Gary Gallagher (University of North Carolina Press, 1998), 97.

5. Quoted in Robertson, op. cit., 71.

6. Quoted in Shelby Foote, *The Civil War: A Narrative, Fort Sumter to Perryville* (Random House, 1958), 506.

7. Henry Kyd Douglas, *I Rode with Stonewall* (University of North Carolina Press, 1968), 138.

8. Quoted in Robertson, op. cit., 154.

9. Quoted in Douglas Southall Freeman, *Lee's Lieutenants: A Study in Command* (one-volume abridgement by Stephen Sears), (Scribner, 1998, 526.

10. Quoted in ibid., 627.

11. Quoted in Robertson, op. cit., 284.

12. Quoted in ibid., 318.

13. Quoted in Hassler, op. cit., 4.

Chapter 13: George B. McClellan

1. Quoted in Frances H. Kennedy, ed., *The Civil War Battlefield Guide* (Houghton Mifflin, 1990), 60.

2. I wish I could say that mine was a truly unique insight, but I later learned that McClellan's best biographer, Stephen W. Sears, had come to the same conclusion, writing in an essay in *Lincoln's Generals*, edited by Gabor S. Boritt, (Oxford University Press, 1994), page 50, "George McClellan was simply in the wrong profession." So, if you won't take my word for it, take his.

3. Quoted in Stephen W. Sears, *George B. McClellan: The Young Napoleon* (Ticknor & Fields, 1988), 65.

4. Quoted in ibid., 94.

5. Quoted in James M. McPherson, *The Battle Cry of Freedom: The Civil War Era* (Oxford University Press, 1988), 360.

6. Quoted in Sears, op cit., 32.

7. Quoted in ibid, 116.

8. Quoted in ibid, 27.

9. Quoted in ibid, 21.

10. Quoted in ibid., 68.

11. Quoted in ibid., 79.

12. Quoted in ibid., 85.

13. Quoted in ibid, 88.

14. Quoted in Warren W. Hassler, Jr. *General George B. McClellan: Shield of the Union* (Louisiana State University Press, 1957), 13.

15. Quoted in Sears, op. cit., 92.

16. Quoted in Hassler, op. cit., 25.

17. Quoted in Sears, op. cit., 103.

18. Quoted in McPherson, op. cit., 360.

19. Quoted in Sears, op. cit., 125.

20. McClellan wrote this to his wife in the fall of 1861, saying that if the Army was inactive that winter, the fault would not, of course, be his.

21. Quoted in Sears, op. cit., 180.

22. Quoted in John M. Taylor, *Duty Faithfully Performed: Robert E. Lee and His Critics* (Brassey's, 1999), 68.

23. Quoted in Kennedy, ed., op. cit.. 60.

24. Telegram (written shortly after midnight) from General George McClellan to Secretary of War Edwin Stanton, 28 June 1862. Stanton did not actually read these words, because the officer receiving the message thought it best to edit them.

25. Both quotes come from McClellan as cited in Sears, op. cit., 183.

26. Quoted in Sears, op. cit., 200-1.

27. This assessment by McClellan was published as part of his "official report of the operations of the Army of the Potomac while under my charge," as submitted on 4 August 1863.

28. Quoted in Sears, op. cit., 322.

29. Quoted in ibid., 128.

30. Quoted in ibid., 324.

Chapter 14: A Cavalry Quartet

1. Quoted in Edward G. Longacre, *Gentleman and Soldier: The Extraordinary Life of Wade Hampton* (Rutledge Hill Press, 2003), 154.

2. Quoted in Walter Brian Cisco, *Wade Hampton: Confederate Warrior, Conservative Statesman* (Brassey's Inc, 2004), 48.

3. Quoted in Longacre, op. cit., 72.

4. John Esten Cooke, *Wearing of the Gray: Being Personal Portraits, Scenes, and Adventures of the War.* (Louisiana State University Press, 1997), 48.

5. Quoted in Longacre, op. cit., 170.

6. Quoted in ibid., 194.

7. Quoted in Cisco, op. cit., 188.

8. Quoted in Longacre, op. cit., 249.

9. Quoted in ibid., 274.

10. Quoted in ibid., 276.

11. Quoted in Roy Morris, Jr., *Sheridan: The Life & Wars of Phil Sheridan* (Vintage Civil War Library, 1993), 4.

12. Quoted in ibid., 1.

13. Quoted in Richard O'Connor, *Sheridan the Inevitable* (Bobbs-Merrill Company, 1953), 16.

14. Quoted in Morris, op. cit., 43.

15. Quoted in ibid, 75-6.

16. Quoted in Frances H. Kennedy (editor), *The Civil War Battlefield Guide* (Houghton Mifflin, 1990), 92.

17. Quoted in Morrit, op. cit., 108.

18. Quoted in O'Connor, op. cit., 136. Other versions of Sheridan's toast and reply are saltier.

19. Quoted in Shelby Foote, *The Civil War: A Narrative, Red River to Appomattox* (Random House, 1974), 136.

20. Quoted in Morris, op. cit., 164.

21. Quoted in ibid., 184.

22. Quoted in ibid., 191.

23. Qutoed in O'Connor, op. cit., 227.

24. Quoted in Morris, op. cit., 256.

25. Quoted in ibid., 258.

26. The official tune of Jeb Stuart's cavalry: "Jine the Cavalry" The chorus is: "If you want to have a good time, jine the cavalry!/ Jine the cavalry! Jine the cavalry!/If you want to catch the Devil, if you want to have fun,/If you want to smell Hell, jine the cavalry!"

27. This was Sam Sweeney, brother of Joe Sweeney, the alleged inventor of the modern banjo, adopted from an instrument used by blacks in the South, which had four strings rather than five, and a different shaped resonator.

28. George Cary Eggleston, *A Rebel's Recollections* (Louisiana State University Press, 1996), 123.

29. Ibid., 114.

30. Pelham left West Point a few weeks before he was scheduled to graduate, in order to join the Confederacy.

31. Quoted in Burke Davis, *Jeb Stuart: The Last Cavalier* (Burford Books, 1957), 73.

32. Quoted in ibid., 93.

33. Quoted in ibid., 155.

34. Quoted in Emory M. Thomas, *Bold Dragoon: The Life of J. E. B. Stuart* (Vintage Civil War Library, 1988), 147.

35. Quoted in Davis, op. cit., 402.

36. Quoted in Thomas, op. cit., 292-3.

37. Quoted in Jay Monaghan, *Custer: The Life of General George Armstrong Custer* (University of Nebraska Press, 1971), 56-7.

38. Quoted in ibid., 35.

39. Quoted in Jeffry D. Wert, *Custer: The Controversial Life of George Armstrong Custer* (Simon & Schuster, 1996), 36.

40. Quoted in Monaghan, op. cit., 79.

41. Quoted in Robert M. Utley, *Cavalier in Buckskin: George Armstrong Custer and the Western Military Frontier* (University of Oklahoma Press, 1988), 19.

42. Quoted in Wert, op. cit., 95.

43. There were rumors that Custer took an Indian mistress and had a child or two by her on the Great Plains. But the honest Injuns—and enemies of Custer, like Captain Frederick Benteen—who spread such gossip spoke with forked tongue, for the dates don't add up; moreover it seems out

of character for Yellow Hair, who was not only devoted to his wife but who had moved from the non-practicing to practicing Christian camp, making a personal commitment to Christ in the Evangelical fashion.

44. Quoted in Monaghan, op. cit., 199 and 201.

45. During the Valley campaign, the mother of James Washington, a young Confederate officer who had been a West Point classmate of Custer's, thanked Custer for looking after her son when he was captured in the Peninsula campaign, giving Custer a button from a coat of George Washington.

46. Quoted in Monaghan, op. cit., 304.

47. Quoted in Utley, op. cit., 149.

Chapter 15: What If the South Had Won?

1. Samuel Eliot Morison, *The Oxford History of the American People, Volume 3, 1869 to the Death of John F. Kenney 1963*, (Mentor, 1972), 354.

2. Quoted in John S. D. Eisenhower, *So Far from God: The U.S. War with Mexico, 1846-1848* (Random House, 1989), 367.

Afterword

1. Jefferson Davis, *The Rise and Fall of the Confederate Government* (abridged, Collier Books, 1961), 562.

INDEX

Index

Index

Other Politically Incorrect Guides™ You Might Enjoy

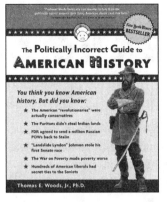

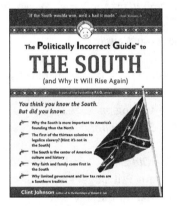
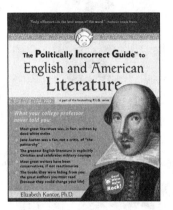

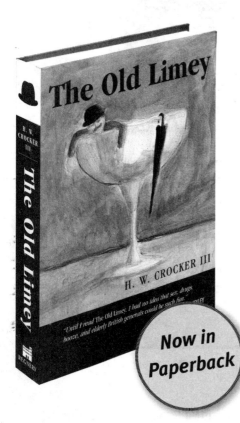
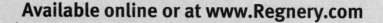